ROYAL INSTITUTE OF PHILOSOPHY LECTURES

VOLUME THREE · 1968–1969

KNOWLEDGE AND NECESSITY

In the same series

THE HUMAN AGENT
TALK OF GOD

ROYAL INSTITUTE OF PHILOSOPHY LECTURES

VOLUME THREE · 1968–1969

KNOWLEDGE AND NECESSITY

MACMILLAN

ST MARTIN'S PRESS

© The Royal Institute of Philosophy 1970

First published 1970 by
MACMILLAN AND CO LTD
Little Essex Street London WC2
and also at Bombay Calcutta and Madras
Macmillan South Africa (Publishers) Pty Ltd Johannesburg
The Macmillan Company of Australia Pty Ltd Melbourne
The Macmillan Company of Canada Ltd Toronto
St Martin's Press Inc New York
Gill and Macmillan Ltd Dublin

Library of Congress catalog card no. 70–105660

Printed in Great Britain by
ROBERT MACLEHOSE AND CO LTD
The University Press, Glasgow

CONTENTS

FOREWORD

I F there is one distinctive feature of contemporary epistemology it is the recognition by many philosophers of the importance of questioning questions before trying to answer them. For example, questions have been asked which seem to call for our somehow *justifying*, but in a very general way, our saying some of the things we do say – about what we see, about other people, about the future, and so on. And many have taken the sort of justification required to be one which, in part at least, is a *causal explanation* of our ideas, experiences, or thoughts. Thus it has been asked, of some of our ideas, whether they are innate, or acquired through things acting on our senses. But in other cases it has seemed that the possibility of causal explanation may mean that, after all, we are not justified. If seeing is an effect in us how can we be said to see, other than in a Pickwickian sense, what is not in us? Or 'How can we take a belief seriously, or consider it seriously as a candidate to be knowledge, if it is no better than a simple physical effect?' (p.132).

By 'questioning questions' I mean, for instance, asking whether questions which seem to call for our justifying what we say, and, moreover, doing so by reference to causal matters, may not really be the expression of philosophical perplexities which no amount of 'justification talk' could remove. In medicine one does not take the patient's word for it as to what is wrong with him. Why should one do so in philosophy?

Take the case of what we say about what we see. The moves in the philosophers' game are well known: the causal story – the representative theory of Descartes and Locke – scepticism – Berkeley's fantastic halfway position, to meet scepticism, between the representative theory and phenomenalism, making God the one spiritual cause of our ideas – Kant's transcendental idealism (the non-spatial, non-temporal unknown supplies the matter, we supply the structure) – Mill's thorough-going phenomenalism, with 'permanent possibilities of sensation' taking over from Berkeley's God and lying doggo until someone comes along with eyes to see and ears to hear – recent versions of phenomenalism in the form of analyses of physical object

vii

statements into 'sense-datum' statements. Until recently few philosophers (Thomas Reid is one remarkable exception) questioned the first move in this progression to subjectivism, still less the notion we have inherited from Descartes, that it is the philosopher's task 'to secure the foundations of human knowledge'.

Let us, briefly, consider the question: Is seeing an effect in us of things outside us acting on our sense-organs?

Perhaps the first thing to note is that one is not committed, by a negative answer to this question, to denying that causation has a place in the analysis of perception. If a person seemed to see in the absence of stimulation of the sense-organs for sight, the eyes, or in the absence of nerve-impulses resulting from such stimulation reaching the brain, he would not, without qualification, be said to be seeing, but perhaps to be having hallucinations, or, if what he reported coincided remarkably with how things were in the world, to be having 'extra-sensory' perception. That our eyes function normally, respond as they normally do to stimulation originating from the object, is part of what we mean by normal vision. We build what is common knowledge about the physical basis of vision into the concept, so that if someone seemed to see under other than the normal causal conditions we could not without qualification say that he saw. But to say that causation is involved in vision in this way is not to say that seeing, itself, is an effect. All that has been built into our concept of seeing is a causal account which starts with the object reflecting light and ends with the brain being in a certain state of excitation.

Next, we must distinguish between 'seeing' and 'seeing-as'. We may so use the word 'see' that a person can truly be said to have seen a stick if he saw it as a snake and it never occurred to him that it might be only a stick. In this use of 'see' 'S saw X' *entails* 'X existed'. In other words, if one knew 'S saw X' one could infer 'X existed' without resort to one's experience of things being constantly conjoined. So, on Hume's use of 'cause', X's existence would not be a *causal* condition of S's seeing X, in this use of 'see'.

Someone who was not content with the sort of involvement of causation in the concept of seeing that consists in the causal account being built into the concept, and who saw the point of the last remark about the sense of 'see' in which the subject 'saw' a stick, although he saw it as a snake, might resort to saying that 'seeing-as' is an effect. He might say that the stick's looking like a snake (or like a stick) – its *appearance* to the observer – is an effect.

At this point it is necessary to distinguish two of the many senses of 'appears' or 'looks like'. In one sense of 'looks like', what an object looks like to somebody is what, on looking at it, that person would take it to be, if he had no reason to think otherwise. In this sense of 'looks', the lines in the Muller–Lyer figure look unequal in length,

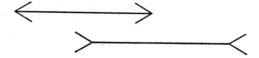

though they are in fact equal. But there is another sense of 'looks like' which is so different that it is seriously misleading to use the same word.

It is sometimes said that a coin, or a round plate, looks round only if seen head-on. Viewed from an angle the coin looks elliptical, the round plate like an oval one. If normal vision were two-dimensional perhaps round plates would look like oval ones in the sense in which the Muller–Lyer lines look unequal – that is, so that if one did not know better one would take oneself to be seeing an oval plate, the sort used under sauce-boats. To people with normal vision round plates viewed at an angle do not usually look like oval ones in that sense of 'looks like'. What, then, is the sense in which they do look oval?

It is a matter of the observer's point of view relative to the object, and the laws of perspective. If, like someone setting out to draw a perspective-true picture of the plate, as it appears to a given point of view, one holds a pencil at arm's length, at right angles to one's line of vision, between one's eyes and the plate, and 'measures' the plate latitudinally and longitudinally, the latitudinal measurement will be greater than the longitudinal one. More simply, if one put a trans-parent screen at right angles to one's line of vision, between oneself and the plate, and drew on it the outline of the plate seen through the screen, the shape drawn would be oval.

I shall call this measurable, objectively-determined appearance of an object to a point of view, its 'optical' appearance.

One can explain some illusions, but not others, by reference to the optical appearance. A straight staff, half immersed, at an angle, in water, looks, from many points of view, as if it were bent or broken at the water line. If one drew the outline of the staff on a transparent screen one would draw a bent or broken line. But in the case of the Muller–Lyer illusion the lines one drew on the screen would be equal in length.

Psychological experiments (R. H. Thouless, *Brit. J. Psy.*, xxi (1931) 339–59, and xxii (1932) 1–30) have shown that unless one uses pencils, screens, and so on, one is likely, in judging what the optical appearance is, to err on the side of the shape the object looks like in the sense in which a round plate looks like a round plate regardless of one's angle of vision. One cannot tell, just by looking at something, whether or not an illusion is to be explained by reference to an optical appearance. Take the case of the so-called 'moon illusion'. The moon looks larger when it is near the horizon than when it is directly overhead. Is this because the optical appearance is larger – perhaps because when the moon is near the horizon it is seen through more of the earth's atmosphere and this has a magnifying effect? One can be sure that the optical appearance is not larger only by measuring it. Our field of vision does not come with a built-in grid for measuring optical appearances.

In the way in which one can be wrong about a thing's optical appearance one cannot be wrong (or right) about how it looks to one in the other sense of 'looks'. Someone may be taken in by the Muller–Lyer illusion, and be wrong in thinking that the lines are unequal. But he is not wrong (or right) about their looking unequal. If we allow ourselves to talk of 'the look' (unequal lines) of the Muller–Lyer lines, this may be said to be false, in that what looks unequal is in fact equal. Then, if someone knew it to be an illusion, there would be a false 'look' but a true belief. But there is a danger in such talk. It suggests that just as there can be representation of the optical appearance, (e.g. a picture) at which we could look, so there could be a representation of 'the look' (e.g. unequal lines) at which we could look. But if anything would be a representation of 'the look' of the lines it would be our treating them as unequal.

Another way of putting this is in terms of the distinction between 'true to' and 'true of'. J. L. Austin, in a paper entitled 'Truth' in the *Proceedings of the Aristotelian Society*, xxiv (1950), writes:

> If, as some also say, a belief is 'of the nature of a picture', then it is of the nature of what cannot be true, though it may be, for example, faithful. . . . A picture, a copy, a replica, a photograph – these are *never* true in so far as they are reproductions, produced by natural or mechanical means: a reproduction can be accurate or lifelike (true *to* the original), as a gramophone recording or a transcription may be, but not true (of) as a record of proceedings can be. In the same way a (natural) sign *of* something can be infallible or unreliable but only an (artificial) sign *for* something can be right or wrong.

In terms of this distinction between 'true to' and 'true of', a representation (such as an image on the retina) of the optical appearance of an object can be said to be *true to* the optical appearance of the object. That is, given particulars about the lens of the eye, etc., one could correlate the retinal image and the optical appearance. But this is *quite* a different matter from S's belief that he is looking at unequal lines, or 'the look' itself, being false. The belief, and the look, are false *of* what is out there. They are false as propositions, not as pictures, are false. I shall mark this feature that 'the look' shares with the belief, and does not share with a representation of the optical appearance, by calling the look the 'epistemic' appearance. Perception would not be how we find things out about the world if there were not epistemic appearances. Or, in plain language, it is only because we see things as being things of a certain sort that we learn about the world by seeing things.

Someone who held 'seeing-as' to be an effect would have to add, to the causal account which ends with the brain's being in a certain state of excitation, 'and the brain's being in a certain state of excitation causes us to see the object as a such-and-such'.

Making use of the 'true to'/'true of' distinction, the difficulty about adding this to the causal account can be brought out as follows. The stimulation of the eyes represents the optical appearance of the object to the point of view occupied by the eyes; and the impulses in the optic nerve represent the stimulation of the eyes; and the state of excitation of the brain represents the impulses in the optic nerve. Throughout we are dealing with something which if true at all, is, *true to* – which does not mean *like* – the optical appearance of the object. Then this is supposed, somehow, to give rise to an epistemic appearance, the object's looking to the subject like a such-and-such, which is *true* (or false) *of* the object. Somehow this last alleged link in the causal chain is one which bridges the *categorial* gap between what is *true to* and what is *true of*. It is as though one could put pictures into one end of a machine, crank a handle, and produce propositions (not sentences, but propositions) at the other.

The Cartesian way of attempting to meet this difficulty is to posit an immaterial substance, somehow located (having its 'seat') in the head, on which can be impressed something – a 'sense-impression' – which is a 'mental' representation of the optical appearance. The 'sense-impression' itself cannot be said to be right or wrong, but about it a judgement is made, somehow 'based' on it: first, to the effect that it is of a certain kind; second, that there is something, of a related kind, which is its remote cause, 'external to' the immaterial substance.

The difficulty exists, of course, only on the presupposition that causation has a place in the analysis of epistemic concepts other than that recognised earlier. The signs that someone makes this presupposition are well known. Foremost is talk of 'the mind' as if it were a part of nature (not that I am suggesting that it is supernatural!), a part about which we know so little that we can unblushingly credit it with a 'structure' which enables it to transform an input which *cannot* be said to be true of the world into an output which *can* be said to be true of the world. Another sign is the inevitable concern with the sceptical problems that beset any attempt to locate epistemic concepts wholly within the causal nexus. It is not too much to say that these problems, and the various 'solutions' to them (Berkeley's idealism, phenomenalism, etc.) have been the major concern of epistemologists for the past three and a half centuries. No doubt they will continue to be so, but perhaps with new reasons given for old answers to misconceived questions.

If R. Edgley, Senior Lecturer in Philosophy at the University of Bristol, is right, then Professor Chomsky is one who gives new reasons for an old answer to a misconceived question. Chomsky, he says, claims support in research in the empirical science of linguistics for 'a theory of psychological *a priori* principles that bears a striking resemblance to the classical doctrine of innate ideas'. Edgley remarks that 'if one thing is clear it is that the classical theory is not.' One source of unclarity is the bewildering variety of meanings that is given to the word 'idea' in the work of Descartes, Locke and others. Are ideas 'sense-impressions' (that is, things to understand which we must first have accepted as meaningful the positing of an immaterial substance, 'seated' in the head, capable of taking and retaining 'impressions' from the sense-organs via the brain), or are they 'principles'? And if they are principles – of inference, perhaps – does having the idea consist in having the *capacity* to see that a conclusion follows from certain premises (which someone might have without being able to say what the principle of inference is), or does it consist in knowing (and so being able to say) what the principle is? In short, is having the idea an instance of knowing *how*, or of knowing *that*? Edgley's contention is that Chomsky illegitimately concludes from his linguistic studies that certain principles are innate in the sense that people know *that* certain things are the case independently of finding them to be so.

Whether he is right about Chomsky I do not know. What I find particularly interesting is his treatment of the question he poses in the section on The Classical Doctrine: 'Experience involves being affected by our surroundings: the type of access to the external world that the mind gets through experience is essentially access provided by causal contact. How, if at all, can this causal relation be conceived if it is to be compatible with its yielding knowledge of that external world?' He does not provide an answer of his own. The nearest he comes to abandoning the notion that seeing is an effect is his remarking, uncomfortably, that 'there seems, then, to be a tension between the truth of an idea and its being the product of the mind's causal interaction through experience with the external world' and that 'we may be tempted to suppose that for the external world to be represented as it really is, independently of our knowledge of it, there would have to be no mind there at all'. I would say: let us yield to this temptation, if by 'the mind' is meant the immaterial substance, posited by Descartes, impressions on which, caused by 'external' material substances, are said to represent the latter.

John W. Yolton, Professor of Philosophy at York University, Canada, wants 'to avoid the misleading implications of terms like "idea", "sense-data", or even Hirst's much better term "percepta" '. He says that 'what is misleading about this sort of term for characterising the nature of perceptual consciousness is that they easily open the door for the matching-question: do my ideas, sense-data, or percepta match or represent physical objects?' He prefers to talk of mental or perceptual contents. 'To perceive a table just is to have mental contents.' Perhaps by 'perceptual contents' he means what I, in my jargon, called 'epistemic appearances'. He says: 'The matching-question is legitimate when we want to determine the veracity of our perceptions, but what is being matched with our perceptual contents does not differ from those contents.' In other words, we check that something is what it looks like by looking more closely, feeling it, etc. Perceptual consciousness is not 'some rare transmuting process able to turn base metals into gold, to transform physical processes into mental contents'. In my Austinian terminology, there is no 'process' of turning what is true *to* our surroundings, what 'represents' them as an effect represents its cause, into what may be true *of* them. Yolton says: 'To reveal the mental nature of perceptual consciousness just is to reveal the nature of seeing, perceiving, etc. To suppose a counter-example of seeing devoid of mental contents would not be to suppose seeing at all.' I said: 'Perception would not be how we find things out about the world if there were not epistemic appearances. Or, in plain language, it is only because we see things as being things of a certain sort that we learn about the world by seeing things.' The difference between us is that Yolton finds himself flirting with idealism. For instance, he talks, as do some phenomenologists, of the development of awareness as being 'the constituting or formation of a world of objects'. I think it is no more than a temporary aberration.

Like Yolton's paper, that by B. A. Farrell, Reader in Mental Philosophy at Oxford University, is half psychology, and half drawing a moral for philosophers. He writes: 'We may soon be getting clearer hints from psychology on how to develop a causal theory of knowledge. When this happens, we may then be in a better position to transport much of this traditional branch of philosophy [epistemology] upstairs into the secure, grant-supported chambers of empirical science.' I am not sure what to make of this. Does he mean that a psychologist, as such, can show that to a philosopher's conceptual question ('Is seeing an effect in us of things outside us acting on our sense-organs?') a certain answer ('Yes') is the right one? Or does he mean no more than we already know – that the psychologist can tell us under what conditions someone will see something as an X, and under what conditions as a Y? He says that for an answer to the philosopher's question 'What is it to see the thing in front of me as a piece of chalk?', 'the obvious place to look is in psychological theory'. Yes, but is it the *right* place? Looking in that place, he says, 'we cease to be traditional philosophers. But, as long as we are clear what we are doing, why should we be concerned about traditional boundaries between subjects? Why bother about them? And if philosophers do move in this general direction, they will simply be co-operating in the business of transforming this part of their own subject into science.' But are we clear what we are doing?

Peter Alexander, Reader in Philosophy at the University of Bristol, is partly concerned to differentiate (*a*) seeing an object, in the use of 'see' in which when you see X it follows that, if X is Y, you see Y whether you realise it or not, (*b*) seeing an object *as* an object of a certain kind, and (*c*) seeing *that* an object is an object of a certain kind. To distinguish it from 'seeing as' and 'seeing that' he calls (*a*) 'simple seeing'. 'Simple seeing', he says, 'is not a sort of seeing different from other sorts; it is involved in seeing of all sorts. We might say that the claim to see simply is a minimum claim involved in all claims to see.' He remarks that 'it is clear that there is some difficulty about reporting my own present simple seeings', but concludes that 'if I can claim to have seen at all then there is something that I myself can correctly claim to have seen, even if it is only a brown moving patch on the plain, and that claim would involve a claim to have simply seen that something.' If by 'correctly' he means 'truly', then I think he has been misled by his own choice of terminology into giving to a question to which Farrell refers, 'Are there any statements of a perceptual character where the risk of error is so minimal that it vanishes altogether?', the answer 'Yes, for example, statements about brown moving patches.' I think this is the only point in his paper with which I have any quarrel. I do not see why there should have to be anything in perception which is immune from the risk of error, in this sense.

The paper by M. R. Ayers, Lecturer in Philosophy at Oxford University, is an ingenious, and I think original and successful, attempt to show that Locke and Berkeley cannot, by use of the principle that, as Locke puts it, 'the objects of the senses do obtrude their particular ideas upon our minds whether we will or no', escape the scepticism about our knowledge of the 'external' world to which their Cartesian 'way of ideas' leads. For Locke the unavoidability of the ideas of sensation is a reason for a belief in 'some exterior cause, and the brisk acting of some objects without me, whose efficacy I cannot resist, that produces those ideas in my mind'. But this anti-sceptical argument, Ayers contends, is circular. For the distinction it requires us to understand between causing an alteration in our ideas by acting in the physical world, and causing an alteration in them by imagining, is one which presupposes 'precisely what the sceptic doubts, that there is a physical world'. Berkeley takes 'what Locke gives as reasons for our belief in an external physical reality, as constituting a *definition* of the concept of reality', but involuntariness is a necessary condition of ideas being ideas of sensation, and the only plausible interpretation of involuntariness depends upon the assumption that human action in the physical world is possible: '*When in broad daylight I open my eyes*, it is not in my power to . . . determine what particular objects present themselves to my view.' Furthermore, the neo-Berkeleyan view of modern phenomenalists, that physical objects are merely theoretical entities, has no answer to Berkeley's dilemma.

Although he criticises answers to scepticism, Ayers is not a sceptic. In the second half of his paper he argues for its being a necessary truth 'that any experience is necessarily the experience of an animal, that is, a physical object'. His argument involves an examination of Strawson's attempt, in the second chapter of *Individuals*, to give meaning to talk of reidentifiable particulars in a purely auditory universe. He sees this attempt as being, like Leibniz's attempt to replace the system of spatio-temporal relationships with one of quali-tative relationships, doomed to failure.

A. Palmer, Lecturer in Philosophy at the University of Southamp-ton, says that he will 'try to show that behaviour is a necessary condition for thinking about movement'. That is, 'if one could not do things like signing a cheque or building a house then one could have no idea of change or movement'. On the face of it, this seems a tall order. The chosen route is via reflection on what it is to perceive and think. The Cartesian account of perception as a reception of particulars, 'sense-impressions', leaves thought, as that which has generality, and can be true or false of how things are, unintelligible. Now, 'one necessary condition for thinking of movement or change is the possibility of having the idea of something being other than it is', and 'thought has to have some generality for it to be possible to think of things as other than they are'. If Palmer could show that thought could have generality only if thinkers behaved – that is, did things like signing cheques and building houses – or if he could show that thinking itself was behaving, he would be home and dry. What he does do is to argue that while 'thinking' is not a performance verb, still less an activity verb, there are parallels between thinking and performances. 'Take as an example "walking to the university". The parallel to the possible non-existence of the object of thought is found by noticing that the correct description of what a person is intentionally doing may still be "walking to the university" even if, perhaps because of a recent fire, the university no longer exists.' This, and other parallels, such as that just as a person doing something intentionally knows what he is doing so a person thinking knows what he is thinking, enable us 'to explain how it is that thought possesses the characteristics it does . . .'. These characteristics which thinking shares with performances are 'intentional characteristics'. Without them 'thought about movements or change . . . would not be possible'. As if this showed that 'behaviour is a necessary condition for thinking about movement', in the sense that unless we could first understand behaviour we could not understand movement, Palmer goes on to draw the conclusion that 'an attempt to account for intentional activity in terms of such movements or change is self-stultifying'.

Wittgenstein in *Philosophical Investigations*, Ryle in *The Concept of Mind*, and Malcolm in *Dreaming* have things to say which it is sometimes hard to understand. To C. W. K. Mundle, Professor of Philosophy at the University of North Wales, Bangor, it seems that 'in each of these books, a version of the verification principle is a suppressed premiss', and consequently that the authors, in spite of their denials, are in some sense behaviourists. For example, what else can Wittgenstein's attack on the notion of a private language be but 'a sophisticated kind of behaviourism'? How else are we to understand *Philosophical Investigations*, 1 304? If I knew of a short answer to these questions, this would be the place for it. I do not.[1]

[1] My 'Being and Feeling', *Proc. Arist. Soc.* (1968–9), 'Sensations of Colour', in *Mill*, ed. J. B. Schneewind (London, 1969) and 'Wittgenstein on the Myth of Mental Processes', *Phil. Review* (1968) have a bearing on them.

In the first half of his paper, David Wiggins, Professor of Philosophy at the University of London, considers the question 'How can we take a belief seriously, or consider it seriously as a candidate to be knowledge, if it is no better than a simple physical effect?' One form this question takes is 'the so-called causal argument for scepticism about perception'. Wiggins writes: 'This argument, which it is rare to see sympathetically treated, finds reason in the complicated mechanical genesis of perception to question the veracity or real representativeness of the end-state of the process of coming to see something.' By 'the end-state of the process of coming to see something' does he mean the state of excitation of the brain which is the effect of something acting on the sense-organs, or does he mean an object's looking like something – say, a piece of chalk – to someone? The former 'represents' the stimulus, the latter can be said to be true if what is being looked at is in fact a piece of chalk. Wiggins says: 'For there to be *perception* of it, the scene I report must itself figure in the explanation and causal ancestry of my visual state.' I think he thinks that the only way causality can be involved in the concept of perception is one which puts seeing in the category of effects. At the beginning of the first section of his paper he writes: 'If we suppose that mind is just one part of nature and that it does not there enjoy any special autonomy or metaphysical insulation from ordinary causality . . .'. He thinks he *has* to suppose this. He is serious when he says that 'if my beliefs are to relate to the world at all, I simply have to lay myself open to the world in order to let the phenomena put their print upon me. How otherwise can my beliefs even aim at a correct account of the world?' I would ask: But how can a 'print upon me' (cf. Descartes's 'sense-impression') be true or false of the world?

R. G. Swinburne, Lecturer in Philosophy at the University of Hull, regards determinism as making a significant claim, as opposed to its being a piece of advice (to go on looking for causes), analyses what would be evidence for or against the truth of the claim, and concludes that the achievements of modern science – quantum theory, in particular – give good grounds for its being false.

Michael Clark, Lecturer in Philosophy at the University of Nottingham, is concerned with the question whether differences in discourse about the future, and about the past and present, 'reflect a logical asymmetry between the past and future beyond the merely defining fact that the future succeeds, and the past precedes, the present time'. The first half of his paper is taken up with a discussion of a view he attributes to Hartshorne about the meaning of statements like 'X will happen'. It is the view that in saying 'X will happen' I am saying something about present conditions and causal laws, so that 'I wonder whether present conditions causally determine that X will happen' means 'I wonder whether present conditions causally determine what present conditions causally determine'. If Clark is right then Mundle should have taken Hartshorne as an example of a verificationist instead of Wittgenstein.

Although 'verificationist' would evidently be a term of abuse for Mundle, 'empiricist', I think, would not. At any rate, when he refers to 'the traditional conception of empiricism' at the end of his paper it is to oppose an empiricist theory of meaning ('a sentence is meaningful for a person only if he can interpret each of the linguistic expressions which it contains in terms of what he himself has observed or experienced') to a verificationist one ('a sentence used to make a statement about a person, P, is meaningful *for anyone* if and only if it is verifiable *by people other than P*'). Other contributors to this collection are as suspicious of empiricism as of rationalism. Edgley, for instance, remarks that 'many contemporary philosophers have been convinced that empiricism and rationalism are equally unacceptable, and that both positions, and the conflict between them, are the result of trying to answer confused, misleading, and perhaps senseless questions'. At the beginning of this foreword I suggested that we should regard with suspicion questions which seem to call for our somehow *justifying*, in a very general way, our saying some of the things we say. Mary Hesse, Reader in Philosophy of Science at Cambridge University, is concerned with the justification of the things scientists say. Traditional empiricists seem to her to have assumed that 'there are statements of some kind whose meaning as descriptions of states of affairs is supposed to be transparent, and whose truth-value is supposed to be directly and individually decidable by setting up the appropriate observation situations'. Such observation statements express what Duhem calls 'practical facts'. About practical facts she writes: 'There is a sense in which they are literally inexpressible. The absence of distinction between fact and linguistic expression here is not accidental. As soon as we begin to try to capture a practical fact in language, we are committed to some theoretical interpretation.' Nevertheless she evidently regards the notion of a 'transparent observation language' as meaningful, for she goes on to consider whether there is such a language, to provide a foundation for scientific theory, or whether scientists should be content with a language in which the predicates are theory-laden from the start. The latter view is the 'new empiricism' of Duhem and Quine. I wonder whether a transparent observation language would

be what one would have if one could transform what, in us, is true *to*
the stimulation of our sense-organs into something which was true *of*
the world. If so, then since the notion of such a transformation is
meaningless, so is the notion of a transparent observation language,
and the denial that there is such a language.

In the second half of his paper, Don Locke, Lecturer in Philosophy
at the University of Warwick, argues, rightly I think, that 'memory
provides each of us with a special privileged insight into his own
identity', in the sense that if I remember (that is, do not merely seem
to remember) breaking the window then I am identical with the
person who broke the window, and I can know that I remember it
'just in virtue of the fact that I remember it'; I do not have to find out
that I remember it in the way others find it out, by asking me. I am
not so sure about what Locke seems to conclude from this, namely
that, in Shoemaker's terminology, memory 'provides a criterion of
self-identity distinct from the criteria we have for the identity of
others'. It depends what he means by 'distinct'. The wording
suggests that memory could be the *sole* criterion of self-identity. But
we usually distinguish between somebody's really remembering
something – being at a party, say – and only seeming to remember it
but really imagining it, by whether *he* was at the party, where 'he'
refers to a *person*, identifiable by bodily characteristics. If we did not,
as a rule, employ some such means to distinguish between real and
seeming memories, I do not know what we could mean by 'remember'. I suppose that, in special circumstances, exceptions to the rule
could be allowed, without 'remember' going out of currency, rather
as, in special circumstances, we allow promises not to be kept,
without putting 'I promise' out of work. But there could not be
nothing but exceptions. Memory and the bodily criterion of personal
identity could not be distinct to that extent.

In the course of her paper on 'Dreaming' Martha Kneale, formerly
Tutor in Philosophy at Oxford University, opposes to Malcolm's
contention 'that no mental activities other than dreaming can occur
during sleep' the case of Coleridge 'who did not merely dream that
he composed a poem beginning "In Xanadu did Kubla Khan a
stately pleasure-dome decree", but who did in fact compose such a
poem in a dream'. I asked Malcolm what he thought of this, and he
wrote:

I am puzzled as to how the example of Kubla Khan is supposed to
prove 'that mental activities other than dreaming may occur
during sleep'. Mrs Kneale says that Coleridge 'did not merely
dream that he composed' Kubla Khan, but he 'did in fact

compose' it 'in a dream'. True enough. This is a distinction we often
make in telling dreams. I might dream that I climbed Pikes' Peak,
but without the actual climbing of the mountain being part of my
dream. But I might have another dream in which I did not merely
dream *that* I climbed Pikes' Peak, but the actual climbing
occurred in the dream: 'I scrambled across boulders, up rock
faces, traversed a glacier, and camped in a small tent near the
summit.' I might dream that I had a conversation with Freud.
But also I might not merely dream *that* I had a conversation with
him, but actually have a conversation with him in a dream. On
telling the dream I would report that I said this and Freud said
that. If the gentleman from Porlock should interrupt me when I
was telling the dream, or if a fire should break out in the house,
then I might not be able to remember the rest of the conversation.
But we have to think of how the word 'remember' is used here, and
not assume that it carries the same grammar as it does in other
contexts. As it clearly does not.

It is no more surprising that a person should compose a poem in
a dream than that he should climb a mountain in a dream or carry
on a conversation in a dream. What is surprising in the Coleridge
example is that when he wrote down the dream-poem it turned
out to be both long and beautiful. Most dream-poems, dream-
proofs, and dream-conversations are not worth preserving.

In any case, we should not confuse composing-in-a-dream with
composing, or believing-in-a-dream with believing. If in a dream
I believed that my wife was a murderer it does not follow that ever,
at any time, did I believe that my wife was a murderer. Coleridge
did compose Kubla Khan in a dream; but it strikes me as being of
dubious correctness to say that he *composed* it. I don't mean that
someone else did.

J. B. Schneewind, Professor of Philosophy at the University of
Pittsburgh, opposes two views of moral knowledge. The first, with
which he disagrees, is that moral knowledge requires there to be first
principles with certain features (they must have a high degree of
generality, allow of no exceptions, not be merely formal, and be such
that other principles derive their validity from them) to serve as
the support for our particular moral judgements. On the second view,
morality is understood along the lines of a science. Rather as, in
science, a law is formulated to cover a set of well-established data
and used to predict experimental results, so, in morality, moral
principles are formulated to systematise our particular judgements,
and enable us to apply our moral beliefs to new situations and prob-

lems. It is very interesting to compare Schneewind's scientific view of morality with Mary Hesse's non-traditional-empiricist view of science.

Terence Penelhum, Professor of Philosophy at Calgary University, discusses what he calls 'theological non-naturalism'. By this term he means, not what someone brought up on Moore's *Principia Ethica* might take him to mean, namely the view that theistic statements are not *analysable into* non-theistic ones, but the view that theistic statements are not *verifiable by reference to* non-theistic ones. Moreover he is concerned not with the 'non-understander', for whom theistic statements are not verifiable because they are not meaningful to him in the first place, but with the atheist, the sceptic and the believer. He suggests that if a sceptic were to find himself after death in a community of persons whose personalities are as they would be if they were infused by grace, ruled over by Jesus in love and forgiveness, he would be irrational if he did not take this as verifying the claims of Christian theism. I am inclined to agree – though perhaps in the light of what I said in the foreword to last year's lectures, *Talk of God*, I should, to be consistent, not do so.

This is the third volume of Royal Institute of Philosophy lectures. The fourth volume, containing lectures on topics in the philosophy of the social sciences, will be published early in 1971 under the title *The Proper Study*.

G. N. A. VESEY

Honorary Director
The Royal Institute of Philosophy

Professor of Philosophy
The Open University

1

INNATE IDEAS

R. Edgley

EMPIRICISM, the philosophical theory that all our ideas and know-ledge are derived from experience, has in recent years been the target of radical and persuasive objections. In the seventeenth century, and for long after, rationalism seemed the only alternative to empiricism, but, like Kant, many contemporary philosophers have been convinced that empiricism and rationalism are equally unacceptable, and that both positions, and the conflict between them, are the result of trying to answer confused, misleading, and perhaps senseless questions. Of all the traditional theories in particular, none, I suppose, has looked to modern philosophers less capable of being revived than the rationalist doctrine of innate ideas: the doctrine that some at least of our ideas and knowledge of things are not derived from outside the mind, through experience, but are present from birth in the mind itself and thus represent the mind's own contribution to our understanding of reality. What Strawson has called 'those old and picturesque debates regarding the origin of our ideas' seemed to have become museum pieces, charming, as antiques can be, but with little relevance to current issues. These complacent attitudes, if that is what they are, have been rudely disturbed by Chomsky and his colleagues. Chomsky has suggested[1] 'that contemporary research supports a theory of psychological *a priori* principles that bears a striking resemblance to the classical doctrine of innate ideas'. In the prevailing situation, the novelty of this suggestion is twofold. It is not only that the theory of innate ideas may be true after all, but also that the support alleged for the ancient doctrine has a distinctively modern look. The research that Chomsky

[1] 'Recent Contributions to the Theory of Innate Ideas', in *Synthese*, XVII 1 (Mar 1967).

claims supports the doctrine is research in the empirical science of
linguistics. The implication is that empiricism is refutable empirically, and more generally that a philosophical dispute such as the
dispute between empiricism and rationalism, once it is made clear,
can be settled by science.

These aspects of Chomsky's theory are novel in the prevailing
situation, but on a longer view it is not only the doctrine of innate
ideas itself that appears as a revival. As Chomsky has shown in his
book *Cartesian Linguistics*, some of his most fundamental convictions
about language, especially those that seem to support the rationalist
position, resemble claims made by earlier thinkers such as Descartes,
the Port-Royal grammarians, and Humboldt. The exciting brilliance
and adventurousness of the revolution he is promoting in linguistics
are in no way diminished by the fact that, like most revolutionaries,
he constantly draws strength from the past. His attempt to solve a
philosophical problem by scientific means also reflects a characteristic of traditional thought, the absence of any sharp distinction
between science and philosophy. What I want to consider is whether,
in drawing from the empirical science of linguistics the philosophical
conclusion that we have innate ideas, he has not revived, besides the
insights, some of the traditional failings responsible for the confusions of 'those old and picturesque debates'. However, on this
point, whatever the value of the distinction between science and
philosophy, a preliminary distinction is essential: it is one thing to
break down barriers between specialisms and specialists, and
another to confuse different issues. Chomsky has said:[1] 'In the nineteenth and twentieth centuries, as linguistics, philosophy and
psychology have uneasily tried to go their separate ways, the classical
problems of language and mind have inevitably reappeared and
have served to link these diverging fields . . . this rather artificial
separation of disciplines may be coming to an end.' There is little to
object to here. Many problems, among them some of the most
interesting ones, could not be raised, let alone solved, within the
confines of any single existing specialism; and more strongly, the
solution of a problem may require considerations of logically diverse
sorts. None of this is incompatible with drawing attention to logical
distinctions and using them to question the propriety of certain sorts
of arguments.

In rough outline, Chomsky's view is as follows. The essential
characteristic of language is its 'creative' aspect, and 'the central fact

---

[1] In the first of his Beckman Lectures at the University of California, Berkeley,
1967.

to which any significant theory must address itself is this: a mature speaker can produce a new sentence of his language on the appropriate occasion, and other speakers can understand it immediately, though it is equally new to them'.[1] The competence of such speakers can be represented by a generative grammar, a system of rules that generate the infinite set of grammatically well-formed sentences of the language. By this competence, a speaker relates the observable physical features of the phonetic signal to a semantic interpretation, and the rules representing this process involve abstract grammatical structures at both superficial and deep levels. These deep structures and rules are very similar from language to language, so that underlying the differences between natural languages are basic similarities, linguistic universals constituting a 'universal grammar' that specifies the form of all possible human grammars. It is these universals that reflect characteristics of the language faculty, that part of the human mind concerned with speech. If this were not the case, the child could not learn his language. For the data on the basis of which a child learns a language, that is, the sentences to which he is exposed, are both meagre in range and degenerate in quality, and no process of inductive generalisation could yield the grammar of the language, with its infinite generative capacity, from such slight evidence. That grammar could be acquired only if the child himself brought to the data those characteristics of mind that constitute, in effect, innate knowledge of the universal form of any possible grammar. There is, says Chomsky,[2] 'little hope that much of the structure of the language can be learned by an organism initially uninformed as to its general character. . . . The child who acquires a language . . . knows a great deal more than he has "learned".'[3]

I. THE CLASSICAL DOCTRINE

How close is the resemblance between these views and 'the classical doctrine of innate ideas'? If one thing is clear, it is that the classical doctrine is not. That doctrine is in fact a set of variations on a theme whose identity is obscure and doubtful; on a number of topics, even in the work of a single philosopher, the doctrine exhibits a bewildering tendency to fluctuate between one alternative and another. Indeed, the overall impression it conveys is itself ambiguous in a characteristically philosophical way: it seems at one moment a

---

[1] *Current Issues in Linguistic Theory* (The Hague, 1967) p. 7.
[2] *Aspects of the Theory of Syntax* (Cambridge, Mass., 1965) p. 58.
[3] Ibid., pp. 32–3.

daring and almost incredible hypothesis, and at the next a resounding platitude.

The following fluctuations are relevant to our purposes:

(i) The notion of what exactly experience contributes to our ideas and knowledge varies between (*a*) a commonplace view that it contributes ideas of smell, taste, sight, and so on, such that what the idea is of is something that can in principle be seen, tasted, heard, etc., and (*b*) a more sophisticated doctrine that experience essentially involves being affected by something in such a way that ideas arise as an effect of this causal transaction. Thus Descartes and Locke, for instance, both employ the former notion in selecting a certain class of ideas for discussion. But the empiricist doctrine that all ideas are *derived* from experience suggests that experience itself does not contribute ideas but only the raw material from which ideas arise.

(ii) It is sometimes claimed (*a*) that only some of our ideas are innate, and sometimes (*b*) that all of our ideas are innate. Descartes, for instance, supposes at one point that some of our ideas draw their 'origin from the senses, and should be placed in the class of adventitious ideas',[1] not in the class of innate ideas. But further thought convinces him that

> no ideas of things, in the shape in which we envisage them by thought, are presented to us by the senses . . . in our ideas there is nothing which was not innate in the mind, or faculty of thinking, except only these circumstances which point to experience . . . nothing reaches our mind from external objects through the organs of sense beyond certain corporeal movements . . . but even these movements . . . are not conceived by us in the shape they assume in the organs of sense. . . . Hence it follows that the ideas of the movements and figures are themselves innate in us. So much the more must the ideas of pain, colour, sound, and the like be innate . . . for they have no likeness to the corporeal movements.[2]

Leibniz too felt the pull of both theses. In the introduction to the *New Essays*, he argues:

> The senses, although they are necessary for all our actual acquiring of knowledge, are by no means sufficient . . . since the senses never give anything but instances, that is to say particular or individual truths . . . necessary truths, such as we find in pure mathematics and especially in arithmetic and geometry, must have principles whose proof does not depend upon instances nor, consequently, upon the witness of the senses. . . .

[1] *Meditations*, III.
[2] *Notes Directed Against a Certain Programme*.

Later we find: 'I even think that all the thoughts and actions of our soul come from its own nature, and that it is impossible they should be given to it by the senses.'

(iii) What is innate is sometimes represented (*a*) as ideas, knowledge, or truths, and sometimes (*b*) as 'natural inclinations, dispositions, habits, or powers'. This latter description is, of course, quoted from Leibniz's introduction to the *New Essays*, and it occurs during the argument in which he seeks to show that knowledge, and therefore innate knowledge, can be implicit and unrecognised and need not, as Locke seemed to assume, be something present to consciousness. Locke's views were directed mainly against the doctrine of innate ideas put forward by the English Platonists, and some of his objections are levelled at a common Platonic metaphor used in presenting that doctrine, the metaphor of truths imprinted on the soul. In replacement of this and Locke's own metaphor of the mind as a *tabula rasa* Leibniz offers, as illustrating the sense in which knowledge can be implicit, existing as a disposition rather than consciously, the image of the mind as a veined tablet, the veins marking out the figure of Hercules so that this figure is innate: that is, the mind's structure is such that this figure rather than any other is disposed to appear in it. It is the abundant imagery of these debates that makes them literally picturesque. But the images are all incoherent, and all for the same reason: they contain no analogue of knowledge, the knowledge, innate or acquired, whose presence in the mind they are supposed to illustrate. Having something in the mind, whether an inscription, a picture, or something partly determined by the structure of the mind itself, does not amount to knowing anything.

(iv) The empiricist thesis is distinguished from the doctrine of innate ideas by being represented as claiming sometimes (*a*) that nothing is innate in the mind and sometimes (*b*) that something is innate, though not enough to account for our knowledge. One aspect of this duality is seen in the dispute engendered by one of the more popular versions of the conflict between empiricism and rationalism, the version representing the conflict as concerned with the question whether in knowing things the mind is passive or active. Empiricists are at one moment supposed to claim that the mind is passive; and at the next moment, in deference to all their talk about operations of the mind, it is allowed that the mind is in their view active - though of course not active enough.

These fluctuations suggest, to put it no stronger, that each party to this dispute is guilty of some fairly radical failures, both in the presentation of its own doctrines and in the understanding of those

of its opponent. A provisional diagnosis would be that much of the
argument involves that professional hazard of philosophical discussion, talking at cross-purposes; though we may suspect that the
nature of the subject-matter itself makes these confusions difficult to
avoid.

In these variations we can, I think, discern two positions, or
ranges of positions, which I shall distinguish as respectively the
dominant and the recessive doctrine of innate ideas. The dominant
doctrine is that some of our ideas are derived from experience and
some are innate, and these innate ideas constitute knowledge of
reality. The recessive doctrine is that all of our ideas are innate, and
these ideas constitute 'habits, dispositions, or powers'. I call this the
recessive doctrine because in maintaining the strong thesis that not
just some but all of our ideas are innate it weakens the notions of
innateness and of ideas to the point at which empiricism can agree –
but without enthusiasm, because this is the point at which triviality
sets in.

To make these variations intelligible, and the connections between
them that give rise to shifts between the dominant and recessive
doctrines, I shall offer a rational, or more or less rational, reconstruction of some relevant considerations. I have no illusions about
historical accuracy; my aim is to identify, in terms that will bear on
Chomsky's argument, underlying pressures that make the positions
indicated at least to some extent plausible.

We have many ideas of and some knowledge about the world we
live in. These ideas and this knowledge exist in the mind, but include
ideas and knowledge of things outside the mind. How is this possible?
Where do these ideas and this knowledge come from? How do we
get them? How are we to conceive of the relation of the mind to the
rest of reality in such a way that the acquisition of ideas and knowledge of that reality is possible?

These questions are vague and confused enough, but one can see
some familiar possibilities shaping themselves in response to them.
The terms in which the questions are formulated invite us to answer
either that these ideas and this knowledge come from outside the
mind, or that they come from the mind itself; and that accordingly
we should turn our attention either outwards or inwards. By turning
to the mind itself, we may be told, we can learn something not simply
about the mind but about other aspects of reality. But the image we
are offered in illustration of this mystery leaves it no less mysterious:
we may read there an inscription saying that God is omnipotent, and
we may thus come to know something about the mind, namely that
it bears the inscription 'God is omnipotent'; but reading it there does

not explain either how we are able to understand the meaning of the message or how we come to know that what it says is true. The message might of course be true, by luck or because of some factor we are unaware of, and provided that it is meaningful; but how we come to understand its meaning and find out that it is true – of these things the image has no illustration. We need to know from philosophers not simply that the mind or soul contains innate truths, but how, if it does contain such truths, we can know that they are truths, and not falsehoods or meaningless gibberish.

The view that our ideas and knowledge come to us from outside the mind raises the question of exactly how this transmission or importation is achieved, and what it is outside the mind that is so transmitted. At an ordinary common-sense level ideas and knowledge can come to us from outside the mind in the shape of information given to us by other people: we get ideas from them in the sense that their ideas are conveyed to us. This is one paradigm of the learning situation that Plato uses as a contrast to the doctrine of innate ideas in the *Meno*; and it is by virtue of this contrast that the doctrine has been important in the philosophy of education, which distinguishes between the Socratic method of questioning the pupil so that he works things out for himself and a procedure in which the teacher transmits ideas to the pupil. However, even if the pupil gets his ideas from a teacher, what actually passes between them is only sounds, the sounds of the teacher's voice that the pupil must interpret as words having this or that meaning; and in any case, the teacher himself must have got his ideas from somewhere. Ultimately and basically, according to empiricism, knowledge about things comes to us more or less indirectly from those things themselves. To have knowledge of something, someone must have contact with or access to either that thing or something from which its existence and nature can be inferred. This contact with or access to the world around us by means of which we get ideas and knowledge is, of course, experience. Our surroundings make their existence and nature known to us through the senses.

Experience of our surroundings essentially involves being aware of those surroundings by being affected by them. But awareness of one's surroundings can be of many different kinds and at many different levels. Typically, empiricists have characterised the awareness involved in experience as awareness in sense-perception of those features the ascription of which is logically least vulnerable, i.e. of those features of which we may legitimately be most certain. The view that any description of what one is aware of in experience must be logically minimal in this sense is the result of refining the distinction between experience and reason in such a way that experience is treated as supplying only the data, the basic premises from which reason infers, or on the basis of which reason constructs, the rest of our knowledge. The doctrine that all our ideas are derived from experience then has a sense in which the derivation referred to is logical derivation. The ambiguity of the word 'idea' allows this doctrine two forms: (*a*) that all our true ideas or judgements (and therefore knowledge) are logically derivable or inferable from the basic data of experience; and (*b*) that all our meaningful ideas are logically analysable into the basic ideas of experience. A weaker version of (*b*), using the notion of idea in (*a*), is that all our meaningful judgements are logically derivable from or incompatible with the basic data of experience. Involved in these claims are views about logical relations between statements and concepts in any field of inquiry whatsoever, e.g. physics, or biology, or mathematics; in a word, any statements and concepts that can form part of the content of our knowledge or belief. But at the fundamental level of the doctrine itself it is inevitable that these views about statements and concepts of any sort should involve in particular the psychological or partly psychological concepts commonly used in formulating the doctrine: the concepts of experience, reason, knowledge, idea, awareness, belief, seeing, recognising, imagining, remembering, understanding meaning, and so on. This is not to say that the issues at this point are necessarily psychological, in the sense of being empirical; they certainly include questions about the logical inter-relations of these psychological concepts.

To represent empiricism in the above way is to represent it as claiming, in effect, that all our ideas are logically derived from a certain sub-class of basic ideas, those constituting the fundamental data provided by experience. These data can be formulated as premises of arguments, or evidence to which we must ultimately appeal in justifying our claims about reality; and experience in this sense therefore already involves the use of thought and words in the recognition and classification of its features. What experience is here contrasted with is reason, i.e. with argument or inference from those first premises. But the doctrine that all ideas are derived from experience is open to a different interpretation: it suggests that all our ideas are derived from something that does not itself consist of ideas at all, but of that from which even our most basic ideas are derived. Experience regarded in this way is contrasted not simply with reason but with thought in general, including understanding the meaning of words and the ability to use them in describing what we experience: experience is then a precondition of thought and understanding, not their most basic parts. The problems raised at this level do not merely engage with psychological concepts, but positively centre on them.

Traditionally, these problems have been raised in their acutest form by concentrating on an aspect of experience I have already mentioned but not taken up. Experience involves being affected by our surroundings: the type of access to the external world that the mind gets through experience is essentially access provided by causal contact. How, if at all, can this causal relation be conceived if it is to be compatible with its yielding knowledge of that external world? The media through which our information about the external world comes, the sense-organs, are on the body's surface; the experience that results seems to be at the periphery of the mind, on one side its physical input, on the other its mental output of ideas and knowledge, derived from it in what now seems to be a causal sense of 'derived'. But the question is now raised: are such ideas derived entirely from experience, or does some other non-experiential source contribute to it? The experience may simply be the occasion stimulating the mind, the mind responding by actively constructing the idea out of its own resources. Descartes's way of answering this question in the passage already quoted is instructive. With experience thought of as the medium through which external things affect the mind, the contrast between innate ideas and ideas derived from experience tends to become a contrast between what is derived from the mind itself and what is derived from the external world. Even ideas of colour and sound are innate because, though we 'envisage' them 'on occasion of certain corporeal movements', i.e. when an external object is affecting our senses, those ideas 'have no likeness to the corporeal movements'. The implication is that the more the ideas *were* like their external causes the more they would be attributable to them and the less to the mind itself. In the extreme, an idea caused entirely by an external object would be entirely like that object.

As a general causal principle this is a ludicrous failure. An idea in the mind would be attributable entirely to an external object only, so to speak, if there were no mind there at all. It is trivially true that no effect is attributable entirely to a single cause identified in any such simple way as in Descartes's example: it must be attributable in part to some of the conditions in which that cause operates. In particular, an effect must be attributable in part to the nature of that in which or to which the effect occurs. Not even the meagre framework of explanation proposed in stimulus-response theory violates that principle. Thus the glass breaks because the stone strikes it, but not simply because the stone strikes it: the glass's own structure makes a contribution to the event, as we imply when we leave a logical space for further explanation, even if we do not actually give that explanation, in attributing the breakage in part to the glass's brittleness. It does not matter how alike the cause and effect are: the effect, and perhaps even its likeness to the cause, are still attributable in part to the nature of that in which or to which the effect occurs. Nothing more alike than the lighting of two matches; but if the lighting of one match causes another to light, the lighting of the second is in part due to its nature and condition, to its being a match rather than, say, an ivory tooth-pick, and dry rather than wet. Ideas, even those derived from experience and thus caused by external objects and events, must be in part attributable to the nature of experience and the mind, and the external item is at most a necessary condition of having the idea. To the extent that the doctrine of innate ideas rests on this consideration it is recessive, and no less trivial than the commonplace schema of causal explanation underlying it.

Why does Descartes introduce into his argument the question of likeness, which in the light of the foregoing remarks seems so irrelevant? The general principle that an effect must resemble its causes might be put in this form: there can be nothing in the effect that is not in its causes. In the *Third Meditation*, indeed, Descartes explicitly commits himself to the view that 'there must at least be as much reality in the . . . cause as in its effect'; and further, 'if we suppose that there is found in an idea anything which was not in its causes, it must of course derive this from nothing' – that is, anything present in an idea must be present in its causes. It is difficult not to hear in this schema of causal explanation an echo of a schema of logical derivation: there can be nothing in the conclusion of an argument that is not in its premises. This schema of logical derivation is truth-preserving, i.e. it specifies a condition under which if the premises are true the conclusion will be true. It seems clear that Descartes's condition of likeness between an idea and its external cause is also a truth-condition: it is an analytic criterion, formulated in a misleadingly concrete way, of the accuracy or truth of an idea. If there is something in an idea that is not in what it is an idea of, i.e. if the idea represents its object as having characteristics that the object does not have, then it misrepresents that object and is thus incorrect or false.

There seems, then, to be a tension between the truth of an idea and its being the product of the mind's causal interaction through experience with the external world. The price paid for regarding all ideas, even empirical ones, as innate in this recessive sense is that innateness is no longer, as in the dominant doctrine, a mark of acceptability; on the contrary, Descartes's list of innate ideas in the passage quoted significantly includes ideas of sound and colour, which he (like Locke after him) regards as defective, because they represent things only as they appear to be, not as they really are. In other words, the mind's contribution to the causal process in which, through experience, it interacts with the external world renders its ideas innate but at the expense of making them subjective. These ideas cannot constitute innate knowledge, since knowledge must represent things as they really are and not simply as they appear to be.

How then is knowledge possible? It may seem that the requirement of objectivity is impossible to fulfil: we may be tempted to suppose that for the external world to be represented as it really is, independently of our knowledge of it, there would have to be no mind there at all. The rationalist alternative to this impossible 'ideal' is to move in the opposite direction: the mind makes a further contribution, employing innate ideas of a different sort. But is this not a jump from the frying pan into the fire? If the mind's role in experience introduces a subjective element, so that in experience things appear to us otherwise than as they really are, how is it that a further mental contribution does not make matters worse rather than better, distorting even further our view of things? The answer is that these are ideas derived not from experience but from pure reason or understanding. This is the dominant doctrine of innate ideas; and this seems to be its essential aspect for rationalism. Rationalism is not simply the claim that we have ideas that are not derived from experience; it is the claim that some at least of these ideas are ideas of reason.

The discussion, it is clear, is working with three major contrasts, not one. The doctrine of innate ideas would be literally the doctrine that some of our ideas are inborn, i.e. we are born with them and have them at the moment that we are born. The alternative to this would be the doctrine that all of our ideas are acquired from birth onwards. The literal doctrine would not strictly be a doctrine about the source or origin of our ideas, but only about how long we have had them. To anyone interested in the question of how we got them various possibilities, some more scientific than others, might suggest themselves: e.g. by genetic inheritance, or by evolution, or as tribal memories, or as recollections of a life before birth (of a life, presumably, in which these ideas, saving an infinite regress, would not be innate). However, to each individual, an idea that he was born with would be an idea that, being already in the mind, would appear to come from the mind itself, rather than from outside the mind,

B

from the external world. We thus have a second contrast, between ideas that come from the mind itself and those that come to us from outside the mind. Now if ideas that come to us from outside the mind are regarded as necessarily coming to us through the causal contact with the world involved in experience, the third, primarily philosophical, contrast is introduced, between ideas derived from experience and ideas of reason. The distinctively rationalist doctrine of innate ideas is the doctrine that these ideas are not merely innate, and are not merely contributed by the mind, but are ideas contributed by that part of the mind distinguished as the reason or understanding.

In the fascinating welter of views referred to and quoted by Chomsky in *Cartesian Linguistics* this essential aspect of the rationalist doctrine of innate ideas gets submerged. The romantic movement, as he observes, was in a fair way addicted to innate ideas and a theory of the mind as creative and actively contributing from its own resources; but to the degree that romanticism was a reaction against rationalism and the value of reason, its allegiance was to a doctrine to that degree different.

What is the significance of the rationalist ascription of innate ideas, at least in the dominant version of the doctrine, to reason? And why is it that in the classification of our ideas in terms of their sources it is the contrast between reason and experience that is the primarily philosophical one? The answer to these questions is adumbrated in my introduction of this essential feature of the rationalist doctrine. If the mind's contribution in the causal process of experience introduces a subjective element into our ideas, we need to be assured that any further contribution will not have the same effect. If ideas can be innate at all, it is, I suppose, in principle possible for any idea to be innate. We might, for instance, be born with the idea that we are more important than anybody else, particularly than anybody else who has a different coloured skin or who lives far away on the other side of the world; or we might have an inborn tendency to think inductively, or to suppose that God must be like us, or like our father; or we might have an innate idea of causality as involving constraint, or of nature as 'red in tooth and claw'. But not any old idea, however innate, will serve the purpose of rationalism. As an epistemological theory rationalism is trying to show how our knowledge of reality is possible: the innate ideas alleged to be involved in this knowledge, therefore, must not be defective by being false or meaningless or incoherent; otherwise the 'knowledge' they contribute to would not be knowledge, but only opinion, or belief, or nonsense. Since, in the dominant doctrine, these ideas cannot be derived from experience, their acceptability is understood in terms of their having their source in the faculty of reason; for to ascribe an idea to reason is to imply that it is justified, as meaningful, or true, or both. Other innate ideas, if any, will be of interest to psychology and to any discipline studying the mind in general. But rationalism is a theory of the mind only to the extent, whatever that is, that it is a theory of knowledge; and thus its task is to explain our knowledge only to the extent, and in the manner, that such an explanation will show our ideas to be justified. Kant makes this point by insisting that the philosopher should show not merely that we have this or that non-empirical idea but also that we have it by right, legitimately.

If the rationalist doctrine that reason contributes to our knowledge is combined with a recognition that experience is also necessary, it may seem to be indistinguishable from the version of empiricism I have already outlined: our knowledge is derived by rational inference from the data of experience. Sometimes, indeed, the debate seems to take a fairly innocuous form about whether both elements are necessary and if so which is the more important. Sometimes rationalists appear to be claiming nothing more dramatic than that reason is the ultimate arbiter, not experience, for any empirical judgement can and should be subjected to rational scrutiny: acceptance or rejection, even of empirical claims, severally or (e.g. in Descartes) as a class, can then be represented as the work of reason. Now if reason works in conjunction with experience it should be possible to isolate by analysis the principles according to which it works, the truths or ideas that constitute the contribution of pure reason independently of experience. But the claim that an idea is an idea of reason in this sense then has a fairly unexciting interpretation: it is an idea that is justifiable without appeal to experience, e.g. because its denial is not merely false but self-contradictory or unintelligible, i.e. one whose truth is guaranteed by its meaning, and is so logically necessary. Many truths have been thought to be of this kind, such as the truths of logic and pure mathematics; and acknowledging this is not incompatible with empiricism, in any reasonably sophisticated form. What empiricists have denied is (*a*) that these truths give us information about reality and (*b*) that knowledge of them is innate.

It seems clear that the fact that these truths are justifiable in this way does not imply that they are innate or are contributed by the mind itself. It does not even imply that everybody, or even anybody, has an idea of these truths: there are no doubt many theorems of pure mathematics, necessarily true and provable, that nobody has yet proved or even had any idea of. The temptation to deny these obvious remarks is the result of confusion. It may be and presumably is the case that the logical and mathematical truths we have already thought of, and which we know to be true, and perhaps even that any truths we know, of whatever sort, imply all the truths of logic and mathematics. But it does not follow that we know, or have any idea, even by implication, that all these (other) theorems are true: what is implied are other logical and mathematical truths, not other knowledge or belief, even implicit. The pattern of implication is as follows: 'Smith knows that p' implies 'p', and 'p' implies 'q'. It is a consequence of this that 'Smith knows that p' implies 'q'. But it is not a consequence that 'Smith knows that p' implies 'Smith knows, thinks, or has an idea (even implicitly) that q'. What is implicit in what we already know is not necessarily what we already implicitly know; it is what, in order to know, we may need to find out by reasoning.

We *may* need to; on the other hand, some implications of what we know are part of the meaning of what we know in such a sense that we are capable of understanding both, but we could not understand both and know the truth of the one without knowing the truth of the other. In this way, one could not know that the figure on the blackboard was a triangle without knowing that it had three sides. But one could know that it was a triangle without knowing that if one of its angles was a right angle the vertex of that angle would lie on the circumference of a circle whose centre was the mid-point of its opposite side and whose diameter was the length of that side. The difference between these two sorts of implications is as vague as the concept of understanding the meaning of something; but failure to draw the distinction is perhaps one source of the temptation to suppose that everything implied by what someone knows to be true he must also know to be true.

It might then be shown that in order to get to know or learn anything at all, whether from experience or by reasoning, we must have some knowledge, at least implicit (in the foregoing sense), that, being presupposed by the very ideas of experience and rational inquiry, cannot itself be acquired in either of these ways. This knowledge would not therefore be shown to be innate in the strong sense of being inborn (though the capacity or potentiality for later acquisition of this knowledge might in fact be inborn); but it would be innate in the weaker sense of not being learned from experience or reasoning.

But would this innate knowledge really warrant the title of 'knowledge', and would it really be rational or derived from reason? The philosopher himself may, like Kant, succeed in justifying it without appeal to experience, and so for him it will be both knowledge and rational: the rationalism of the rationalist philosophers is to a considerable extent their own rationalism, a characteristic of their philosophical method rather than a feature ascribable to the laity in their search for knowledge. For as far as the laity are concerned, what is innate are certain basic ideas which logically speaking rank as assumptions and which, being no better than assumptions, render doubtful the rest of the so-called knowledge that is built on them.

Kant's rejoinder to this Cartesian argument is to distinguish between empirical inquiries on the one hand and transcendental or philosophical ones on the other. But his way of drawing the distinction shows that the argument continued to haunt him. It may seem an odd coincidence that in our pre-philosophical inquiries we happen to make the correct assumptions, i.e. that the ideas implicit in our view of things happen to be the ones that turn out to be philosophically justifiable after all. We may explain the coincidence, and so make it seem less like a bit of astonishing luck, by attributing it to God's honesty or pre-established harmony or some other matter that eliminates the luck, if not the astonishment. Kant, properly shunning such artificial aids, argues that these ideas are correct and necessary in a strong sense, because they constitute conditions of intelligibility such that without them things would be inconceivable and the notions of knowledge, experience and reason meaningless. He cannot, however, resist the temptation of explaining how it is that this is so. Drawing on a consideration already present in the work of his predecessors, but unlike them resting his case there, he calls upon the third of the three contrasts involved in the discussion, the contrast between what is contributed by the external world and what is contributed by the mind, and explains the basic ideas as conditions of intelligibility by attributing them to the structure of the mind itself. Transcendental arguments reveal our transcendental psychology: the ideas necessarily implicit in any pre-philosophical inquiry come not from reasoning or experience but from our own mental structure. The ideas of the laity are shown to be acceptable by showing that our minds are so constituted that it would be impossible for us to conceive of things without employing these ideas.

However, the implication of this doctrine is that if our minds had a different structure what is now impossible would be possible, and our view of things would be different, and different in such a way that not both views could be correct, representing things as they really are. Apart from the fact that on Kant's own theory this alleged possibility is strictly inconceivable, the effect of this transcendental psychology is to undermine the acceptability of the doctrine as an answer to the question how the basic ideas can, from a logical point of view, be anything other than assumptions, reducing all the so-called knowledge involving them to their own logically inferior status. This question can be answered by showing that without these ideas nothing would be intelligible; it is no answer to claim that we can't help thinking in this way. Of course, if we couldn't help thinking in this way our thoughts might happen to represent rather than misrepresent things as they really are; but we could never know that they do and the possibility that they do not would remain logically open. Kant's reply to this objection is in effect to accept the point, pressing his transcendental psychology to its logical conclusion in idealism, i.e. subjectivism. By his Copernican Revolution, in which things are required to conform to our thought about them, rather than our thought to things, he rules out the possibility of our knowing things as they really are and contends that our knowledge is only ever of things as they appear to us to be. We are thus back where we started from, though not without having learned something on the way: the doctrine that some aspects of our thought about things external to the mind are contributed by the mind itself, whether innately or not, and whether they are ideas of colour or basic ideas of reason or understanding, looks like the start of a slippery slope leading to a position from which knowledge of that external reality is inexplicable.

2. CHOMSKY'S THEORY

Let us return to our earlier question: how close is the resemblance between Chomsky's theory and the classical doctrine of innate ideas? One resemblance is clear: it shows some tendency to fluctuate between a dominant and a recessive version. In identifying what is innate as ideas he moves sometimes towards the dominant doctrine that these constitute information or knowledge, and sometimes towards the recessive doctrine that these are simply an aspect of mental structure. In conformity with this latter recessive interpretation, Chomsky usually represents empiricism, and even behaviourism, as claiming not that we have no innate ideas but that we have some, that is, some innate mental structure; though in Chomsky's view not enough to account for our knowledge. However, in one combination of features Chomsky's theory is peculiar: in general he clearly does not agree with the recessive doctrine that all our ideas are innate; but on the other hand, the ideas that he contends are innate are some of them highly contingent and thus very unlike the ideas of reason alleged to be innate in the dominant doctrine. I shall argue that Chomsky fails to show that what is innate is knowledge; but that given this modification, it is its peculiar combination of the characteristics of the classical variations, a combination in which it differs from and does not resemble the classical doctrine, that constitutes one of the chief merits of Chomsky's theory and saves it from both the incoherence of the dominant version and the triviality of the recessive version.

In the Beckman Lectures, Chomsky ascribes to one of his critics, Hilary Putnam, an attitude that he finds typical of empiricism in general: namely, 'a curious distaste for the conclusion that the mind has intrinsic structure, as does every known organism or physiological system'. Of course, this distaste seems curious, not to say perverse, from that point of view from which the mind is seen in profile, as a system causally interacting with its environment: not only 'every known organism or physiological system' but everything whatsoever has intrinsic structure in the sense that in its interaction with its surroundings anything it does or that happens to it is attributable in part to its own characteristics. But, as my rational reconstruction of the historical argument has shown, there is a tension between this point of view and the requirement that if those products of the mind's interaction with its surroundings that the epistemologist is specially interested in, ideas, thoughts, impressions, experience and so on, are to be acceptable or accurate, and thus if they are to constitute knowledge, they must represent the mind's surroundings as they really are, not simply as they appear to be. Any mental structure that contributes something of itself to the shaping of these products may be an obstacle to the satisfaction of that requirement; and in this light the empiricist 'distaste' for mental structure can be seen not as 'curious' or simply perverse but as a cautious economy. Creativity is no doubt a good thing. But a reporter who invents his story is not doing his job.

How then can we think of mental structure, which is essential, in such a way that it permits an undistorted view of things? How can reality, its dumbness notwithstanding, be allowed to speak for itself? For a start, accuracy of representation must not be confused with total similarity between the representation and what it represents: simply as a representation, e.g. an idea or an impression, it must have characteristics that the thing or situation it represents perhaps does not and cannot have; ideas are very different from physical objects, events, states and situations, and that difference will be attributable to the nature of the mind. These necessities of representation, as we can call them, need not distort because with respect to the question of accuracy of representation they are merely formal characteristics: they do not affect the content of the representation and so do not make things appear otherwise than as they are. In this way the mind, in its interaction with its environment, will perform, by virtue of its structure, the causal function of converting its input into something different, namely ideas and knowledge; but it will effect this conversion without introducing into the content of these ideas and knowledge anything of its own structure. What the mind contributes to our ideas of reality does not itself consist of ideas of reality.

This distinction between form and content is, of course, vague, but the mind's awareness of reality has been given some shapes, both literally and figuratively, that can be seen as attempts to avoid the implication that the mind itself contributes anything of the content of knowledge in the essential features of its representations. Thus a *tabula rasa* is not without structure; its structure is such that it receives information without adding to it. The mind should be transparent to reality; like good quality window glass its structure allows the view to be transmitted unaltered, as if it were not itself there. The mind is a mirror; not a distorting mirror, but one whose structure enables it to reflect things as they really are. Whatever their other shortcomings, one of the most conspicuous defects of these models is that in economising on the mind's contribution, they are too parsimonious. What the mind represents, according to these models, it represents as it really is, without distortion or addition. But it represents far too little of reality – generally, in fact, only its visual features. Underlying this limitation is another: knowing is depicted as a kind of seeing or perceiving. In general, traditional empiricism tends to claim not only that anything we know about reality must be perceptually testable, and perhaps reducible to perceptual judgements, but also that knowing and judging are themselves reducible to perceiving or having perceptual images. In the twentieth century this latter tendency has been counteracted in particular by recognition of the importance of language and its essential role in thinking, having ideas, and knowing things. Now language is certainly contributed by the mind, and to the extent that knowledge is expressible in language our knowledge may reflect that contribution. But again, empiricists have in effect argued that this is not a substantive contribution determining the content of our knowledge. The common claim that the rules of a language are conventional can be seen in this light. Part of this claim is that the differences between languages may reflect informative and interesting differences between the minds of one linguistic group and the minds of another;

but to the extent that statements in one language are translatable into those of another, these different features do not enter into the content of anything that is said or thought. More generally, languages place no necessary restriction on what can be thought. The only essential features common to all languages are structural features of a logical kind, basic analytic principles allowing deductive inference from one assertion to another. These can be represented as truths, but in such a form they will not be truths about reality, since they give no information about reality.

Chomsky thinks that classical empiricism ascribes these deductive principles, and perhaps inductive principles, to the mind, as reflecting its innate structure, or as constituting 'analytical mechanisms or inductive principles or mechanisms of association';[1] and presumably he agrees with this ascription, his objection being that further principles or mechanisms must also be attributed to the mind as innate. What is the significance of this ascription? His general approach to his problem, and in particular that aspect of it most deeply committed to breaking down the barriers between philosophy and psychology, renders the answer ambiguous. The problem, he says, is the problem of designing an input-output device, the input being data and the output knowledge. To do this 'we first attempt to determine the nature of the output in many cases and then to determine the character of the function relating input to output . . . this is an entirely empirical matter . . . quite analogous to the problem of studying the innate principles that make it possible for a bird to acquire the knowledge that expresses itself in nest-building or in song-production'.[2] His conclusion is that the device incorporates various theories;[3] but in the course of his linguistic investigations he also notes[4] 'that we are . . . using the term "theory" . . . with a systematic ambiguity, to refer both to the child's innate predisposition to learn a language . . . and to the linguist's account of this'. This ambiguity, of course, answers to the fluctuation between the dominant and recessive doctrines on the question of what exactly is innate, knowledge or a disposition of some sort. Let us for the moment consider its effect on the idea that analytical principles are attributable to the mind as reflecting its innate structure.

Suppose somebody argues: 'If the river burst its banks, the rainfall must have been unusually heavy; and the river did burst its banks. So the rainfall must have been unusually heavy.' This is an analytically valid argument, and the principle of the inference is *modus*

---

[1] 'Recent Contributions', p. 9. [2] Ibid., pp. 2–3.
[3] Ibid., pp. 7–8. [4] *Aspects*, p. 25.

ponens: 'If *p* and if *p* then *q*, then *q*.' The validity of the argument, and the truth of the principle, are not empirical matters. Let us now consider the person who argues in that way as an input-output device, with the premises of the argument, or data, as input, and his knowledge of the conclusion as output. What can we say about the character of the function relating input to output? Consider a question that sounds more familiar: if he knows the premises and knows the conclusion on the basis of those premises, i.e. because he drew it from those premises, can we say that he knows the analytic truth that is the principle of the argument? It seems to me that this too follows, and is again not an empirical matter. He may not be able to formulate what he knows on being asked, but he would at least know it implicitly in the sense already outlined. However, it is important to notice exactly what it is that is not an empirical matter in this latter case. What is analytic is that if he knows the premises and knows the conclusion because he drew it from those premises then he knows the analytic principle of *modus ponens*. But though this is analytic, and though the principle he implicitly knows is analytic, the fact that he knows that principle is not analytic. This is an empirical fact, and its empirical content is psychological, i.e. about his mind. That he knows it tells us something about his mind: not much, but a little, since he might have been an idiot, or a babe-in-arms, or a dog, so that having a mind does not entail having the knowledge; this is knowledge a sane person has, though perhaps only implicitly, when he comes to the age of reason.

Thus to say that somebody knows a certain analytic truth tells us something about his mind; and his knowledge, one might say, being knowledge, is in his mind. But these commonplaces cannot be all that is meant by arguing that to account for the fact that people get to know things by reasoning we must regard the structure of their minds as incorporating analytic principles; whatever anyone knows, whether something analytic or empirical, the fact that he knows it tells us something about his mind, and that knowledge is of course, being knowledge, in his mind. What more, then, is being claimed? Do we not have here, lurking in an obscurity that is understandable but hardly decent, an attempt to explain how it is that someone can have knowledge that is both non-empirical and not discovered by reasoning? Let us ask: what is it that is being said to be innate and to reflect the structure of the mind – knowledge of analytic principles or the analytic principles themselves? Given that an analytic principle can be regarded as a theory, in what sense is that theory *incorporated* in the device? Traditionally it was said sometimes that knowledge of truths, and sometimes that the truths themselves, are innate; and the commonest representation of this latter view is in the metaphor of truths inscribed on the soul, the information coming literally from inside, not outside, the mind. Nothing as unhelpful as this is possible today, of course. But Kant's refinement may still be with us, though in the cruder form of the suggestion that not only synthetic *a priori* but even analytic principles reflect mental structure: it is because the mind has the structure it does have that analytic principles are true and can be known to be true innately, neither from experience nor by reasoning. If this is the doctrine, it repeats, in cruder form, Kant's monumental error. It implies that as a logical possibility our minds could have had a different structure, not simply in our not knowing these analytic principles but in our having (and knowing) different ones, such that our present principles would have been false; and this is logically impossible.

The point can be made in another and perhaps clearer way. How on earth, it might be asked, could a principle such as *modus ponens* reflect or be a principle of mental structure? There are, for example, principles of atomic structure or of anatomic structure, and we could say that atoms and bodies are, or are modelled by, devices that incorporate these principles or theories: and this would presumably mean not that atoms or our bodies know these principles or theories, but that we know them and that these principles accurately describe, and perhaps explain and predict, the structure of atoms and bodies; so that (the structure of) atoms and bodies could be said to conform to these theories. Now the principle that if p and if p then q, then q clearly does not have that relation to minds and mental structure: if it describes, explains, or predicts anything at all, it is not upon minds in particular that it bears in these ways. However, this principle has a form that does relate it in a special fashion to minds, its form, namely, as a principle of derivability or deducibility: from the fact that p and if p then q, it is deducible (or inferable) that q. Deducing, inferring, drawing conclusions, arguing, and so on, are things that people do (in a broad sense of the word 'do'); and the fact that somebody draws a conclusion tells us in particular something about his mind, i.e. 'deduce', 'infer', 'conclude', etc., are psychological verbs. Thus, as atoms and bodies can conform to principles of atomic and anatomic structure, so also people's minds, in the inferences and deductions they make, in a word, in their reasoning, can conform to analytic principles; and just as atoms or bodies can conform to, without knowing, the principles that the physicists or anatomists know, so laymen in their reasoning can conform to, without knowing, at least explicitly, the principles that the logicians know. Analytic principles might then seem to reflect, or be principles of, mental structure in a way analogous to that in which atomic or anatomic principles or theories reflect, or are principles of, atomic or anatomic structure; and minds could be said to incorporate analytic principles as atoms and bodies could be said to incorporate atomic and anatomic theories. If we design a model of an atom, a body, or a mind, the sense in which the appropriate theories are incorporated will seem even stronger: the model is designed consciously to conform to those theories, so that the theories themselves are more or less literally built into the model, a situation we might illustrate metaphorically by saying that the theories are inscribed in that device.

I do not know whether this analogy is at work in Chomsky's thinking on the subject, but it is almost certainly present in some of the traditional versions of the doctrine of innate ideas. It is in any case indefensible. In neither of its possible forms does an analytic principle describe, explain, or predict the structure of our minds or the course of our reasoning. In that form in which it does relate specially to our minds its bearing on them is not descriptive, explanatory or predictive, but normative: *modus ponens*, for example, says that from the fact that p and if p then q, it may legitimately or correctly be deduced or inferred that q. Sometimes our reasoning conforms to principles of this kind, sometimes it does not, sometimes it contravenes such principles. Of course, our reasoning cannot both contravene these principles and have knowledge as its output; and our knowledge is sometimes the output of such reasoning. Concentrating on this normative form of analytic principles, we may suppose that as norms in general are simply conventions we are as free to vary these rules of reasoning as we are to vary the rules of tiddlywinks. The doctrine that these are principles of deep psychological structure quite properly rejects this conventionalism; but on the wrong grounds. For though it implies that we are not free to vary the rules, it does so for this reason, that it is psychologically impossible for us to do so. But this in its turn implies that it is at least logically possible, given a different psychological structure, that these norms should have been different, and therefore that their non-normative versions should have been false; and this is logically impossible.

The general conclusion to be drawn from these considerations reveals a reversal of the normal roles of dominant and recessive features in the doctrine of innate ideas. In the case of simple analytic principles of inference, the dominant doctrine that what is innate is our *knowledge* of them, in the sense outlined, is unobjectionable and unexciting; the doctrine that the innateness of our knowledge is due to the innateness of the principles themselves, as reflecting or being principles of our psychological *structure*, is adventurous but incoherent. This incoherence is the effect of taking up the point of view from which the mind appears in profile, as an input-output system, and consequently treating the conceptual apparatus of the recessive doctrine as providing an explanatory framework for the phenomena of the dominant doctrine.

The version of empiricism I have outlined finds a place for deductive inference but not for induction. Radical empiricism rejects induction as a valid kind of argument, and if Chomsky is right this type of empiricism would be even less capable of accounting for our knowledge than a type admitting induction. Significantly, this does not prohibit radical empiricism from allowing either innate ideas, even an innate idea of induction, or ideas actively created by the mind. Hume argues that though induction cannot be justified as valid, we have a natural and perhaps innate tendency to think inductively. Popper sees the rejection of induction precisely as freeing the mind, and enabling us to conceive of it as free, for that creative activity in the invention of its own ideas that is supposed to be denied by classical empiricism and affirmed by rationalism. There is no paradox here, only the characteristic empiricist drive towards scepticism. For Hume, our belief in induction is simply a belief, not knowledge, and inductive arguments lead to belief, not knowledge. For Popper, the ideas the mind creates do not amount to knowledge but only hypotheses or conjectures; and even under stringent empirical tests, however firmly we may come to believe them, they still fall short of knowledge.

In view of this, can considerations of the sort Chomsky adduces be regarded as a refutation, and an empirical one, of empiricism itself? It may be true, as he claims, that these empiricist theories cannot account for our knowledge: the character of the function they assign to the input-output device, i.e. the intrinsic structure they attribute to the mind, is not sufficient to show that the knowledge we have would result as the output. Now that this is so seems to be a matter of logic rather than an empirical matter; though the topic is the 'psychological' topic of what characteristics we need to attribute to the person's mind if, given that he has some data as his input of knowledge, he is to derive other knowledge as output from it, the failure of empiricism in this respect seems to be its failure to meet a certain logical requirement, namely that what he knows as output, the content of his consequential knowledge, should follow from what he knows as input, the content of the data, in accordance with whatever principles are ascribed to his mind; this seems to mean that the data we have do not entail what we consequentially know. The failure of empiricism even with induction would consist in the logical fact that this principle is still not logically sufficient to generate what we consequentially know from the data.

Objections of this logical type to empiricism are of course well known, to empiricists as well as to their critics. Do they amount to refutation? The typical empiricist reaction, as Hume and Popper illustrate, has been towards scepticism; it tends to deny that the output of 'knowledge' really is knowledge, and argues that our claims to such knowledge are not justified; the most that we can claim is probable belief, and perhaps no more than a degree of conviction without even benefit of probability. Now it may be and probably is the case that empiricism is wrong about this. Many contemporary philosophers would argue that empiricism is wrong about the data we have, and in particular that it cannot be as meagre and fragmentary as the sense-data or sense-impressions of classical empiricism, or as homogeneous as the purely physical data of behaviourism. Many would argue that empiricism is wrong about what knowledge is, and in particular that it sets impossibly high standards for its attainment. But whether right or wrong, sceptical empiricism rejects the very problem as Chomsky poses it, with output knowledge of this or that kind treated as a datum, and philosophers in general, whether empiricists or their critics, at least reserve the right, as these arguments show, to question the terms in which that problem is set up. We should perhaps, in a Kantian spirit, not protecting the specialism of our own trade union but simply distinguishing one topic from another, treat the philosophical discussion as transcendental and Chomsky's as empirical: as an empirical scientist he is fully entitled to employ concepts like that of knowledge in their ordinary and scientific ways, while the philosophical task is to analyse such concepts and show how, if at all, they are justified. To the extent that this Kantian approach assumes that concepts in ordinary and scientific employment cannot be repudiated by philosophical considerations, sceptical empiricism is already rejected. But the argument for rejection takes place on ground that Chomsky's problem presupposes: ground that the empiricist forces us onto, by accepting the substance of Chomsky's criticism, but as an objection to our claims to knowledge in general, not to empiricism itself.

If we allow knowledge of certain basic analytic principles to be innate in the sense already outlined, but reject the idea that this innateness is to be understood in terms of the way these principles reflect psychological structure, how, it might be asked, is such knowledge to be explained, when it is of truths that are neither empirical nor discovered by reasoning? A modern empiricist answer might be that this knowledge is implicitly acquired in the process of learning to think and reason, and that this is implicit in the process of learning a language. In learning the meanings of words we in effect learn certain simple analytic truths; for these truths are simple in this way, that knowing them to be true is a necessary condition of understanding their meaning. Empiricists have commonly regarded this account as a reduction and deflationary, i.e. as showing that the admission that some knowledge is innate commits us to nothing more extraordinary than admitting that we learn a language. Innate ideas, which seemed to be strange potentates ruling from the mind's mysterious hinterland, are revealed as intimate acquaintances of even the most ordinary chaps. Here Chomsky appears and reopens the debate at the very moment of the empiricist triumph. How extraordinary is learning a language? What exactly does it involve? What explanation can we give of how we learn a language? Far from getting rid of innate ideas, in the sense of unmasking their old familiar faces, learning a language, he claims, positively requires these powers, powers innate yet exotic, and certainly unsuspected. For what we know when we know a language has such a rich and complex structure that the data we are exposed to in learning a language would be logically inadequate to generate that knowledge without the aid of strong innate principles.

It is in being part of a theory of language learning that Chomsky's doctrine of innate ideas is most decisively distinguished from the rationalist doctrine he claims to inherit. The distinction has two connected aspects, and both are related to the fact that the classical doctrine, in its chief exponents, Plato, Descartes, and Leibniz, has no particular connection with linguistics. Descartes certainly says things about language that resemble parts of Chomsky's account, but as Chomsky himself reveals in *Cartesian Linguistics*, these occur in Descartes's arguments about the differences, and in particular the evidence of the differences, between mind and matter, and thus between human beings and machines (including animals); for Descartes at any rate, there is no step from Cartesian linguistics to the doctrine of innate ideas. The first difference, then, is that the classical doctrine represents innate ideas as ideas of or about not language but some reality independent of language or any other human artifact: things eternal and immutable, or God, mind and matter, or principles of inference. The second difference is that, as I have already pointed out, the classical theory, if it is to support the distinctive doctrine of rationalism, needs to attribute innate ideas not to the mind in general, or to the language faculty in particular, but to the reason. It is not enough to show simply that these ideas are not derived from experience. Thus the ideas identified as innate by the dominant doctrine, whether eternal and immutable ideas, or clear and distinct ones, or principles of inference, reveal their identity not simply by being not derived from experience but by being in some sense logically or rationally necessary: their denial may be self-contradictory, or unintelligible, or they may be necessary if any knowledge, or any rational knowledge, is to be logically possible at all. Chomsky's claim, however, is that our innate ideas at least include some that are contingent. As he has repeatedly emphasised, the universal grammar that reflects our innate language capacity is a rich and articulated structure, and the class of possible grammars that it defines is not the class of grammars that are merely logically possible in the sense of being self-consistent or intelligible. It is not even the class of grammars that are necessary from a utilitarian point of view for organisms of about our size and mobility, and with our interests and aims: the grammatical form that a language must have is not simply the form that it must have in order to function efficiently as a medium of human communication. The constraints are much more severe, and are imposed by necessities of a general biological or psychological kind.

This feature, constituting the second difference between Chomsky's theory and the dominant doctrine distinctive of rationalism, is regarded by Chomsky himself as one of the most interesting and important characteristics of his account; and it is easy to see why. It means that the universal grammar, and the psychological theory alleging that this grammar reflects our innate mental structure, have high information content and are far from degenerating into the vacuousness that traditionally threatens such claims.

The gap that this aspect opens up between Chomsky's theory and rationalism is evident from the fact that this is one important respect in which Chomsky's views link up with the theories of biologists about innate and instinctive tendencies and capacities in animals. I have quoted his reference to nest-building and song-production among birds, and he more than once places his views in this general context.[1] This seems unexalted company for the innate ideas of rationalism. But part of Chomsky's point is presumably that just as a bird has an innate tendency or capacity to sing a highly specific kind of song, so that a thrush hatched and reared in isolation from other thrushes will nevertheless sing the song characteristic of its species, so all natural languages exhibit specific uniformities

[1] See also E. H. Lenneberg, 'The Capacity for Language Acquisition', in *The Structure of Language*, ed. Fodor and Katz (New York, 1964).

that reflect the innate contribution of each child to the language-learning situation. It is perfectly possible to conceive of and construct a language lacking these features: the artificial language of Russellian logic, for instance, has a phrase-structure grammar that is uncharacteristic of natural languages. Such a language would be very difficult or even impossible for a child to learn as a first language, because its grammar would not answer to those innate species-specific mental capacities that enable the child to master any natural grammar with such ease and on the basis of such formally inadequate evidence. But in principle, at any rate, anything that could be said in a natural language could be said in an artificial language: the innate contribution is to our knowledge of the language and not to the content of our knowledge of any non-linguistic reality.

Put in this way, and in the context of biological theories about innate or instinctive tendencies and capacities in animals, Chomsky's theory is a plausible, illuminating, and informative hypothesis; but it is a hypothesis about innate tendencies, or capacities, or mental structure, or even, if you will, about innate information in some technical sense such as the word may have in, say, information theory. This is not sufficient to show that what is innate is knowledge. Chomsky talks of both innate knowledge and innate structure indifferently. But the difference is important if the theory is a theory of innate ideas that is to be essentially incompatible with empiricism. We can see this if we consider Hume's treatment of induction. Hume in effect agrees with Chomsky that in order to account for the output we must ascribe principles of induction to people; and there seems no reason why, as an empiricist, he should not allow other innate principles of 'human nature' to be similarly attributable. What his empiricism forbids him to allow is that such principles should be innately known to be true; they are at most beliefs, and the output also, therefore, is belief, not knowledge. To the extent that Chomsky treats his ascription of these principles as a matter of psychology, interpreting it in terms of some general psychological concept such as mental structure, his position on this matter differs from Hume's only in degree, that is, only on the question of how many and what principles are needed to account for the output. To distinguish his doctrine from empiricism, Chomsky must show that what is innate is not simply some disposition or capacity, nor, more specifically, mental structure, and not even, more specifically still, Hume's natural beliefs, but knowledge. We have here, from dispositions or capacities at one extreme, to knowledge at the other, an order of attribution of ascending logical strength: that is, these concepts are ordered by conditions of increasing stringency governing their application. Birds no doubt have a disposition to sing or build nests in a specific way, and this disposition is perhaps innate: Chomsky's reference to this disposition as expressing knowledge seems venturesome, not to say reckless. Where the disposition or capacity involved is a mental one it may reach the level of being a belief but still, as Hume maintains, fall short of rational or justified belief, and shorter still of knowledge.

Empirical concepts in general are inexact or vague by comparison with the idealised concepts of pure logic or mathematics; and among empirical concepts those that are psychological or partly psychological tend to be vaguer than most. This means that though there are clear central cases that are paradigms for the application of the concepts, and clear central cases to which the concepts paradigmatically do not apply, between these two areas of clarity their application is more or less faltering and uncertain. Typically, correct application is determined by a range of criteria, and in the area of uncertainty some of these criteria are fulfilled and some are not. With psychological concepts this situation is radically complicated by the problem of other minds, i.e. by the asymmetry between first-person and second- and third-person uses of psychological words. These second- and third-person uses seem like second- and third-class uses, since they require as criteria behavioural, and in general observable, characteristics that seem logically less than adequate. When these second and third persons are, so to speak, not persons at all, but dogs, birds, or fish, whose behaviour may fulfil some of the criteria but does not include their use of these words, in the first or any other person, we have what we might call an essentially disputable area of application. When someone is able to use and understand words and so make statements, the concepts of belief and knowledge become clearly applicable, because what a person believes or knows can be identified as what he says. But for what he says to be something that he knows, more stringent conditions must be fulfilled than for it to be something that he believes.

What are these more stringent conditions? Let us consider a clear central case of knowledge that is not of some directly observed fact. If someone claims to know that it will snow tomorrow, what distinguishes this from a claim merely to believe that it will snow tomorrow? First, it must be true that it will snow tomorrow. Second, he must not only believe but believe with that degree of conviction that amounts to being sure or certain. Third, his certainty must be justified not simply by its being true that it will snow, nor even by there being good reasons for thinking that it will snow, but by his having good reasons for being certain – reasons good enough, that is, to exclude reasonable doubt that it will snow tomorrow. Fulfilment of these conditions would make this a paradigm case of knowledge.

If we had any innate knowledge it would necessarily fail this third condition, for this condition entails that the knowledge in this paradigm case is learned or discovered or inferred. The failure, moreover, would be total: the claim to knowledge would not just be inadequately supported, it would not be supported at all. But if what is alleged to be innately known were something so basic or rudimentary that it was from a logical point of view unnecessary for it to be justified, because, for example, it was involved in the very notion of justification, or because it could not be understood without its truth being accepted, this third condition would be inapplicable. The innate ideas of the dominant doctrine distinctive of rationalism are of this sort. Chomsky's universal grammar is not. The very contingency of its principles, which is one of its chief merits as grammar and which gives the associated psychological theory its informative content, is, in combination with their generality, an obstacle to its being both innate and knowledge; for since it leaves open as logically possible other forms of grammar, a claim that this was known to be the form of all natural grammars could hardly be justified in the absence of any considerations ruling out, as at least unlikely, some of the other logically possible candidates. The linguist may rule these out, by appealing to the evidence. The child learning the language cannot, and if he could, his knowledge would not be innate. For him, other logically possible grammars are ruled out not logically, by relevant considerations, but psychologically. He can't help thinking as he does. The conclusion he comes to happens to be right, but from a logical point of view he has jumped to it. What is innate is from this point of view not knowledge but prejudice.

There is, of course, a good explanation in Chomsky's theory of how it comes about that the child happens to be right. It is not sheer luck or coincidence or a matter of God's grace or pre-established harmony. For the cunning of Chomsky's theory, by comparison with the classical doctrine, is that his innate ideas are ideas about language, which is a human product; and it is therefore plausible to suppose that the structure of this product will have features reflecting aspects of the human mind that are characteristic of the species, and that other human minds, having these characteristics, will in the learning situation automatically, from tenuous data, reconstruct the language according to the same model. Because the language that provides the input to Chomsky's language acquisition device is itself the output of language production devices there is a pre-established harmony, of an entirely natural and plausible kind, that explains how the learner's reconstruction inevitably tends to match the original. However, this explanation is not available to the child as a consideration justifying his confidence, and if it were that confidence would simply be a part of the child's evidence, not innate knowledge.

This objection faces us with the typical threat of scepticism. If the language-learning situation is this, that on the basis of inadequate data we jump to a conclusion in accordance with our innate prejudice, how can the conclusion be said to be known? Yet surely scepticism at this point is ludicrously academic? If we know anything, we know our language. It seems to me that so far as Chomsky has any argument for the strong claim that what is innate is not merely mental structure, and not merely Humean natural belief, but knowledge, it is this: that anything less would not account for the fact that the output of the language-learning situation is itself knowledge. In other words, Chomsky shares an important area of common ground with sceptical empiricism. Empiricism establishes sceptical conclusions by arguing in accordance with the following principle: if someone knows that something is the case on the basis of, or in consequence of, certain evidence or data, it follows that he must already know, explicitly or implicitly, whatever else (if anything) is necessary for what he consequentially knows to be logically derivable from what he already knows in conjunction with the data. Since the evidence is inadequate, he must know some suppressed major premise from which, in conjunction with the evidence, his consequential knowledge logically follows. Chomsky's input-output version of this is: if someone knows that something is the case on the basis of, or in consequence of, certain facts as input, we must, to explain that output of knowledge in terms of that input, ascribe to the person himself principles that are necessary to generate logically that output from that input. So far as there is any argument in Chomsky for the specific claim that what is innate is knowledge, rather than for the general claim that what is innate is psychological structure, it seems to depend on identifying his principle with the empiricist principle. Hume, doubting that we can have the innate knowledge required, uses the principle to throw doubt on our claims to consequential knowledge. Chomsky, taking our consequential knowledge as a datum, in effect seems to use the principle to show that we must have the required innate knowledge.

The weakness of this procedure is twofold: this condition on knowledge is too stringent even in normal cases; and the situation of the child learning his first language is anyway far from being a normal case of the acquisition of knowledge.

On this first matter, it is odd, on the face of it, that Chomsky should insist on such stringent conditions for consequential knowledge and allow such lax conditions for innate knowledge: to know a language a child needs not only the data but also knowledge of the general form of any human grammar; but he can apparently know the general form of any human grammar without so much as a scrap of evidence. Hume at least was consistent on this point. However, given his principle and a refusal to doubt commonplace claims to knowledge, the stringency and laxness of Chomsky's conditions on knowledge can be seen clearly as two sides of the same coin. If we try to account for knowledge by tightening up the standards to an almost impossible pitch in one place, we shall have to relax them beyond reason in another: as in other contexts, the price of a Puritanical exterior is an interior where anything goes.

It might be objected that my paradigm example of knowledge, though setting standards less stringent than Chomsky's for consequential knowledge, is still too rigorous to model the child's acquisition of knowledge of the language. The answer to this is that the example is, and was presented as, one central case of knowledge; there is no implication that its conditions are necessary for all cases. One good reason for not treating the child's acquisition of language as a central case of this sort is that until the process of acquisition has gone far enough to give the child a fair mastery of the language, he occupies, with the birds, bees and fishes, that area where the application of the concepts of belief and knowledge is essentially disputable. Even more disputable are the concepts of reasoning and inferring involved in my paradigm example. Positively inapplicable are the concepts in terms of which Chomsky models the child's acquisition of language — the concepts of forming hypotheses about linguistic structure and testing them against the evidence. Chomsky is, of course, fully aware that this picture of the child as a scientific genius is only a formal reconstruction of the language-learning situation. But it is only in the context of this picture that Chomsky's input-output principle can be plausibly identified with its counterpart in sceptical empiricism, the input represented as data or evidence, the process represented as the forming and testing of hypotheses against the evidence, and the consequential knowledge of the language represented as inferred from, or logically based on, the data, which then become the child's reasons justifying his claim to know the language. It is only in this context that the child's innate contribution can with any plausibility be identified as knowledge: the concept of knowledge here is part of the formal reconstruction, not literally applicable.

For the child to be correctly and literally described as knowing the language we do not need to interpret the picture literally. But as we relax the third condition in my paradigm, the condition requiring that the person to whom knowledge is ascribed should have reasons justifying his assurance, the application of the concept demands, in compensation, more stringent conditions of other kinds. The first condition, or some analogue, is tightened up, and we require not simply that the person concerned should believe what is true, or more generally get something right, on one occasion, but that he should continue to get things of that same sort right on other occasions: one and the same skill or competence is then attributed to him as being exercised on these different occasions, i.e. his getting these things right is an exercise of knowledge. The claim that this is knowledge is further strengthened precisely if the causal or quasi-causal explanation of how this competence was acquired appeals to facts that, if they were attributable to the person concerned as his reasons justifying the claim to knowledge, would logically support that claim. In this way, for example, a woman may be said to know intuitively or instinctively that her husband is worried or anxious. The force of these adverbs 'intuitively' and 'instinctively' is to imply on the one hand that the worry or anxiety were not directly observed in any publicly checkable sense, and on the other hand that she did not reason it out, come to the conclusion, or infer, that her husband was worried or anxious. We ascribe to her an intuition or instinct for things of this sort if she tends to be right about them on different occasions; and this 'faculty of knowledge' can be explained, and confirmed as knowledge, if on this occasion, for instance, she thought that her husband was worried or anxious because of the way he looked at her or because of the set of his shoulders as he walked or sat. The word 'because' here introduces a fact that is neither simply an explanatory cause of her thinking that he was worried or anxious, nor her reason for thinking that he was worried or anxious. But in being a fact that would have been her reason, and in her circumstances of close acquaintance a good one, if she had not only noticed it but had drawn her conclusion from it, the fact, in explaining her thought, also helps to justify it as knowledge. This is not a central case of knowledge, but it is sufficiently like a central case to make the application of the concept reasonable.

The same is true, it seems to me, of the child's knowledge of the language. The chief criterion for the application of the concept of knowledge in this case is the fact that the child is able to use words correctly, i.e. that he can get things right in a variety of situations. Support for this application of the concept is provided by the further fact that the child has been taught the use of words, i.e. that he has been exposed to the input data, and that these data constitute positive evidence that he could, if he were a scientist, cite in justification of his claim to knowledge. If this evidence is not only not evidence to him, in the sense in which he literally uses it to test hypotheses, but is moreover from the point of view of a formal reconstruction logically inadequate to generate what he consequentially knows, an explanation of the child's competence that links input to output through a mental structure that the child shares with all other language users will confirm rather than undermine the characterisation of the output as knowledge; for it will confirm the important practical implication of this characterisation, that the child's ability to use words correctly was not just a fluke but will survive in unforeseen circumstances in the future. This will not be a central case of knowledge; but in fulfilling these laxer conditions, which are, so to speak, natural analogues of the stricter logical conditions, it will be considerably closer to the centre than Chomsky's alternative of innate knowledge.

2

PERCEPTUAL CONSCIOUSNESS

John W. Yolton

IN his contribution to *Human Senses and Perception*,[1] R. J. Hirst has made a number of important suggestions about perceptual consciousness. (i) He has emphasised the need to describe 'what the percipient is or may be conscious of' from the percipient's own point of view (p. 294). This mode of description is contrasted with stimulus or neurological description. Perceptual consciousness of one object is distinguished from perceptual consciousness of another object 'only by or on the evidence of, the person concerned' (p. 295). The method of obtaining descriptions of perceptual consciousness is either to question a percipient or to reflect on our own experience. (ii) The second important point stressed by Hirst is that the end product of perceiving is 'the conscious experience of external objects' (p. 303). Such an obvious point is often lost sight of in behavioural, dispositional, or neurophysiological analyses. (iii) The third and final suggestion made by Hirst to which I want to call attention is the usefulness of a genetic hypothesis to explain and account for perceptual consciousness. Hirst feels that perceptual consciousness is 'unanalysable at the conscious level', meaning (*a*) that it is 'a unitary awareness of objects or scenes' and (*b*) that the 'various interacting unconscious activities' which coexist with awareness 'cannot be brought forward into consciousness' (p. 305). The various analytical theories of perception (e.g. the traditional empiricist, the sense-datum) have been designed to break perceptual consciousness into its components. This has resulted in their being false to perceptual consciousness. A genetic explanation of awareness has several advantages, prime among them being its ability to explain the complexity and development of awareness.

[1] By G. M. Wyburn, R. W. Pickford, and R. J. Hirst (Edinburgh and London, 1964).

A major difference between analytic and genetic accounts of perceptual consciousness is that psychological data and theory are usually irrelevant to the former but of great use to the latter. Philosophers of perception are too prone to ignore psychological data and theory. I do not want to become involved here in the question of how, if at all, philosophy is related to psychology in the analysis of consciousness. I do not know whether such analyses as do use the contributions of psychology can be said to be empirical, whether the philosopher treating of mental events is describing facts any more or any less closely than the psychologist. That the philosopher concerned with perception and knowledge should not always limit his analysis to logical, conceptual, or justificatory questions but should sometimes find factual studies relevant to his analysis, may not be a popular notion among philosophers. Nevertheless, there have been philosophers who thought it wrong to separate conceptual from factual questions, who have looked to the sciences for suggestions and support. Psychology of learning can be usefully relevant to philosophy of knowledge. One might easily come to see the relevance of some psychological data and theory simply by noting that human perception and awareness is a learned and developmental phenomenon. The development of awareness can hardly be examined or fitted into philosophical systems without some attention to learning theories and genetic psychology.

One can think easily of psychologists who have been aware of the relation between psychology and philosophy: Piaget's genetic epistemology arising out of his studies of children; Merleau-Ponty's application of psychology to a philosophy of man and perception; phenomenological psychologists (Buytendijk in Holland is a leading figure) whose descriptions have frequently presupposed certain philosophical questions and issues.[1] Hirst also gives an interesting construction of some of the probable preconscious factors behind and concomitant with perceptual awareness. But, curiously, Hirst insists that these unconscious factors are brain activities, not psychic or mental events (pp. 305, 310), even though he talks of these activities as being sensory and interpretative. I find this point in Hirst curious, since he has been so insistent upon what I take to be a very important recognition, that perceptual consciousness is *conscious*. However, Hirst wants to work within an identity theory where neural activity and perceptual awareness are two aspects of one process. He stresses the differences between first- and third-person perspectives but also holds out the usual identity theorist's hope of the third-person

---

[1] I have examined these and other psychologically oriented accounts of perception in *Thinking and Perceiving* (La Salle, Ill., 1962).

perspective eventually replacing any need of relying upon the first. I do not want to debate the identity theory, though I should simply say at the outset that I consider the propositions which I have cited from Hirst count against any claim that perceptual consciousness *is* brain activity. Hirst does not, I think, subscribe to such a simple identity claim. He recognises that reductionism can at best reveal the *brain-correlates to* sentience, not sentience itself (p. 311), yet he prefers to talk about brain activity in sensory and awareness terms. He even goes out of his way to say that 'the eyes and brain in themselves cannot see or get views of anything, only the person can do this' (p. 311). In part, from the fact that awareness cannot be analysed or broken down *by* awareness, Hirst seems to conclude that we cannot postulate conscious processes not discovered *in* awareness. His goal seems to be to find a way of talking about a scale of perceptual consciousness from *pure sentience*, which is a reduced perception (p. 314), though *literal perception*, to various forms of *enriched perception* where the 'resultant contents of consciousness may differ widely from the object or scene present to the senses' (p. 314). I think Hirst's talk of sensory activity of the brain attempts to capture pure sentience. Pure sentience is not available in awareness and hence has to be reconstructed.[1]

The features of perceptual consciousness which I want to stress can be summarised by saying that perceptual consciousness is mental and that it has unconscious antecedents. I want to suggest that there are reasons for thinking of some of those unconscious or preconscious antecedents as already being mental, that Hirst's reduced perception of pure sentience is a form of awareness. There are some distinct advantages to accepting such a reconstruction since, if the unconscious antecedents were only physical and neural, we would still be confronted with the usual problem of how consciousness can emerge from the non-conscious or non-mental. If some of the unconscious antecedents of perceptual consciousness are themselves mental, we no longer have the problem of explaining the origin of awareness solely from physical processes. Understanding what it means to speak of perceptual consciousness as mental is also helpful for seeing what is misleading in the controversies over direct and indirect realism.

[1] Professor Hirst has been helpful in discussion with me in clarifying his views. It is clear that I would like to turn his recognition of the first-person perspective and of the mental features of awareness against the identity theory, while he has attempted to assimilate them to that theory. Quite apart from the question of how we interpret the three propositions in Hirst's account which I have cited, Hirst's work (both in *Human Senses* and in *The Problems of Perception*) should be warmly praised for its close association with and use of psychological data. In that way, he has made important contributions to the philosophy of perception.

I. FROM CRYPTO-CONSCIOUS PROCESSES TO SIGNIFICANT ENVIRONMENT

Conscious organisms do not, of course, fall fully conscious from the womb. Both phylogenetically and ontogenetically, the conscious members of the species arrive at consciousness by a slow process from earlier levels of response to and encounter with the environment. Starting with man in the world, the organism in its environment, the basic category is that of *encounter*, to use some pragmatic and phenomenological vocabulary. There are several varieties of encounter. (i) There are those physical encounters which happen to the organism, just as they happen to inanimate objects: things buffet one another. (ii) Add a receptive apparatus – neural and physiological – that is, make the organism alive and animate, and we pick up a new set of encounters or, better, the old set of encounters becomes registered in a new way. The first sort were registered through the behaviour of the affected objects: the stone, bumped, moves. Physical forces may still move the live organism, but these forces will be recorded in some form or other in the inside mechanism of that organism. Reaction takes place, but only after going beyond the surface of the organism, or reaction takes place at the same time as the recording. It is this record in the organism which leads eventually to avoidance action by the organism.

Now (iii) if we add to the physiological and neural apparatus another aspect of the living creature, what we call consciousness, we find another dimension of the encounters of the organism with an environment. A description of the first level of encounter would be found in physics, where the laws of motion and force are formulated and the behaviour of bodies is studied and predicted (e.g. astronomical bodies). A description of the second level of encounter would be found in physiological psychology, where the structure and operation of nerves, cells, muscles, neurons are studied, together with their effects on or correlations with behaviour. A description of the third type of encounter, that of consciousness, can be found in certain introspective psychologists (e.g. Brentano, Husserl, the Würzburg group) and in some of the recent work of phenomenological psychologists. A fundamental feature of this third level is *meaning*. In fact, perhaps encounter here – conscious encounter – *is* meaning: the response to a meaningful (i.e. interpreted) stimulus. What is meaningful is very likely a result of the second level of encounter, of what sorts of stimuli are recorded by the inside mechanism of the organism as well as the specific ways in which they are recorded.

Consciousness requires the working of the neurophysiological apparatus, but that working is a necessary, not a sufficient, condition for awareness. In those organisms which are conscious, and which record their encounters in conscious and meaningful terms, there are other factors responsible for the way these encounters are interpreted. The transformation of the neurophysiological messages into significant units is controlled by factors on the side of consciousness rather than factors on the side of neurophysiology.

The conscious level of encounter is preceded by a pre-predicative and preconscious level.[1] The pre-forming factors structuring conscious levels of experience are not all of a neurophysiological nature. The transition from level (ii) to level (iii) is probably filled in by various preconscious operations. Freud and other depth psychologists have made us aware of the role of post-neural but still preconscious forms of reactions. The messages from the encounters which lies below the threshold of consciousness have probably been readied for their conscious translation, both by neurophysiological mechanisms and by a number of diverse psychic sets or dispositions operating in any given organism's preconscious recording channels. Any account of experience must recognise the preforming role played by these preconscious processes in the conscious translations and interpretations of the earlier encounters. There are some analogues on the earlier levels to what takes place in the conscious interpretations of the stimuli. We must be cautious, however, not to be misled by these analogues into thinking that the structure and form of encounter is identical throughout the various stages and levels of development.[2]

Between the fully conscious and the neurophysiological recordings in the inside mechanism of the organism, there stand crypto-conscious processes and factors. The movement in the development of the infant organism from the earliest to the conscious levels of encounter may be gradual, but there are some striking differences. The transition from the neurophysiological level to the preconscious and conscious levels is a radical and unique transition. The common meaning to the term 'encounter' on all levels is something like (as Piaget suggests) 'assimilation of and adjustment to the environment'. But even the environment changes as we go from one level to another. We could say that there is a stable and fixed environment, what we ordinarily call the 'world of physical processes and things'. What one

---

[1] For a fruitful discussion of this level of awareness in Merleau-Ponty's analysis of perception, see Charles Taylor and Michael Kullman, 'The Pre-Objective World', in *Essays In Phenomenology*, ed. Maurice Natanson (The Hague, 1966) pp. 116–37.

[2] See my 'The Form and Structure of Experience', in *Acta Psychologica* (1963).

experiences is that world. But before we can even speak about that world, before the phrase even makes sense, we have to have made sense of our encounter. One might say that the environment of the organism is twofold: the *pre-environment*, the world within which the organism develops to consciousness, and the *significant environment*, the world we finally come to know consciously. As a result of some particular ontology, at the philosophical level of being-in-thought, we may come to relate significant to pre-environment. But in the life of the growing infant, the pre-environment plays a silent role. It is the significant environment which this organism first comes to know and to be aware of: this world is a product of awareness. It is improper or misleading to speak of an awareness *of* the significant environment. It is more proper to speak of the content or the meaning of one's awareness.

2. THE PRE-ENVIRONMENT AS THEMATISED

The development of awareness from pre-environment to significant environment is aided by many physical and neurological processes of the organism. The nervous system and the brain are important, though not the only non-conscious factors in the genesis of awareness. The sense-organs, the muscles, chemical substances like hormones, and the integration of all these, together with the impulse-carried information transmitted to the brain, are all causal factors standing behind the overt behaviour of the living organism. What animal behaviourists call 'instinct' may be a name for the integrative role of some of these non-conscious ingredients. It is difficult to correlate instinct with awareness, primarily because instinct has been studied thoroughly only in animals, but also because whatever move the human organism makes through instinct to awareness is rapid and difficult to isolate. The human organism must react to stimuli in ways similar to non-human animals, but even to discover what unconscious cues the human organism uses in its motor behaviour, e.g. in balanced walking, is very difficult. Unconscious cues might be defined as those sign stimuli not controlled by mental factors; but to discover such sign stimuli in complex motor behaviour requires the same patient experimentation as Tinbergen and Lorenz have conducted on animals. In general, just when and to what extent instinctual (and other internal physical) factors function in human behaviour is still unexplored. Whether instinct is to be thought of as entirely neurophysiological, or whether it acquires, leads to, or is influenced by some psychic (perhaps emotive) tone is also difficult to decide. The French psychologist Albert Burloud (who was much concerned during his life with the connections between psychology and philosophy) preferred to speak of *tendencies* and *sensibility* operating in a context of significance. The lived world of the organism is alive with meaning: it is 'thematised'.[1] The concepts of significance, meaning, and thematisation are not entirely clear and precise as used by Burloud (and by phenomenologists), but what he is suggesting is that the responses to stimuli by the human organism are not reflex or physiological responses entirely. There are some psychic elements involved. The thematisation is controlled by internal factors, 'sensibilité' being one of these. The 'conscience sensible' for Burloud comprises both sensation and emotion, it is 'a state of spontaneous awareness in which there is an immediate relation of subject and object' (p. 7). Such a response is that of undifferentiated awareness, what he elsewhere calls the 'infra-consciousness'.[2] The sensibility is closely linked with instinct or what Burloud calls 'tendencies'. Needs are an important determinant in the development of these tendencies of the organism. Needs are reflected in intellectual as well as physiological processes, but the essential trait of a psychological process (as opposed to a physio-logical one) is its 'thematic' character (p. 28). Thematisation takes place prior to intellectual or conscious awareness; it is what might be called the awareness of the body. 'There is a discernment of need preceding and preparing the discernment of intelligence, a discern-ment which is at work in the heart of vegetative life. Need is thus one of the two means – the other is sensation – by which the mental is articulated in the physiological' (pp. 34, 35). Burloud argues that this sensory and emotional response, embodied in fear, frustration, attention, is preconscious but still mental. There is

> the existence of an emotional thought, blind, stranger to reflection, quite anterior to intellectual thought, but nevertheless composed (as is intellectual thought) of transposable relations; abstract thought lacking concepts but having implications. Emotional thought has latent ideas which are not conceived in themselves, which do not go beyond sensible or immediate awareness, but which do not cease to enrich themselves and the feelings on which they are projected [p. 169].

[1] *Psychologie de la Sensibilité* (Paris, 1954). Translations from Burloud are my own.
[2] *De la psychologie à la philosophie* (Paris, 1950). I would urge philosophers to examine the work of Burloud. It is rich in psychological information and sensitive to philosophical issues. I would even say that the two books I have referred to here are more important for philosophers of perception and knowledge than the work of Piaget.

Recognition is a central operation in this bridge from neuro-physiological response to conscious response. Burloud insists that recognition depends on 'certain unconscious archetypes which precede the immediate organisation of perception' (p. 140). Money-Kyrle has advanced the same notion from the psychoanalytic perspective: 'The very perception of a situation involves the projection into it of a meaning derived, in part from conscious or preconscious memories of similar situations, in part from primary or near primary symbols which belong to our innate endowment'.[1] Response to primary symbols, e.g. the breast, is one of the ways in which the pre-environment is thematised. Another thematising factor introduced by psychoanalysis is that of *fantasy*.[2]

The thematisation of the organism's world is biological and psychological, the distinctively human thematisation resulting from the latter. The human organism has tendencies to think or feel in certain ways in specific situations. The suggestion of psychoanalysis is that the first psychic responses are to certain primary symbols of vital significance to the organism. 'Thus, at the beginning of post-natal life the only external sense patterns to be perceived at all may well be primary breast symbols and then only when the infant is under the influence of anxiety aroused by hunger, discomfort or some other cause.'[3] These sense patterns are perceived because they are of importance to the needs of the organism but also because the infant has already had a rudimentary mental life involving this sort of symbol, the fantasy life. The fantasy life consists of responses, on the psychic level, to the operation of stimuli upon the instinctual structures.[4] The innate patterns of the fantasy life constitute perception when they are projected into the sensory field. Objects that have never been sensorily encountered before are recognised because of

---

[1] *Man's Picture of his World* (London, 1961) pp. 83, 84.

[2] I should point out that my brief borrowings, in what follows, from psycho-analysis come from Melanie Klein and her followers. I am far from being an expert or even an informed reader in the Kleinian theory. The work and theory of this group is, however, especially relevant to perceptual consciousness because it offers us a very interesting analysis of the early stages in the child's development of awareness. I am not particularly wedded to the Kleinian analysis of the pre-conscious, but it is an interesting charting of the preconscious areas as mental and psychic. For those who find the Kleinian theory too fantastic (as many do), I would offer Burloud's analysis as more reasoned and more easily acceptable. In any event, I cite the Kleinian account as illustrative only, as one way to characterise the earliest years of infant awareness in psychic terms.

[3] Money-Kyrle, *Man's Picture of his World*, p. 47.

[4] Money-Kyrle, 'An Inconclusive Contribution to the Theory of the Death Instinct', in *New Directions in Psycho Analysis*, ed. Klein, Heimann and Money-Kyrle, p. 500.

their similarity with the objects of the innate fantasy life. Fantasy life becomes the first level of experience in the conscious or psychic sense. Fantasy is not just an image, but neither is it 'an elaborate *mise en scène* or coherent dramatisation'.[1] It would be too cognitive to speak of 'knowing' at the fantasy level; feeling is closer to the probable nature of that experience. It is intimately bound up with the total connative and emotional tone of the organism. Susan Isaacs defines fantasy as 'the mental corollary, the psychic representative, of instinct'.[2] Instinct itself is 'a borderline psychosomatic process'.[3] The fantasies of this early level of experience are part of the unconscious in adults (that to which some psychotics retreat), almost the whole of the unconscious in infants.[4] An inner world precedes and is projected onto the outer world. 'The inner world is exclusively one of *personal* relations, in which nothing is external, in the sense that everything happening in it refers to the self, to the individual in whom it is a part. It is formed solely on the basis of the individual's own urges and desires towards other persons and of his reactions to them as the objects of his desires.'[5]

Fantasy thought, like Burloud's emotional thought, is pre-verbal. This fact makes talk about it difficult without violating its pre-verbal quality. Being pre-verbal it is also non-verbal. It may be impossible for those who have not been in the psychoanalytic situation to appreciate the evidential value of the data upon which the concept of fantasy life is based. It would be misleading to say that psychoanalytic theory, in this and other respects, is merely explanatory, but just how much descriptive content it can be allowed to have is unclear. The concept of fantasy lends itself easily to the philosophy of mind, for it provides an important bridge between preconscious and conscious levels of experience. It is tempting to say that this concept has full descriptive value. But since what it purports to describe is pre-verbal and only indirectly accessible, we must be cautious. The over-intellectualisation of fantasy by a number of the writers in the volumes mentioned above (and Melanie Klein herself is the best example of this) tends to discredit the concept of fantasy as a descriptive term. Susan Isaacs is well aware of the problem encountered in the attempt to characterise in words a stage in our

[1] Joan Riviere, 'On the Genesis of Psychical Conflict in Earliest Infancy', in *Developments in Psycho Analysis*, ed. Riviere, pp. 49–50.

[2] Susan Isaacs, 'The Nature and Function of Phantasy', in *Developments*, p. 83.

[3] Ibid., p. 99.

[4] Paula Heimann, 'A Contribution to the Re-Evaluation of the Oedipus Complex – The Early Stages', in *New Directions*, p. 24.

[5] Riviere, 'The Unconscious Phantasy of an Inner World Reflected in Examples in Literature', in *New Directions*, p. 350.

mental life which is pre-verbal. She insists that what she says about the content of fantasy does not capture the original character of the fantasy.[1] Meanings, Isaacs points out, are 'far older than speech'.[2] She is careful to separate experience from our verbal description of experience. But her strongest claim for the pre-verbal nature of fantasy life is taken from hysterical conversion symptoms:

> In these familiar neurotic symptoms, ill people revert to a primitive pre-verbal language, and make use of sensations, postures, gestures, and visceral processes to express emotions and unconscious wishes or beliefs, i.e., phantasies. . . . Each detail of the symptom turns out to have a specific meaning, i.e., to express a specific phantasy.[3]

The behaviour of children in play has been one of the prime sources for the Kleinian theory, as indications of the nature of such pre-verbal experiences. But even here, the tendency is to take the verbal interpretation recovered in analysis as the correct description of the experience. It *may* be the correct description viewed from the level of language. The problem is how to characterise what the quality of the experience was when it occurred. Isaacs points out the difference between a pain felt at this early level and the later interpretation of that experience as the feeling of a 'bad' mother who has not removed the pain. 'The pain itself is positive: the "bad" mother is a positive experience undistinguished at first from the pain.'[4] Or again, 'When the infant misses its mother and behaves "as if he were never going to see her again", it does not mean that he then has discriminative notions of time, but that the pain of loss is an absolute experience, with a quality of sheer "neverness" about it. . . .'[5] The standard locutions, from which Kleinian talk of introjection and projection is derived – 'taking things in with our ears', 'devouring things with our eyes' – are, Isaacs suggests, 'conscious metaphors' representing 'unconscious psychic reality'.[6] The difficult question is how much is the interpretation of these play experiences influenced by the Kleinian theory. What seems clear – certainly tempting – is that every individual goes through a stage of psychic development which is pre-verbal and non-discursive. Moreover, these stages seem to have many close similarities to those verbalised by the Kleinian theory. The actual nature and content of the unconscious fantasies may not be capable of verbalisation, but that they do have something to do with the basic instincts, the objects of the infant's *Umwelt*, his internal feelings, psychic sets, seems warranted.

[1] 'The Nature and Function of Phantasy', p. 84.
[2] Ibid., p. 87.   [3] Ibid., p. 90.   [4] Ibid., p. 97.   [5] Ibid.   [6] Ibid., p. 109.

The more specific the attempt to indicate the psychic content of the psychoanalytic level of experience, the more prone it is to the charge of over-intellectualisation. Burloud's support for psycho-analytic factors in early experience is less encumbered with complex theory than that of the Kleinians. He guards against over-intellec-tualising the early years of the infant's psychic life. For example, he suggests that we must make room in our analysis of the infant for an immediate, conscious experience of privation and frustration. The experience of privation is that 'of a connection between a need and the event which blocks it'.[1] This connection has just as much reality as the sensations between which it holds: 'The need is itself only a felt relation . . . between a privation or a lack, manifested by internal sensations, and the object which is capable of satisfying it' (p. 165). Infant 'angoisse' is 'an organic constriction accompanied by sensations' (p. 166). For the infant to feel himself menaced by the loss of something is surely, Burloud stresses, not for him 'to think, even obscurely and confusedly, the abstract concept of danger'. Rather, 'it is to experience in one experience, correlated with each other, the one penetrating the other, a feeling of possession and a feeling of privation' (p. 166). What the Kleinians refer to as 'pro-jection' is also put by Burloud in less intellectual terms. He suggests, in line with his notion of the thematisation of experience, that the *form* of these early experiences of frustration is retained and trans-posed into new situations which resemble the early ones. Thus:

> The theme of the privation of the mother is nothing more, in origin, than the emergence into immediate awareness of a kind of abstract souvenir of experiences of frustration, their *emotional form* ready to be reanimated in other experiences of the same kind and to cause to flow again on those experiences the emotional tone with which it is charged [p. 167].

3. SIGNIFICANT ENVIRONMENT AS PERCEPTUAL CONSCIOUSNESS

There are several different sorts of events taking place in relation to the living organism, particularly in its move from the pre- to the significant environment. The significant environment emerges as a result of (*a*) the actions of certain physical events in the cells, neurons, muscles, etc., events largely of a chemical and electrical nature; (*b*) the physico-biological structure of the organism with its

---

[1] *Psychologie de la sensibilité*, p. 165.

set dispositions to respond in specific ways to specific stimuli; and (*c*) certain rudimentary psychic events – feelings, affects, fantasy, or images – which mark the earliest form of experience of the organism. The end result of these various factors is the defining of a style of life of that organism. The disposition-sets and the physiological structure of the organism, in conjunction with the external stimuli, control the reactions of the organism from the start. Very soon the psychic events begin to exert an influence on behaviour also. The organism's lived world is first the environment of effective stimuli; then it is the environment as experienced, as felt, as fantasied; later as thought and interpreted. Bodily behaviour, both overt and internal, integrate with the primitive psychic experiences to form the first significant environment.

We do not, on the theory just advanced, have to account for the origin of awareness out of purely physical processes: the mental is there from the start. Awareness in the conscious sense emerges from preconscious but mental factors. On this theory, the beginnings of awareness are internal, in the emotional and fantasy life. Features of that fantasy life are projected outward in perception. What is perceived is, in part at least, triggered by the vague psychic needs and expectations of the fantasy life. This theory is not saying that all conscious perception is anticipated by unconscious fantasy; it is useful for us primarily as a way of accounting for the emergence of awareness. In this way, it does not by-pass the question of the relation between brain activity and perceptual consciousness, but it suggests that that relation cannot be conceived as a one-to-one relation nor as a simple translation from impulse to conscious content. The total organism in its lived pre-environment has to be viewed as the antecedent to perceptual consciousness. The notion of the perceiver as mind and body *is* misleading if taken in a straightforward way. There are physical and mental features, but there are also grey areas where the two tend to merge together. The live organism is aware from the start, in some sense of 'aware' which is much less than or different from 'conscious awareness' but also other than 'responsive to stimuli'.

A number of advantages accrue to this way of viewing the early stages of perceptual consciousness. The response of the organism has always been recognised as limited by the capacity of its neurophysiological equipment: the range of stimuli is further restricted, in the beginnings at least, by basic needs and interests of the organism. These needs and interests have psychic controls as well, in the way in which the theory I have just sketched suggests. If perceptual consciousness begins with a response to the familiar (as Money-Kyrle's adaptation of Kleinian theory says, and also as, in a quite different way, H. H. Price's analysis of recognition in *Thinking and Experience* suggests), there is a problem of explaining how any feature of the environment could appear familiar for the first time. The paradox of recognition – that the first recognition is already re-cognition – is resolved by the theory I have summarised: what is perceptually recognised *is* familiar in some of its features (perhaps only in the common emotional form) because it fits or is reminiscent of ingredients of the fantasy-content. Emotional tone colours our psychic life, both at the preconscious and conscious levels.

Another advantage to the theory I have presented is that, in stressing that some of the antecedents to conscious perception are themselves mental, we are able to strengthen the important point that what phenomenologists call 'constituting a world' – the formation of the significant environment – is cognitive. This point is readily available to us simply by attending to our own experience of being aware, but it receives an added reminder from the analysis of the emergence of awareness adumbrated here.

Finally, appreciating the possibility that the consciously perceived world is anticipated and formed by prior conscious or quasi-conscious processes can help to show us what is wrong with asking whether the world as known and perceived represents the world as it is. Again, we can arrive at this conclusion by other means but there is some advantage in seeing that the world as consciously perceived (the significant environment) has been influenced by quasi-conscious processes. The rejection of direct realism (of the view that the world is exactly as I perceive it to be) has been made for various reasons – relativity of perception, illusions, time-lag between stimuli and awareness – but one can seriously ask what is being asserted or rejected in this controversy. In one very important way, this controversy is misleading. To perceive a table just is to have mental content. I use this awkward phrase 'mental content' in an attempt to avoid the misleading implications of terms like 'idea', 'sense-data', or even Hirst's much better term 'percepta'. What is misleading about this sort of term for characterising the nature of perceptual consciousness is that they easily open the door for the matching-question: do my ideas, sense-data, or percepta match or represent physical objects? If the matching-question is ever possible, it is so only at an abstract metaphysical level. It is far from clear what would be meant by asking the matching-question at the perceptual level.

Talk of ideas or sense-data leads us to think of awareness as having a special sort of objects – mental objects – which are the immediate contents of awareness, which may or may not correspond to something in the environment. I do not want to deny that one can ask ontological questions about the status of mental contents, however they may be described. What I want to suggest is that giving them an ontological status leads to viewing them as separate from, and hence as possibly misleading for, physical objects. If our awareness of physical objects is had via these immediate objects of awareness, all the traditional problems of the knowledge of body quickly arise. If, on the other hand, we see the development of awareness as also being the constituting or formation of a world of objects, it may be more difficult for us to separate awareness and object. In one sense, what could be more easy than to distinguish my perception of body from the body that I perceive? It is only one of those metaphysical moves which affirms their identity (idealism) or their radical difference (realism). In another sense, this distinction may not be possible. What I have in mind is distinguishing the *body of my perception* from the *body perceived*. That is, if what I mean by a table just is the object of my perceptual awareness, can I possibly mean or understand anything other by 'table'? Sometimes when we talk of direct and indirect realism, we are lured by an implicit concept of object which gives it a perspective of its own, in which it has properties of its own, different in kind from the properties we perceive. If direct perception of the desk is a perception which differs in all ways from perception as we know it, what would it be like, how are we to understand it? If the desk's real properties differ (or may differ) from those I am aware of when I perceive, what kind would they be? This last question might be answered by talking of microscopic or imperceptible properties. If direct realism is the perception of imperceptible qualities, then our perception is not (and of course cannot be) direct. If the real properties of the desk are perceptible properties but not the ones we do perceive, what can we say about properties that are perceptible but are not perceived?

There is a powerful truth in Berkeley's insistence that we cannot mean by sensible thing anything other than the sort of sensible contents we have in sensing and perceiving. The matching-question is legitimate when we want to determine the veracity of our perceptions, but what is being matched with our perceptual contents does not differ from those contents. My question is whether the shape, size, position, or colour are as I take them to be. When I discover that I have been deceived, I have not discovered that the object lacks shape, size, position, or colour; only that these were not quite as I took them to be. I have not, through my discovery, gone beyond my perceptual contents; that, as Berkeley argued, is something I cannot do, it would violate the very meaning I have of desk,

table, chair. I can mean or understand objects to be nothing other
than they have been constituted by me in my significant environment as being.

When we watch the learning process in children, it is tempting to
think we are witnessing objects affecting their awareness or the
infant coming to see the objects that are in the environment. We
watch the movement of his eyes, then see the smile and say 'now he
sees me', thinking that the *me* that is seen existed in the environment
prior to his seeing. The physiologist reads his machines or peers
through to the back of my eye-ball, noting the movement of muscles,
and thinks he has discovered how perception comes about. In truth,
neither our behavioural observations of the infant's reactions nor the
more sophisticated discoveries of the physiologist or oculist have
made any discovery about perception. The electrical-chemical
changes observable in the child's eyes are correlatable with light-
ray stimuli refracted and reflected from surfaces: both are physical
events. When we as perceivers observe those electrical and chemical
changes in rods and cones, note the muscle movements, measure the
angle and degree of reflection, our role as perceivers of those events
obscures from us the fact that we are, as it were, strangers from
another world (the conscious world) observing foreign (i.e. physical or
non-conscious) phenomena. The obfuscation is due as much to our
forgetting that even those phenomena we are observing lose their
physicality when perceived.

This last statement sounds too paradoxical, as if perceptual
consciousness were some rare transmuting process able to turn base
metals into gold, to transform physical processes into mental contents. There are several ways in which we can take the paradox
and mystery away, without losing sight of the truth about perceptual
consciousness. We could follow a metaphysical turn and say that the
physical-mental distinction is one drawn from within the significant
environment, that having achieved perceptual consciousness by the
ways depicted here, we then go on to extrapolate back into the pre-
environment. This way is an involved and tortuous one which may,
in the end, force us to accept the label 'idealist'. I think, however,
that there is a simple truth here. The physicality that objects lose
when perceived is some supposed condition outside the orbit of
awareness. We easily and rightly distinguish the processes in my eye
and optic nerve from the perceptual awareness the oculist has of those
processes. This is a distinction *within* the significant environment.
When the sceptic says the world may be other than it seems, may
not even be there at all, he has made the impossible move off and
beyond perception, has at least forced us to think we have some

understanding of how there might be a world other than it seems. *Our* world could not be other than it seems in the sceptic's wholesale way, since our world, the only world we can know or conceive, can only have the qualities and properties we have learned through perception. To suggest that our world might be other than it seems, is to suggest that our world might be a different world. But the world that there is *is* the world unfolded in our awareness, including the electrical, chemical, and other physical processes we find correlated with our perception. If there is any alchemy at work in perception, it is the alchemy which changes a live organism into a perceptually conscious one. What our brief foray into the preconscious area has done is to suggest that there is no *fundamental* change in the development of awareness, that the development is a refinement and extension of a common condition.

4. CONCLUSION

Stressing the conscious, mental features of perceptual consciousness has seemed to some to reinforce those idealistic metaphysicians who say that the mental cannot know the physical, that only ideas can be like ideas. How, the question runs, can that which is mental reveal the properties of the physical? My answer has been to say that perceptual consciousness is not a matter of the mental revealing the physical but rather that perceptual consciousness is our way of having a world. To call attention to the processes involved in, but antecedent to, awareness is just to reveal what is involved in the development of awareness. Similarly, to reveal the mental nature of perceptual consciousness just is to reveal the nature of seeing, perceiving, etc. To suppose a counter-example of seeing devoid of mental contents would not be to suppose seeing at all. Perceptual consciousness *is* 'the conscious experience of external objects' but the words 'of' and 'external' in this phrase do not mark an epistemic gap bridged by consciousness. We do not start with consciousness and then find objects. The emergence of consciousness and the emergence of the significant environment are one and the same. The response to meaningful stimuli on the third level of encounter marks the earliest formation of the perceptual world.

The elaboration of perceptual consciousness beyond its first emergence has been undertaken by a wide variety of philosophers and psychologists. I have endeavoured to bring those writers together in one constructed theory in my monograph, *Thinking and Perceiving*. In this paper, I have (*a*) emphasised the mental and meaning character of awareness, (*b*) indicated how the recognition of perceptual consciousness as meaning-response moves us out of and away from questions of realism and idealism, and (*c*) suggested some ways in which the early levels of perceptual consciousness might be reconstructed from specific psychological data and theory.

3

A PSYCHOLOGICAL LOOK AT SOME PROBLEMS OF PERCEPTION

B. A. Farrell

I SHALL attempt something rash in this paper. I shall draw your attention to some past and current work on perception by psychologists and others. I shall concentrate on work in vision and hearing. This outline will occupy the first part of my lecture. I shall then go on, in the second part, to suggest that this scientific work has certain philosophical implications. This whole attempt is a bit rash for obvious reasons. It is not easy to outline fairly and accurately past and current work in any branch of science. I am very liable, therefore, to do an injustice to the efforts of psychologists and others in this field. What makes matters more difficult for me is that I also have to show that this work is of philosophical interest. What has led me to embark on this perilous enterprise is a hunch I have developed in recent years. I have the hunch that philosophers who are interested in perception would do well to pay rather more attention than (perhaps) they have been wont to do in the past to the work and discourse coming out of the scientific laboratory and similar places.

I

I begin, then, with an outline of some scientific work and thought in this field.[1]

When one puts on scientific spectacles and takes a look at man's capacity to see and hear, one is constrained, in the first instance, to

---

[1] I am indebted to Messrs. N. K. Humphrey and P. E. Bryant, and to Mrs Anne Treisman for their help in the preparation of the first part of this chapter.

regard a human being, not as a mind or as a person, but as an organism. One thinks of physical energy of different sorts and properties impinging on the organism, and being absorbed and transduced in various ways by different parts of the body – parts which are built to do this job. These parts are the receptors – the eyes in the case of light energy, the ears in the case of energy from atmospheric disturbances. Now a great deal of knowledge has been accumulated over the last hundred years about the minutiae of these special parts of the body, and how they deal with the physical energy for which they are especially adapted. But it is only in recent years that we have come to understand certain essentials about the way in which the eye is built to deal with the energy coming from material things, and therefore so built as to enable us to perceive them. This understanding has been achieved as the result, in particular, of two things: (i) the exploration by various workers into animal reactions to shapes, contour contrasts, and so on; and (ii) the development of 'single unit' analysis. Let me explain this by means of an example.

Consider the already classical work of Hubel and Wiesel on the eye of the cat.[1] What they did was to record from single cells in the striate cortex of the animal. They stimulated the retina with a spot

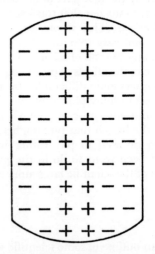

FIG. 1. *Retinal receptive field of a single unit in the cat striate cortex. This figure is based on data in Hubel and Wiesel (1962). The unit is stimulated by light falling on the area marked by plus signs, and inhibited by light falling on the area marked by minus signs.*

[1] D. H. Hubel and T. N. Wiesel, *J. Physiol.* (1962) 160.

of light, and found what points in the retina affected the firing of a particular striate cell. In this way they mapped the receptive field in the retina for a single cell in the striate cortex. They found that there were different sorts of receptive fields in the retina. One of them can be schematically depicted in the way shown in Fig. 1. Here we have the retinal field for a striate cell where the cell is fired by light falling on the area marked by plus signs, and is inhibited by light falling on the area marked by minus signs.

It seems clear that this field is adapted to deal with input from a vertical bar shape against a dark background. The cat's striate cortex also possesses retinal fields where the bright bar shape is oriented in various ways, where the bar shape is dark against a bright background, where a bright bar is set at a particular angle against a dark background, and so on. There are certain retinal units that allow for some very simple generalisation – what Hubel and Wiesel call 'complex units' (Figs. 2 and 3). There are others that

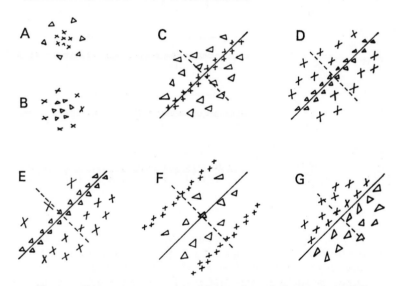

FIG. 2. *Common arrangements of lateral geniculate and cortical receptive fields. A, 'On'-centre geniculate receptive field. B, 'Off'-centre geniculate receptive field. C–G, Various arrangements of simple cortical receptive fields. X, areas giving excitatory responses ('on' responses); Δ, areas giving inhibitory responses ('off' responses). Receptive-field axes are shown by continuous lines through field centres; in the figure these are all oblique, but each arrangement occurs in all orientations.*

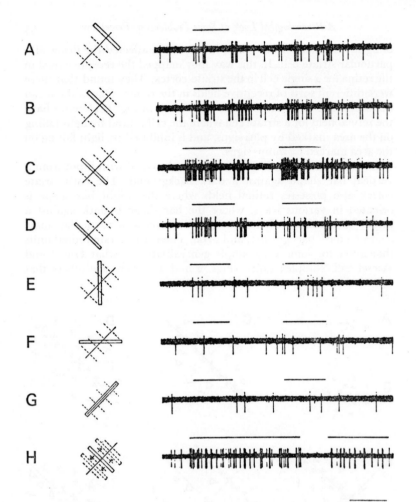

FIG. 3. *Responses of a cell with a complex field to stimulation of the left (contralateral) eye with a slit ⅛ × 2½°. Receptive field was in the area centralis and was about 2 × 3° in size. A–D, ⅛° wide slit oriented parallel to receptive-field axis. E–G, slit oriented at 45 and 90° to receptive-field axis. H, slit oriented as in A–D, is on throughout the record and is moved rapidly from side to side where indicated by upper beam. Responses from left eye slightly more marked than those from right. Time 1 sec.*

respond to a bar or edge in a particular orientation as long as it ends at a certain point – the 'hypercomplex units'.

It seems, then, that the retina is mapped by units that fire when the incoming energy has some particular feature and impinges on a particular part of the retina. The situation appears to be that the eye is built to distinguish certain features of the light energy reflected by material things in the world, and hence certain features of the things themselves (for example their edges and orientation). If we wish to be fashionable, we can say that at this first stage in the working of the visual apparatus, the energy input is processed by being analysed into certain constituent features - features that it is necessary for the organism to take account of, in order for it to make a successful adaptation to the material objects, which are the immediate source of the energy input.

But this is information about cats and also about monkeys (where similar findings have been made). What about human beings?

Salapatek and Kessen have shown that day-old babies can scan with eye movements a coloured triangle on a contrasting field. The evidence suggests that the human eye is also built so as to distinguish from the outset certain features of the light energy coming from material things – namely, features produced by corners and lines, and sharp contours separating dark and light. Bower worked on somewhat older infants – from four to nine weeks – and found that they can, and do, distinguish a number of features of the input from visual figures, for example, the orientation of lines and size. Fantz has discovered visual preferences in primates and human babies. These preferences were, for example, for three-dimensional and shaded patterns rather than flat, plain ones.[1] All this work may still be exploratory and not conclusive for one reason or another. But it is obvious that the results are very much in line with what has been discovered about the eye of the cat and the monkey. This consistency, along with the evolutionary and morphological analogy between infrahuman primates and ourselves, does suggest quite strongly at the present time that the visual systems of *both* do work in the same sort of way at the peripheral stage of processing – the stage which we have been considering.

But we cannot remain at the periphery. Thus, when a rat is presented with an inverted and uninverted triangle in a visual discrimination problem it analyses the energy input into the

[1] P. Salapatek and W. Kessen, 'Visual Scanning of Triangles by the human new-born', *J. Exp. Child Psychol.* (1966) 155–67; T. G. R. Bower, 'The Visual World of Infants', *Scientific American*, ccxv (1966) 80; R. L. Fantz, 'The Origin of Form Perception', *Scientific American*, cciv (1961) 66.

constituent features relevant for solving the problem. (See the pair in Fig. 4.) But it shows us that it has solved the problem by showing us that it has learnt to connect the input from the constituent features of the triangles to reactivity which is successful. Observe, however, that though the rat has the machinery in its receptors to deal with the input from the triangles, it may not have the machinery to deal with the input from the two bottom figures (e and f) in Fig. 4, for it cannot solve the discrimination problem posed by them.[1] In contrast, a monkey can deal with these. Indeed, comparative

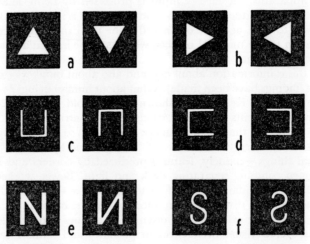

FIG. 4. *Figures used by Lashley to test for discrimination of symmetrical patterns.*

psychologists have failed to find any comparable limits to the monkey's power of visual pattern discrimination.

On the other hand, consider the oddity problem. This is the problem of choosing the odd item from an array. A monkey can distinguish vertical and horizontal lines, circles both large and small, and so on; and it is able to pick out the odd shape from an array of four (as in the left-hand figure in Fig. 5). But when presented with three verticals and a horizontal (as in the right-hand figure in Fig. 5) it cannot pick out the horizontal. This recent finding by Humphrey[2] suggests very strongly that the input in the oddity problem is dealt with, not only at the periphery, but also at a later

[1] K. S. Lashley, *J. Gen. Psychol.* (1938) 18, 123.
[2] N. K. Humphrey, *Personal Communication.*

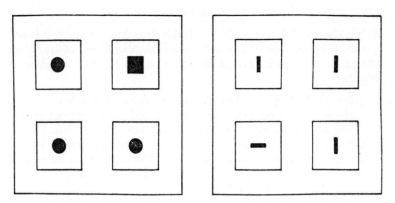

FIG. 5

stage in the transmission of the input. Whereas the monkey has the machinery at this later stage to classify the input from the shapes in a way which can then lead to successful learning, it lacks the necessary machinery to classify input from the straight lines in the same sort of way. In short, the monkey lacks the machinery to enable it to identify the horizontal as the odd one out – in some very primitive but sufficient way.

Assuming, then, that the human infant starts off life with the same sort of input analysers in the visual periphery as do infrahuman primates, what happens as he grows up? Let me pick out one feature of interest. Consider some of the reports of children's behaviour by Piaget in *The Child's Construction of Reality*. Whatever difficulties there may be about Piaget's methods of inquiry, and the tiny sample he explored, and so forth, the reports he offers us remain highly suggestive. To begin with, the child seems to exhibit *no* special behaviour in respect of material things that disappear as such. Between three and six months the child begins to grasp what he sees, and in general to co-ordinate his visual and tactile worlds. But he remains unable for some time to do the elementary thing of finding the object he wants by removing another masking object:

OBS. 25. So also Jacqueline, at 0:6 (28), opens her mouth on seeing the bottle approach. When it is near her, within reach, I hide the bottle with my hand. Jacqueline kicks in anger and impatience; it does not occur to her to remove my hand, but she stares at it with an expression of intense expectation and desire. All this occurs as though the bottle seemed to her to emanate from my hand and as though this emanation having just disappeared, she expected it to reappear.

57

When the child is able to deal with this situation, however, it is not yet able to take account of movements or displacements of the object that are visible to it. This is shown in one of Piaget's well-known reports:

> OBS. 44. At 0:9 (17), just after having discovered a box under a cushion (see OBS. 34), Laurent is placed on a sofa between a coverlet *A* on the right and a wool garment *B* on the left. I place my watch under *A*; he gently raises the coverlet, perceives part of the object, uncovers it, and grasps it. The same thing happens a second and a third time but with increasing application. I then place the watch under *B*; Laurent watches this manœuvre attentively, but at the moment the watch has disappeared under garment *B*, he turns back toward coverlet *A* and searches for the object under that screen. I again place the watch under *B*; he again searches for it under *A*. By contrast, when for the third time I again place the watch under garment *B*, Laurent, whose hand is outstretched, raises the screen at once without turning to *A*; he finds the watch immediately. I then try a fourth time to put the watch under *B*, but at the moment when Laurent has both hands in the air; he watches my gesture attentively, then turns and again searches for the watch in *A*!

> OBS. 45 . . . On the whole it may be said that, between 0:9 (17) and 0:10 (16) when the object is moved from an initial position *A* to a later position *B*, Laurent searches for it in *A* much more often than in *B*. When he searches for it in *B* it is often because the movement of prehension directed toward *B* was already made and thus is merely extended.

The next stage is reached when the child *does* take account of sequential movements of a thing, but only when these are visible. In other words, it is no longer foxed by the *A–B* problem in OBS. 44 and OBS. 45. But as soon as 'the simplest possible of invisible displacements' are introduced, the child fails:

> OBS. 55. At 1:6 (8) Jacqueline is sitting on a green rug and playing with a potato which interests her very much (it is a new object for her). She says 'po-terre' and amuses herself by putting it into an empty box and taking it out again. For several days she has been enthusiastic about this game.
>   1. I then take the potato and put it in the box while Jacqueline watches. Then I place the box under the rug and turn it upside down thus leaving the object hidden by the rug without letting the child see my manœuvre, and I bring out the empty box. I say to

Jacqueline, who has not stopped looking at the rug and who has realized that I was doing something under it: 'Give papa the potato.' She searches for the object in the box, looks at me, again looks at the box minutely, looks at the rug, etc., but it does not occur to her to raise the rug in order to find the potato underneath.

Finally, the child reaches the stage where it is able to solve this sort of problem by taking account of the invisible displacements of material things.

What does all this suggest? It suggests that the input from a material thing is processed in some hierarchical way, and that maturation and learning are necessary in order to establish the machinery for this processing. These reports about the child also suggest that we postulate that the machinery of the organism comes to classify, or (to talk Americanese) to categorise or conceptualise the input from a material thing in the Piaget situations. It does this in such a way as to give us sufficient evidence and good reason to say the following of the child: at the final stage which Piaget distinguishes here, the child can identify a visually presented thing, in some very primitive way, as permanent or independent. We must observe, however, that if Piaget's work here and elsewhere is to be accepted (see his *Play Dreams and Imitation in Childhood*), then what the child has achieved at this point is still very limited indeed. For one thing, we cannot be sure that the child has even got to the point where it can identify an individual material thing as *a particular* thing. For it is doubtful whether the child at this stage can exercise the categories (of concepts) of *a class* and *a member* of a class; and until it can do so, it cannot handle input so as to identify a thing as *a* thing.

Let us now take a quick glance at quite a different part of the whole field. Consider the topic known as auditory masking – that is, where a subject is required to hear a tone (say) when accompanied by noise. The standard task of the subject here is to decide, for example, whether a tone has been presented on any occasion or not; and, if so, whether it was, for example, a high note or a low one. In his work on this topic Treisman[1] was led to suggest that the input is handled in a hierarchical way by an analytic tree; and that at each point in the tree there was a decision device which enabled a decision to be made between, for example, tone or noise, high tone or low tone, and so on. A decision at one of these points was necessary to enable the subject to report, for example, tone or noise. Treisman went on to take a further and important step. He suggested that a

---

[1] M. Treisman, *J. Acoust. Soc. Amer.*, xxxv 8 (1963) 1256.

piece of decision machinery worked as a signal detection device, to which statistical decision theory could be applied. This suggestion enabled him to order the experimental data in an illuminating way, and to use the model of an analytic decision tree for very precise predictive purposes.

This is not the place to explain the details of statistical decision theory – even if I were competent to do so. For our purposes, the essence of it is this. The activity of the decision device is represented as falling along an axis *x*, on which axis any presented signal (signal noise, or SN), or, in the absence of a signal, noise (N), will produce a certain value *xi*. Repeated presentations of the signal would produce a certain distribution on *x*, round some mean and with a certain

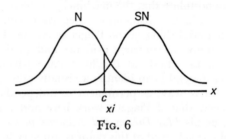

FIG. 6

distribution. Likewise for the background Noise (N). So we find ourselves with two partially overlapping curves something like those in Fig. 6. Finally, we suppose that the decision device is in a certain state in respect of inputs, such that, if the value *xi* produced by an input is *above* a certain value *c*, the input will be accepted as a signal; if *xi* is below value *c*, it will be rejected as a signal. The value of *c* is known as the criterion or cut-off point used by the decision device. Fig. 7 is a diagram of Treisman's model of this aspect of the auditory perceptual system.

Now this model is only concerned to cover simple auditory input. But much more complex material can be handled – at least in part – in the same sort of way. For example, Broadbent[1] has tried to explain what it is that accounts for the fact that we hear common words more easily than uncommon ones – what is known as 'the frequency effect'. The hypothesis he has offered recently (in contrast with his earlier view) is that the frequency effect is due to a response-bias on our part. That is to say, our decision machinery operates with a criterion placement for common/uncommon words, which favours

---

[1] D. E. Broadbent, *Psychol. Rev.*, LXXIV 1 (1967) 1; D. E. Broadbent and M. Gregory, *Nature*, CCXV (1967) 58.

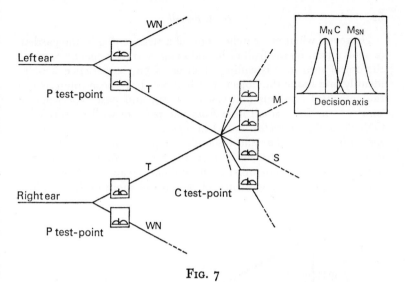

FIG. 7

(WN=white noise; T=tone; N=noise; SN=presented signal; M=masking tone; S=signal tone. In the box (top right) M_N=mean of N, M_{SN}=mean of SN. This illustration shows the hierarchy of test-points, each working as a statistical decision device with a criterion.)

letting through the common words. The frequency phenomenon is not to be explained by reference to the character of the input. Broadbent then followed this up by looking into the perception of emotionally toned words. It is well known that if, for example, a person is presented with an obscene word over a noisy telephone, he is less likely to report it correctly than if he is presented with a socially acceptable one. This fact poses an interesting problem theoretically and clinically. Can we explain it by supposing that these obscene words are like uncommon ones? That is, is it simply that there is a response-bias against them? The result of Broadbent's inquiry so far goes against this supposition. It seems that there is something in the nature of the obscene words themselves that prevents them getting through and allowing us to hear them. As Broadbent wrily remarks, it could be said that 'Freud was right after all'!

I mention this work on hearing to try to show quickly how psychologists can go in search of the *sort* of internal machinery that is involved in the later stages of processing. It is illuminating and sometimes very surprising to see how much light the careful study of behaviour can throw on what would otherwise seem to be quite inaccessible – namely the details of our internal machinery when we are alive and at work.

However, when one catches sight of a strange dog in the garden, or spots a pear on the fruit dish, and so on, and then goes on to name the object seen, one is calling upon one's past experience here to identify and name the object. Psychologists have been interested in the empirical relations between the input and past experience in 'store'. Consider a small item from one piece of work of this kind. Oldfield and Wingfield[1] looked into the latency, or delay, times in the naming of familiar and unfamiliar objects. The quickest way of getting a glimpse into this work is to present a film of the objects used, and to invite a member of the audience to act as subject. What is done is to show a sequence of pictures of more or less familiar

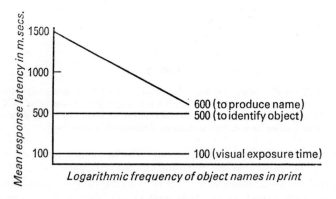

FIG. 8

objects. These are shown at two different speeds – first at the slower speed, and then (in a different order) at a faster speed. The task a subject has to perform is to name them aloud as quickly as he can. [Dr Wingfield's film was shown at this point in the lecture.] What strikes the ordinary subject in a demonstration of this kind is that he can and does identify the object before he can and does name it. He sees what it is before he can tell us. The relevant results of Wingfield's work were as follows. The object had to be exposed to the subject for approximately 100 m.secs. before he could identify it correctly. By giving the person the name of the object first before the picture, it is possible to determine the time required for him to decide whether it is this object or not. This amounted to another 400 m.secs. So it takes

[1] R. C. Oldfield and A. Wingfield, *Quart. J. Expt. Psychol.*, xvii(4) (1965) 273; A. Wingfield, 'Identification and Naming of Objects' (D.Phil. thesis, Oxford Univ.).

about 500 m.secs. (in the experimental situation) for a subject to conceptualise the visual input and so to see the object as, for example, a chair. The remainder of the time is required for him to get the name out of store and into the effectors (see Fig. 8).

But this work on perception is confined to the intact, normal organism – even though it may be functioning in odd experimental situations. As we all know, further insight into normal functioning can often be obtained by studying the pathological or abnormal organism. As an example, consider the work of Humphrey[1] on the destriate monkey. It was known that, when the striate area is ablated, monkeys seem to be blind in most of their ordinary behaviour. It was also known that under strict testing they exhibit some rudimentary visual powers (for example, they are sensitive to total luminous flux). What Humphrey did was to train a destriate monkey to find the experimenter's hand for food in any part of the field in front of his cage. He then found that, when the hand was held stationary, the monkey reached at random. But when the hand was moved, the animal reached at once in the right direction, and soon learned to reach for it accurately and promptly. Systematic testing was done with one-inch square wooden blocks and flashing lights, and the same findings were made. Then, in further testing, the surprising finding was made that the monkey would reach to a stationary sound source without previous training, and that he performed in respect of sound sources as if they were visual objects. The findings are quite striking when seen on film. [Dr Humphrey's film on these animals was shown at this point.] The problem, of course, is to explain these phenomena. One suggestion is that the monkey retains the machinery to allow him to react to certain changes of input, irrespective of whether these are visual or auditory.

It is instructive to compare these animal data with an old, clinical report on humans. Riddoch[2] examined a number of cases in World War I of visual defects due to injury of the occipital region. His first case is typical. Lieut-Col T. missed seeing pieces of meat on the left side of his plate, but in a good light could tell if an object were moved in his left half-field. When travelling by train, he could see nothing but vague movements on looking out of the window on his left. The moving somethings had no distinct shape, and were colourless. The nearest approach to colour that could be attributed to them was to say that they were a shadowy grey. It is interesting to note how consistent these reports are with Humphrey's findings

[1] N. K. Humphrey, 'Two studies in the neuropsychology of vision' (Ph.D. thesis, Cambridge Univ.).
[2] G. Riddoch, *Brain*, XL (1917) 15.

on the monkey; and how they fit into the view of perception that is growing out of current scientific work.

I have now given you some examples of psychological work and discourse. What do they add up to? Allow me to be very bold and to try to sum up in a few sentences the general view that seems to emerge from the current drift of scientific work. When one investigates human perception by the methods of science, one is concerned throughout with the flow and processing of energy in and by a human organism. This processing seems to have a hierarchical character. For the normal adult, it involves treating the input at *some* stage in a certain way, of which the public manifestation is such that it is correct to say (for example): 'He has applied some concept to (for example) the item presented.' The human organism also comes to tie inputs and its processing of them to certain sorts of output. It does so largely as the result of interaction with the environment. The ways in which the mature human organism conceptualises the world around it is determined (in part at least) by what has gone into store as the result of past interaction. This store is open to modification in the light of 'failures in pay-off' when interacting with the world. The complexities of the parallel and higher-level processing involved here are very formidable indeed, and quite beyond our grasp at the moment. But the general plan is clear enough in outline to show how the whole business of perception may be subsumable, in principle, within the scope of natural science and the corpus of scientific knowledge.

II

Now let us turn to look at what philosophers have made of the subject. To do this is like entering another world – one that seems to be remote from science, somewhat anachronistic in character, and struggling to escape from the thrall of its own past.

A. M. Quinton begins his well-known article in *Mind* – 'The Problem of Perception' – in the following way:[1]

> The problem of perception is to give an account of the relationship of sense-experience to material objects. This relationship has traditionally been seen as logical, a matter of showing how beliefs about objects can be established or supported by what we know in immediate experience. For, it is held, only our knowledge of experience is direct, immediate, by acquaintance; what we know

[1] A. M. Quinton, *Mind*, LXIV 253 (1955).

or claim to know about objects is indirect, derivative, by inference from what we know directly. Consequently if our beliefs about objects are to have any secure foundation, it must consist in what we know directly, by acquaintance, about sense-data. From this starting-point philosophers have gone on to present varying accounts of the type of inference involved.

When one looks through psychological spectacles at the traditional answer Quinton outlines, it is clear that it runs quite counter to the view of perception which is coming out of the work in science. To begin with, what is meant by 'immediate experience'? When a subject in Wingfield's experiment identified and named the object 'chair' in the picture of a chair, his 'experience' was not 'immediate' in the sense that it took no time. On the contrary, it took him 500 m.secs. to identify the presented object as a chair, and 100 additional m.secs. or more to name it. Of course, it was immediate in the sense that the subject did not hesitate about the object, and gave the answer at once. But this was because the experimental situation did not attempt to give the subject conflicting cues, which might lead him to see the object as a chair and also (perhaps) as a bed or a ladder. And *this* sense of 'immediate' is not the one with which the traditional answer is concerned at this point.

The reply could be made, however, that when the traditionalist speaks of immediate experience, he is not speaking about seeing a chair, or even a picture of one. He is speaking about seeing coloured patches, hearing sounds, and so forth. These are what a person knows immediately. Very well, but in what sense? Not instantaneously, obviously. Apart from the fact that the neural transmission of input takes time, the input is processed (probably) through a decision tree. The completion of this hierarchical progression represents part of what occurs when the person identifies what is presented to him as a red patch. It is clear that, if the traditionalist does want the instantaneous use of 'immediately', then this use has no application to the human organism, and is therefore of no service to him.

Perhaps he means by 'immediate experience' what is unlearned, hence untainted by his own past experience, and hence uninfected by error. But this will not do either. It is very tempting, no doubt, to suppose that when an infant of a few days or weeks looks at a red circular patch, it is aware of a red circle, and so can be said to have immediate experience of seeing red, or of something red, or the sensation of red, or something of this sort. But this temptation amounts to a psychological howler. It may well be the case that the human infant is born with the specific machinery necessary to pick up the light inputs of the spectrum. If so, it is quite possible for the human child to learn to tie differential activity to these inputs – which would help to explain how it is that, for example, it can come to learn to choose a red ball and not a green one. But all this does not oblige us to postulate that the young child *also* processes the input by *conceptualising* it in the ways necessary to enable it to show us that it can identify the ball as red. The child has still to go through further maturation (no doubt), and also learn that this is a red ball and not one of another colour. Hence it runs counter to psychological work and discourse to suppose that the young child has an immediate experience of seeing red, or what not, which is not dependent on past experience and so is free of error. This sense of immediate experience seems to have no application either to the human organism.

Nevertheless, it could be argued, this sense of 'immediate experience' is getting at something real and important. Let us agree that the child has to learn to see the redness of the ball. What he sees here contrasts with what he sees in seeing the ball. For the former is seen or experienced non-inferentially, the latter inferentially. To say this is to say that the child sees the redness directly, he has knowledge of it by acquaintance – whereas he only has knowledge of the ball indirectly, or derivatively, by inference from what he knows directly in acquaintance. Because of this, his knowledge that he is seeing red is incorrigible; his knowledge that he is seeing the ball is not incorrigible.

An obvious difficulty with this defence of traditionalism is to give a psychological meaning to expressions such as 'direct seeing' and 'knowledge by acquaintance'. The traditionalist seems to use them to handle concepts which do not appear in the psychological view of perception we sketched above. Looked at in the light of this scientific view of the matter, these concepts seem to be of doubtful validity. Consider, for example, the contrast here between 'direct and indirect' perceptual knowledge of things. It just will not do at all to say that, whereas the child sees the redness of the ball directly, it sees the ball derivatively by inference from what it sees directly. This will not do for at least two reasons. (*a*) It seems to be the case that the child gives us evidence for saying that it sees the ball *before* it sees the colour of the ball. But if seeing the ball comes before seeing its colour, the former can hardly be said to be derived by inference from the latter. (*b*) When we recall how Piaget's children dealt with the simple problems posed by moving and hidden material things, it seems quite wrong-headed to say that these children were doing any inferring at all from coloured patches to physical things. What the child is doing here is relying on his maturation-cum-experience to set going different ways of dealing with the input. At first it can only deal with it in a restricted manner, such that it does not give us evidence, in its public reactivity, of reacting to a thing as a thing, with permanence and so on. Later, the child comes to deal with input in a less restricted way, such that it *does* give us evidence of reacting to a thing as a substantial entity, in some very primitive way. Whereas, in the early stages, it is quite misleading to say *simpliciter* that the child sees the ball, it is less misleading to say this at the end of the period we are talking about. But this change is not the outcome of an *inferential* achievement. To suggest that it is is to run quite counter to the psychological picture of perception I sketched in the first part of this lecture. So it is not clear what psychological sense can be given to the expressions 'direct' and 'indirect' knowledge in the context we are considering. This way of defending the traditional answer is also inadequate.

But I can hear some contemporaries protesting about my concentration on traditionalism. 'The traditional view of perception', they may say, 'is pretty passé these days. So why bother about it? That it conflicts with the current psychological outlook is hardly surprising, and perhaps not very interesting. What would be more interesting would be to explore the connections between the current psychological outlook in this field and some topics and discussions in the philosophy of perception that are *not* passé.'

This is not a request that I find easy to meet. In the first place, if we do reject the traditional view *in toto*, it is not immediately clear what there is left in the problem of perception for the philosopher to handle. I am inclined to think that we philosophers are a bit confused about this matter. Mr Quinton exhibits some of our confusion very well. As we saw, he begins his article by saying that 'the problem of perception is to give an account of the relationship of sense experience to material objects'; and the traditional doctrine has viewed this as a logical relationship. One of his main conclusions, however, is as follows:

> The relation between experiences and objects, then, neither is nor should be logical. On the contrary it is causal, a matter of psychological fact. Our beliefs about objects are based on experience in a way that requires not justification but explanation.

But if the problem of perception is to give an account of the relation between sense experience and material objects, and this relation is a causal one, etc., then presumably the problem of perception collapses into a scientific and, specifically, a psychological problem.

Which means that Mr Quinton will not be required to write any more articles on perception for *Mind*!

But, of course, philosophers do raise all sorts of questions about perception, some of which do not seem to fall within Mr Quinton's formulation of the problem. If we are to try to show how psychological work is related to current topics in the philosophical world, we have to remember that these topics are probably not all of the same sort, and hence that psychological work will be related to them in different ways. All I can do here is to select, somewhat arbitrarily, a couple of examples by way of illustration.

We all know that one of the aims of the traditionalist was to try to tease out the incorrigible from the corrigible in our perceptual knowledge of the world. Now it is clear that, if this enquiry is pursued in a traditional fashion, and resort made, for example, to the concept of sense-data, then this way of pursuing the search for the incorrigible will probably run into psychological trouble. But it is possible, perhaps, for us to pursue this search in ways which would avoid this trouble. Thus we could pose the problem by asking: Are there any statements of a perceptual character where the risk of error is so minimal that it vanishes altogether? It seems open to us, *prima facie*, to examine and answer this question without necessarily running into psychological trouble at all – at least in the early stages of our inquiry. For example, when one looks at Austin's *Sense and Sensibilia*, it is possible to maintain that his argument about incorrigibility is, at most, only connected very remotely with psychological inquiry, if it is connected at all.

But not all current topics in the philosophy of perception are of this sort.

Some years ago Woozley[1] described the theory of knowledge as 'that branch of philosophy which has for its study the nature of cognition and its objects'. Recently he has been taken to task by Willard[2] for his treatment of the whole matter. According to Willard, Woozley considers *the* problem of epistemology to be the description of the 'objects' of cognition; and an all-pervasive feature of Woozley's book is the conviction that 'a relation obtains between a cognition and what it is a cognition of' – whether these 'objects' be those of ordinary sense perception, or of knowledge, or of false beliefs, and so on. Now Willard claims that this pervasive conviction is 'a crucial error' – there is no such relation; and he supports this claim by various arguments characteristic of a philosopher. (For example, if there were such a relation between cognition and its objects, then

[1] A. D. Woozley, *Theory of Knowledge* (London, 1949).
[2] D. Willard, 'A Crucial Error in Epistemology', *Mind*, LXXVI (1967).

we would be aware of certain things which we are not in fact aware of.) Willard suggests that 'it would be better to describe cognising as a "referential quality" of persons'.

When this discussion is viewed through psychological spectacles, it takes on a somewhat quaint and anachronistic appearance. It may well be the case that Willard is right in his examination of our ordinary concepts and of Woozley's use of 'cognising' etc. The relations between these concepts, and so on, may be such as to give us good reason to say that it is false to suppose a relation obtains between a cognition and what it is a cognition of. The trouble, however, is that this good reason may not be sufficient. For the network of ordinary concepts we use here, and to which Willard is appealing in particular, may mislead us about the nature of the situation that Woozley is trying to talk about. If we consult the current psychological picture of perception, an argument could be developed quite easily for saying that this is, in fact, the case. Assuming that Willard is right about our ordinary concepts, then they *do* indeed mislead us here, and Woozley is trying to get at something authentic when he concentrates on the cognitive relation. For example, it could be argued that, when Smith sees an oasis in the distance, there certainly *is* an important and complex relation between the input and the final internal achievement by Smith, in which he pigeon-holes it as an oasis – whether the contingencies of nature then reinforce this pigeon-holing or not. This sort of relation is under constant study in the scientific world, as we can gather from the current psychological picture about perception. All of which suggests that Woozley's position is congruent in this respect with current science, and that Willard's criticism of him runs counter to it.

On the other hand, where Woozley's account of the matter seems quaint today is in his view of the nature of epistemology. It is said to be the 'study of the nature of cognition and its objects'; but it is a study which relies only on the empirical knowledge already embodied in the concepts and beliefs of ordinary life, and which is logically independent of any further empirical inquiry whatsoever. This view of the matter will hardly do any more. Thus, Woozley's own examination of the ordinary concepts of remembering and imaging, and the concepts connected with judging may be, and in my opinion is, a good example of philosophical work. But it is easy to argue that his account of remembering is pre-Bartlettian in character, and his account of judging quite out of date in the light of Chomsky and all that. So we cannot take it for granted that our ordinary concepts plus our philosophical techniques are good enough to give us answers which are *really worthwhile having* about our perceptual and epistemological achievements. One of the instructive things about Willard's recent criticism of Woozley is that it brings out indirectly how very near parts of traditional epistemology are to the point of being kicked upstairs into science – to use one of Austin's felicities. We may soon be getting clearer hints from psychology on how to develop a causal theory of knowledge. When this happens, we may then be in a better position to transport much of this traditional branch of philosophy upstairs into the secure, grant-supported chambers of empirical science.

Consider another example. At this year's Joint Session[1] Locke asked this question: 'What is it to take what one perceives to be e.g. a piece of chalk?' And he considers that one, or the important matter to settle here is this: 'How far taking-to-be is a combination of perception and thought' – how these two 'are blended'. Now this is a useful question to pose, and the symposiasts (Locke and Quinton) both contribute to make the issue clearer than it was at the outset. But surely it is also a somewhat naïve question to pose at the present time, and to expect that by philosophical techniques we will obtain helpful answers to it. The danger is that the question and our answers will mislead us in more ways than one. Thus, the question presupposes that the very distinction between perception and thought is an important and useful one to draw here. But it may not be. Recall the work of Treisman and Broadbent on taking an auditory signal to be this or that, or taking a word to be an obscene one or not. Where is the 'perception', and where is the 'thought', and how are they combined in *these* cases? It should be clear at once, surely, that as soon as we begin to look carefully into what happens when I take something to be a bit of chalk, the ordinary discourse concepts of perception and thought crumble in our hands. The question of how they are combined now looks much less interesting, if not a bit pointless. It looks rather like asking in the sixteenth century: 'How is my-being-angry a combination of my innate heat and my breathing?'; or 'How far is my taking what I perceive to be a piece of chalk a combination of animal spirits and the incorporeal principle, which, according to Jean Fernel, is the source of all bodily activity as well as thoughts?' Naturally, it is easy for us today to see the pointlessness of *these* questions. But it is a little difficult, perhaps, for those of us who are not in close touch with contemporary science to realise that the question Locke put about perception and thought, and others of a like nature, may also be somewhat pointless and for somewhat similar reasons.

---

[1] D. Locke, 'Perceiving and Thinking', *Proc. Arist. Soc.*, suppl. vol. XLII (1968).

I hasten to add that I do *not* wish to say, or imply, that the philosophical analysis Locke and Quinton give us in this symposium *does* actually run into psychological trouble at any place. Whether it does do so or not is a matter of detail, into which I shall not inquire. However, Locke does develop a certain line on some matters, which is instructive to all of us. It is instructive because it is difficult to see how he, or anyone else, can adequately develop and support this line without ceasing to be a philosopher and plunging into psychological theory.

Very briefly put, Locke argues that for me to take something to be a piece of chalk is, in part, for me to see it as a piece of chalk. 'What then', he asks, 'is it to see the thing in front of me as a piece of chalk?' He appears to have some difficulties in answering this question. At one point he writes as follows:

> No doubt it is true that if one man sees something as *x* and another sees it as *y*, then this difference can be brought out in their different reactions to it, if they do react to it. But this does not seem a satisfactory account of the difference between them, since they may very well not react to it at all. This difference seems to be an actual difference, not merely a hypothetical one. Moreover seeing it as e.g. a piece of chalk is a timetable occurrence, something that happens when, as, you see it. This alone is enough to show that seeing something as *x* cannot be analysed solely in terms of possible reactions and attitudes.

He then goes on to argue that to see something as a piece of chalk is to see it as falling under the concept of piece of chalk; but he does not say much more about what this means.

Now, in emphasising the notions of seeing-as and concept application, Locke seems to me to be speaking in a way that is wholly congruent with current psychological thought and work. I hope the psychological outline I presented in the first part of this lecture makes it clear why I say this. (And, of course, other philosophers, including myself, have also emphasised the notions of seeing-as and concept application or exercise.) But when Locke asks: 'What is to see as?', he tries to answer this question by the standard moves we philosophers have learnt to make. How far can these take him? Clearly, he can only extract from the ordinary notions of see as, and related notions, what they already contain. But it is clear from his quoted remarks that he would very much like to know what the *actual* difference is between one man seeing something as *x*, and another seeing it as *y*. Now it is very unlikely that by the use of philosophical moves *alone* we will ever get a good answer to this question. For the ordinary concept of see as, and others connected with it, contain little about these actual differences. What they may contain of relevant categorical import will be too thin to give us anything approaching a definitive answer. Obviously so. Our ordinary concepts here have arisen to enable us to handle the public, the personally reportable, and the dispositional aspects of human functioning. In any case, moreover, we do not in fact know yet what the actual internal differences are, in which Locke is interested. So how *can* our ordinary concepts help us? What is more, the whole notion of seeing-as creaks when we are faced by the data of Riddoch's patients and Humphrey's destriate monkeys. Do they 'see as' here or not? And if they do, what, and how, do they 'see as'? We are uncertain what to say here. So Locke must look further afield for an answer to his question.

The obvious place to look is in psychological theory. Here we will not find answers anything like good enough at present to deal with Locke's questions about seeing-as, and similar questions that can be raised about applying a concept. The sketch I gave of psychological work on perception is adequate enough, I hope, to show just how difficult it is going to be to provide satisfactory answers to them. On the other hand, I also hope the sketch I gave is good enough to show us how, if we do turn to psychological theory, we may be able to keep moving along the road to a satisfactory answer. For it is then possible to make relevant statements about the *actual* states of affairs and differences between them when a person sees something as *x* and not as *y*. This, after all, is what Treisman and Broadbent are really doing in part. But in making these statements we are obviously theorising in a way where what we say becomes subject to the canons of scientific adequacy; and we cease to be traditional philosophers. But, as long as we are clear what we are doing, why should we be concerned about the traditional boundaries between subjects? Why bother about them? And if philosophers do move in this general direction, they will simply be co-operating in the business of transforming this part of their own subject into science.

At the beginning of this lecture, I said that I have the hunch that philosophers of perception would do well to pay more attention to the efforts and discourse of scientific workers. I hope that I have done something to explain and justify this hunch.

4

INFERENCES ABOUT SEEING[1]

Peter Alexander

IN his book *Attention*, Professor Alan White says 'When you see *X*, it follows that if *X* is *Y*, you see *Y* whether you realise it or not.'[2] If, in passing through Paris, I saw a tall complex iron structure and that structure is the Eiffel Tower, then I saw the Eiffel Tower whether I realised it or not. I accept this, but because recent philosophical writings and discussions[3] have cast doubt on the validity of the inference-pattern

I saw *x*; *x* is *y*; so I saw *y*

and certain related patterns, it is clear that we cannot be content with this unvarnished statement. Various entertaining examples are produced to show that some instances of this pattern are invalid and therefore that the pattern itself is invalid. If I saw Jones at noon and at noon Jones was bribing Smith then, it is alleged, I cannot conclude that I saw Jones bribing Smith. Similarly, it is said, from the facts that I saw a man in the far distance and that that man was my father, I cannot conclude that I saw my father in the far distance; from the facts that I saw a foot and that that foot was Lloyd George's I cannot conclude that I saw Lloyd George.

---

[1] This is a revised and expanded version of a paper read at a meeting of the American Philosophical Association, Western Division, at Minneapolis in May 1966. I am indebted to Professor Frederick L. Will, who was the Commentator on that occasion, for helping me to see how my argument needed modification.

[2] Alan R. White, *Attention* (Oxford, 1964) p. 54.

[3] Some examples, but not necessarily the view I am criticising, are to be found in: G. E. M. Anscombe, 'The Intentionality of Sensation', in *Analytical Philosophy*, ed. R. J. Butler, Second Series (Oxford, 1965); R. M. Chisholm, *Perceiving* (Ithaca, N.Y., 1947); F. Ebersole, 'How Philosophers See Stars', *Mind* (1965); J. L. Austin, *Sense and Sensibilia* (Oxford, 1962) pp. 98 ff. Other examples have been suggested by P. Geach and, in conversation, by Paul Ziff.

It seems to me that this raises problems about both inference-patterns and seeing; the controversy itself needs clarifying before we can come down on one side or the other. This is not a mere parlour game, because it is claimed that the invalidity of such inference-patterns has implications for various philosophical approaches to the problems of perception and knowledge.

Certain ways of arguing for the invalidity of inference-patterns have a tendency to show that *no* inference-pattern can be valid, that is, to destroy the idea that it is valuable to talk of general patterns of inference. This is a danger we face if we take unanalysed everyday inferences to be instances of a certain pattern and take them to be, in their unanalysed state, invalid. However, short of rejecting all inference-patterns, if there is any *point* in saying that an inference-pattern is invalid there must be some inference-patterns that are valid and so, perhaps, some specifiable conditions under which the pattern in question is valid. If we start from the assumption that some inference-patterns are valid then we must be prepared to show that alleged counter-instances to them are not in fact counter-instances. This may involve the analysis of unanalysed inferences. In the present context it may involve us in either closer specification of the ranges of *x* and *y* or a closer attention to the possible uses of 'saw'. I think most people agree that some instances of the inference-pattern in question are acceptable but some people want to say that others are not. This appears to raise two general questions which we would do well to keep distinct as far as this is possible.

(i) What are the general conditions of the validity or invalidity of such patterns?

(ii) Is there anything about seeing that might explain the differences between examples which seem superficially similar?

I wish at least to begin an examination of the second question, but in the course of it I shall have to make some remarks about the first. I shall restrict my discussion almost entirely to the pattern

$$\text{I saw } x; x \text{ is } y; \text{ so I saw } y$$

where 'saw' is used transitively and in the visual sense. That is, I shall not be concerned with seeing in the sense of seeing the point of an argument or seeing what somebody means.

I take it that a good many instances of this pattern are valid and that this is generally accepted. We frequently say such things as 'I saw a buffalo but I didn't at the time realise what it was' and we may say this even when the animal was in full view and clearly seen. Such statements no doubt involve such inferences as

I saw an animal of a variety then unknown to me;
that animal (I am credibly informed) was a buffalo;
so I saw a buffalo.

That there are many acceptable inferences of this sort suggests that there is *some* valid inference-pattern to be found. On the basis of these examples alone, the general pattern I have chosen to discuss seems the obvious candidate; the problem arises because some unacceptable examples are said also to be inferences of this pattern.

I. CONDITIONS FOR INFERENCE-PATTERNS

I am concerned only with deductive inferences and inference-patterns; I shall take it that an inference-pattern is valid if and only if every instance of it is valid and that an inference is valid if and only if it is truth-preserving.

If we consider an inference-pattern of the form

$$x > y; y > z; \text{ so } x > z$$

it is often thought to be a truism to say that two necessary conditions for its validity are

(*a*) that each variable be substitutable by the same expression throughout, in any one application;

and

(*b*) that any logical constant (here ' $>$ ') be used in the same way at each of its occurrences.

These are, I think, rules we usually adopt.

It is tempting when we come to consider the pattern

$$\text{I saw } x; x \text{ is } y; \text{ so I saw } y$$

to adopt the same necessary conditions, treating 'saw' as a logical constant. However, as I shall argue, in connection with such inferences there are difficulties about accepting (*b*) as a necessary condition and, as we can see at once, (*a*) is not a necessary condition of the validity of either inference-pattern.

The reasons for saying that (*a*) is not a necessary condition can be brought out by two examples.

If we substitute in

$$x > y; y > z; \text{ so } x > z$$

one positive whole number for x on its first appearance and any greater positive whole number for x on its second appearance we obtain a valid inference if, for example, y and z are each substituted

D

by positive whole numbers in a regular way throughout. Thus the inference

$$4>3;\ 3>2;\ \text{so}\ (4\times 3)>2$$

is valid. Similarly, in

$$\text{I saw } x;\ x \text{ is } y;\ \text{so I saw } y$$

we may substitute y by a noun with a modifier on its first appearance and by a noun without that modifier on its second appearance and obtain a valid inference. Thus the inference

> I saw an animal;
> that animal was an American bison;
> so I saw a bison

is also, I claim, valid.[1]

We might attempt to modify this rule by saying that it is a necessary condition of validity that there be some common element in what is substituted for each occurrence of a given variable and then providing more precise rules for different kinds of case. Thus for

$$x>y;\ y>z;\ \text{so}\ x>z$$

we should have some such condition as that what is substituted for x on its second occurrence must be not less than what is substituted for it on its first occurrence, whereas what is substituted for y on its second occurrence must be not greater than what is substituted for it on its first occurrence, and so on.

However, this project introduces such enormous complexities as to cast doubt upon the value of the attempt to state inference-patterns at all. It is, therefore, fortunate that my chief concern here does not commit me to stating necessary conditions for the validity of the general inference-pattern which will allow as valid any unanalysed inference which appears superficially to be an instance of the pattern.

What concerns me much more is the stating of conditions which will allow the identification of instances of the pattern so that we are able to decide whether an alleged counter-instance is really an instance of the pattern in question. I am concerned with the question whether there is any plausible interpretation of the pattern which will allow us to say that many valid inferences and no invalid inferences are instances of it. I therefore propose to state conditions, similar to those I have mentioned, which are necessary in order that an inference may be said to be an instance of a given pattern, rather

[1] I am grateful to Professor Will for drawing my attention to this point. The word 'modifier' has to be interpreted with care. Thus 'I saw a fruit; that fruit was a half-tomato; so I saw a tomato' is invalid. The test for a modifier, where m is a modifier of y, is that in place of 'an $m\,y$' we can say 'a y which is m'.

than necessary conditions for the validity of inferences or patterns.

The first condition is this: given an inference, it is a necessary condition of its being an instance of a certain pattern that it can be obtained from that pattern by substituting each variable by the same expression throughout. This is a condition which, I think, we would generally accept and is essential if we are to avoid complications which would make general inference-patterns useless. Thus

$$x>y; y>z; \text{ so } x>z$$

has as one of its instances

$$4>3; 3>2; \text{ so } 4>2$$

but not

$$4>3; 3>2; \text{ so } (4 \times 3)>2.$$

If the last inference is valid this is not because it is an instance of the valid inference-pattern quoted but because it is an instance of some other valid inference-pattern. Consequently, if it is invalid it shows nothing about the validity or invalidity of the quoted inference-pattern.

When we use symbols for constants we usually accept condition (*b*), that each symbol be used in the same way at each appearance, as a necessary condition of validity. It would be absurd to say that

$$((p \supset q) \cdot p) \supset q$$

is invalid if we have taken ' $\supset$ ' on its first appearance for material implication and on its second appearance for entailment. As I have said, however, it will emerge that we cannot accept this condition for 'saw' as a necessary condition of the validity of the pattern

I saw x; x is y; so I saw y.

Instead, the second condition for which I shall argue is that, given an inference, it is a necessary condition of its being an instance of a certain pattern that in the inference and the pattern the use of 'saw' be the same in corresponding positions.

In what follows I have allowed that y in the inference-pattern may be substituted by either a noun-phrase or a noun with a subordinate clause. It might be thought that the difference between validity and invalidity hangs on which of these we choose. This seems plausible in relation to the inference

> I saw John at time t;
> at time t John was a man blinking;
> so I saw a man blinking.

This inference seems valid if the conclusion is understood as

> so I saw a man who was blinking

but invalid if it is understood as

> so I saw a man's blinking.

However, compare this with the inference

> I saw John at time *t*;
> at time *t* John was a man winning a race;
> so I saw a man winning a race.

Even if we understand the conclusion as

> so I saw a man's winning of a race

it is not clear that the inference is invalid since it makes sense to say that I saw this even though I did not realise that this was what he was doing. The two examples are contrasted because there are movements associated with, and partly constituting, the winning of races which I would be taken to have seen but no movements associated with blinking, other than the blinking itself, which I could be said to have seen without seeing the blinking.

2. DIFFERENT USES OF 'SAW'

We frequently use the form 'I saw *x*' to mean that I saw something *as x* or that I saw *that* something was *x* rather than to mean that I saw something that was *x*. In the ordinary way, if I said, without any further explanation,

> I saw Jones picking Smith's pocket

I would be taken to mean that I saw that this was what was going on, that I discovered it just by looking, that this is how it looked to me. However, I may say

> I saw a spectroscope

and mean

> I saw something which (I am told) is a spectroscope

or

> I saw something as a spectroscope

or

> I saw that something saw a spectroscope.

If it is important to distinguish these we normally use whichever more precise form is appropriate, but we very often do not do so when there is no risk of confusion or when there is no need to stress one meaning rather than another.

There is, however, a use of the verb 'to see' which makes it perfectly proper to say that I see colours and shapes, tables and chairs, spectroscopes and burettes, blackmailers and men born in Wisconsin, and events of all sorts, even when I do not recognise them for what they are. There are also situations in which we can contrast this use with uses which stress *seeing that* or *seeing as*. I may see a yellow colour without either seeing that it is yellow or seeing it as yellow; I may see a spectroscope without either seeing that it is a spectroscope or seeing it as a spectroscope. I shall introduce a terminological device for marking this use; I use 'simple' or 'simply' with some part of the verb 'to see' for that use in which my seeing x does not entail either my seeing that something is x or my seeing something as x. Thus, if I simply saw x I may not have seen it as x and I may not have seen that it was x. I do not wish to say that simply seeing x is not seeing x as something but only that it may not be seeing x as x; it seems likely to me that seeing something is always seeing it *as* something.[1]

Thus it is not inconsistent to say 'I saw my father' and 'I did not see my father', referring to the same occasion, if by the first I mean that I *simply* saw my father and by the second I mean either 'I did not see that the man was my father' or 'I did not see the man as my father'. These last two statements are, of course, different. Seeing *that* a man is my father involves seeing in the man enough of my father's characteristics to recognise him, as well as his being my father, but seeing him *as* my father does not involve either of these. If the man was not my father I would be mistaken in my claim to have seen that he was my father but not necessarily in a claim to have seen him as my father. I may see a man as my father without seeing that he is my father. There are even certain circumstances in which I may see that a man is my father without seeing him as my father although here we are inclined to put 'seeing' in quotation marks. 'You are no father to me', a Henry James heroine might say, and the whole point of the remark would be lost if she were not saying it to her father.

Simple seeing is not a sort of seeing different from other sorts; it is involved in seeing of all sorts. We might say that the claim to see simply is a minimum claim involved in all claims to see. If I have seen at all then there is something which it is correct to say I simply saw. If I claim to see x I may be mistaken because what I saw may not fit the description 'x' but there must be something which it would be correct to say I saw, if I saw at all, and probably something which it would be correct to say I saw even if I don't know what it is. This is to say that I simply saw that thing.

For example, if I saw what looked like a cow and claimed to see a

[1] See G. N. A. Vesey, 'Seeing and Seeing As', in *Proc. Arist. Soc.*, LVI (1955-6).

cow when the animal in fact was a buffalo it can be said that I saw a buffalo and this is to say that I simply saw a buffalo. It is clear that there is some difficulty about reporting my own present simple seeings. If I neither see the animal as a buffalo nor see that it is a buffalo and I do not know by any other means that it is a buffalo then I have no grounds for claiming simply to see a buffalo. However, if I can claim to have seen at all then there is something that I myself can correctly claim to have seen, even if it is only a brown moving patch on the plain, and that claim would involve a claim to have simply seen that something. There may be many things which other people can correctly say I am simply seeing even if I cannot, and which I may later be able to say I simply saw. Whenever I simply see *x* then I see *x* even if, at the time or later, I am not able to report it in that way. In this sense, other people may be able to say things about my seeing, or the objects of my seeing, which I am unable to say.

One of the things I am urging is that whenever a person is correctly said to see something there are things which he can correctly be said to have seen, whether he knew it or not at the time, and this is simple seeing. Thus, any true statement of the form

$$I \text{ saw } x$$

or

$$He \text{ saw } x$$

entails the existence of *x* if it is a report of simple seeing.

Summarising, we may say that '*A* saw *x*' reports merely simple seeing if and only if

(*a*) it reports seeing;
(*b*) it does not entail '*A* saw that something was *x*';
(*c*) it does not entail '*A* saw something as *x*';
(*d*) '*x*' applies to something that was seen whether or not *A* could apply it.[1]

My contention is that this corresponds to one everyday use of the verb 'to see'. Since 'I saw *x*' is sometimes used to report simple seeing and sometimes to report *seeing that* or *seeing as*, it sometimes entails and sometimes does not entail 'I simply saw *x*' depending upon how 'saw' is being used. However, it always entails that there is at least one *y* such that it is correct to say 'I saw *y*' just because whenever I can correctly claim to have seen, there must be something that I saw, although 'something', here, has to be interpreted fairly widely.

[1] J. F. Soltis in his book *Seeing, Knowing and Believing* (London, 1966) uses the notion of 'simple seeing' but describes it differently.

3. SOME ALLEGED COUNTER-INSTANCES

I now wish to consider directly some examples of inferences which have been taken as counter-instances to the pattern

I saw x; x is y; so I saw y

and which have consequently been taken to show that this pattern is invalid. I wish to argue that, however interesting these examples may be, they can be understood in such a way that they are not counter-instances to this pattern and that if they are understood in such a way that they appear to be counter-instances they can be regarded as instances of a different pattern. Putting it in an alternative way, the inference-pattern may be seen as concealing several different inference-patterns which can be distinguished only with attention to the possible uses of 'saw' in it.

I shall first consider four examples which differ from one another in more or less important respects.

Example 1 :   I saw a duck;
that duck was a lame duck;
so I saw a lame duck.

This is the most trivial of my examples and would perhaps not be seriously regarded by many as a counter-instance. Let us suppose that the duck, when I saw it, was standing still. This can be con-trasted with the buffalo, which I saw whole and in a good light from close range but not knowing that it was a buffalo. I can be presumed to have seen enough of the characteristics of the animal to enable me to recognise it as a buffalo if I had known what buffaloes are like. I did not, however, see enough of the characteristics of the duck to enable me to recognise it as lame. *Seeing that x is y* requires (*a*) seeing certain characteristics of x and (*b*) knowing that those characteristics are sufficient conditions for its being y. In the buffalo case, (*b*) was unfulfilled; in the lame duck case (*a*) was unfulfilled. A person explaining to me what a buffalo is would have to enumerate only those characteristics I saw, so it seems reasonable to say that I saw a buffalo. On the other hand, I did not see all the characteristics of the duck which a person would have to enumerate to tell me what a *lame* duck is. There is perhaps some slight pressure to say that I did not see a lame duck because I did not actually see everything necessary for me to recognise it as such. The pressure is weak because we do not always take this to be a necessary condition of seeing and also because I might easily have seen everything necessary if, for example,

I had encouraged the duck to walk. I saw a duck, I even saw a lame duck, but I did not see that it was lame. Seeing more characteristics which I might perfectly well have seen would have constituted seeing that it was lame.

It seems perfectly reasonable to say that I did see a lame duck, meaning that I simply saw a lame duck. This is not a counter-instance to the general pattern if it is interpreted thus

$$\text{I saw } x; \; x \text{ is } y; \text{ so I simply saw } y$$

and that is a perfectly possible interpretation. It may be noted that here it does not matter whether 'saw' in the first premiss means 'simply saw' or 'saw that something was'.

If this is taken as a counter-instance the conclusion must be understood to mean 'I saw that something was a lame duck' or, at least, 'I saw something as a lame duck' and my contention is that the pattern

$$\text{I saw } x; \; x \text{ is } y; \text{ so I simply saw } y$$

is a different pattern from either

$$\text{I saw } x; \; x \text{ is } y; \text{ so I saw that } x \text{ was } y$$

or

$$\text{I saw } x; \; x \text{ is } y; \text{ so I saw } x \text{ as } y.$$

I also contend that each of these is a possible interpretation of

$$\text{I saw } x; \; x \text{ is } y; \text{ so I saw } y.$$

Example 2: I saw a man in the far distance;
that man was Smith;
so I saw Smith in the far distance.

This example is different owing to the indeterminateness of things seen in the far distance. I could presumably see the man in the distance clearly enough to recognise him as a man but not clearly enough to recognise him as Smith. I did not see enough of Smith's characteristics in the man to recognise him as Smith and, moreover, I could not have seen them with the naked eye, given that he remained at that distance; I could not both see that the man had them and see him in the far distance. There is rather stronger pressure here to say that we have a counter-instance. I would probably be less hesitant about saying that I saw the buffalo or the lame duck than about saying that I saw Smith. Nevertheless it is not just false to say 'I saw Smith'; I did see him even if I did not recognise him and even if I did not see him as Smith. That is, I may say 'I saw Smith' if I mean 'simply saw' and this is so even though it may be less misleading to say that *what* I saw was Smith.

As in the last example, it seems that if this is taken as a counter-instance it is being understood as an instance of the pattern

$$I \text{ saw } x; x \text{ is } y; \text{ so I saw that } x \text{ was } y$$

or

$$I \text{ saw } x; x \text{ is } y; \text{ so I saw } x \text{ as } y$$

rather than of the pattern

$$I \text{ saw } x; x \text{ is } y; \text{ so I simply saw } y.$$

Example 3: I saw Jones;
  Jones is a blackmailer;
  so I saw a blackmailer.

This is more complex than the previous examples because, it may be said, there is a sense in which I cannot see blackmailers but can see ducks and buffaloes, because the necessary characteristics of black-mailers include some which cannot be just seen, cannot be dis-covered just by looking. These include a man's having certain motives, his forecasting of probable outcomes of words or deeds and his assessing of what makes and breaks reputations. You would probably *not* regard me as a blackmailer on hearing me say to the Chairman 'If you give me £10 I will destroy this paper' if you knew that the paper in question was the one I am reading, that the Chairman had a strong desire not to hear it, and that it had cost me £10 to get here. You *would* be likely to regard me as a blackmailer if you discovered that the paper was a letter written by the Chairman, the publication of which would destroy his reputation in some way. This would involve my issuing some sort of threat and an estimation of the possible outcome of my publishing the letter, depending upon some view about people's attitudes to what it contained, and so on. These are not characteristics which could be discovered just by looking, as a certain kind of hoof or head are characteristics of buffaloes which can be discovered by just looking.

This might lead one to say that one cannot (visually) see that a man is a blackmailer as one can (visually) see that an animal is a buffalo, and to move from there to saying that one never, really, *sees* a blackmailer. This would be to insist on taking 'seeing' always as 'seeing that'. The pressure may be stronger here to say that the inference does not work but even here it is perfectly sensible to say that I can simply see a blackmailer because it is sensible to say that I can see a blackmailer without recognising him as a blackmailer. Indeed, if the argument were correct, the choice would be between saying this and saying that it is never correct to say 'I saw a black-mailer', which seems perverse.

Frank Ebersole, in his paper 'How Philosophers See Stars',[1] discusses a question which relates to this example. Suppose that I see two exactly similar chocolates, one of which happens to have a white centre and the other of which happens to have a pink centre. I only discover this later by cutting them open; I could not even then say, referring to my original seeing of the chocolates, 'I saw a pink-centred chocolate.' Ebersole briefly discusses the conditions under which such inferences work. He compares with this the case of a new student of biology who sees an unfamiliar mechanical device. He later learns that it is a microtome and he also learns what it does. He is then entitled, Ebersole thinks, to say 'I saw a microtome', referring to his original seeing. This is acceptable, he thinks, although the similar statement about the pink-centred chocolate is not, because in that case 'What one learns . . . does not affect what one saw because . . . it cannot affect what one sees in the future' (p. 525). I doubt if this will do, for two reasons. (*a*) One may learn the name of a microtome without learning what it does and still be entitled to claim to have seen a microtome not because what one has learnt affects what one sees, not because one sees anything more or different, but because one has learnt that what looks like that is called a microtome. Similarly, one might say one has seen a pink-centred chocolate if the box was labelled 'Pink-Centred Chocolates' although one sees nothing more after reading the label. (*b*) In the case of the blackmailer one has learnt that Jones does things which one didn't realise that he did. One does not see anything more or different in looking at Jones although one may then say 'I see Jones differently now; I see Jones as a blackmailer.' Here, however, one again feels that 'see' needs quotation marks.

Example 4:   I saw Jones at time *t*;
               at time *t* Jones was a man bribing Smith;
               so I saw a man bribing Smith.

This example is related to the last one because a blackmailer is a person who performs, or has performed, a particular kind of action; this example stresses the action rather than the agent. If one thinks that this is plausible as a counter-instance, that may depend upon the belief that one cannot just see, by looking, that a man is performing a certain sort of action as one can just see, by looking, that he is making the physical movements involved in that sort of action. I can discover by looking that one man is handing another some money but I cannot discover by looking that he is bribing him. What is

[1] *Mind* (1965).

also required is some knowledge of the intentions of the briber and his estimate of the intentions of the bribed; they have entered into some non-gentleman's agreement, which is not the sort of thing that can be seen. Of course, what is seen may constitute evidence that they have entered into such an agreement but that they have done so cannot be just seen. They may put on a performance which is sufficiently good to fool any onlooker, but if they have not entered into the right sort of agreement then no bribe has passed, whatever else has passed.

The argument would, if pressed, have the consequence that there is no sense in which actions, as distinct from movements, can be seen. This seems excessive. Again it seems reasonable to say that one can simply see actions; it makes perfectly good sense to say 'I saw him taking a bribe although I did not realise at the time that this was what he was doing.' If we accept this, the general inference-pattern is not shown to be invalid as long as the conclusion involves only simple seeing.

Another example which is superficially similar to this last one, but which is alleged to be a clearer counter-instance, has been put to me by Professor Frederick Will. If 'saw' in the inference-pattern means 'simply saw' throughout then 'it is true that if Jones is a magician and I saw Jones then I saw a magician. But it is not true that if I saw Jones at time *t*; and at time *t* Jones was extracting a card from his sleeve (or, more prosaically, scratching his ankle, or winking at Smith), then I saw Jones doing one of these things.'[1] This is certainly a more difficult example for me to accommodate to my view.

Perhaps the difference between this and the bribery example rests on this: saying that I saw Jones extracting a card from his sleeve, because it refers to something which could be just seen, discovered just by looking, carries the suggestion that I saw *that* Jones was extracting a card from his sleeve. Since we cannot discover just by looking that Jones was bribing Smith, the claim to have seen Jones bribing Smith does not carry with it the suggestion that I saw *that* this was what Jones was doing. It might be that in Will's example *what is being said* becomes clearer if we put the inference in this form

I saw Jones at time *t*;
at time *t* Jones was extracting a card from his sleeve;
so I saw Jones, who was then (*or*, while he was) extracting a card from his sleeve.

This seems valid because it makes it clear that the final claim can be

---

[1] I quote this, with permission, from Professor Will's unpublished comments read at the Minneapolis meeting.

understood as a claim that I simply saw Jones extracting a card from his sleeve and thus not to entail that I saw the card's being extracted.

This may appear to beg the question; whenever I am faced with a counter-instance I reinterpret it so that it no longer looks like a counter-instance, the only reason for so doing being that I wish to save the inference-pattern. If this were all I was doing, that would be a sound objection, but it is not all I am doing. The question is whether inferences which appear to fit the pattern but which also appear to be invalid can be given a plausible interpretation, doing no violence to what we would mean by them, such that *either* the inferences can be shown not to fit the pattern *or* they can be shown to be valid. An unanalysed everyday inference is given as a counter-instance to the pattern; an analysis of the inference is given which shows it to be valid. This form of argument cannot be rejected in general but only by showing, for example, that the proffered analysis is implausible for some reason or other. I do not think my analyses are implausible.

One of the problems here concerns the effect of contexts, including linguistic contexts. I think it is clear that we sometimes understand 'I saw *y*' in one way if it is used as the conclusion of the kind of inference in question and in a different way if it is uttered in isolation. For example, if I said 'I saw President Eisenhower', in isolation from any such inference and without further qualification, I think I would normally be taken to mean that I saw President Eisenhower, *knowing who he was*. But if I said

> I saw a man playing golf;
> that man was President Eisenhower;
> so I saw President Eisenhower

I would probably not be understood in the same way. The very fact that it is necessary to state the inference suggests a particular interpretation of the conclusion which, if the inference were not stated, we should normally express by saying 'I saw President Eisenhower although I didn't realise it at the time'. The bare statement 'I saw President Eisenhower', without the inference or any qualifications, might be understood in this way but it would not normally be so understood.

There are some more bizarre examples, which can be more easily disposed of, but which are sometimes raised in this connection. They are related to such familiar questions as whether my seeing part of, or one side of, a thing entitles me to claim to have seen that thing. I see a tomato on the kitchen shelf, that is, without being able to walk round it and without turning it round to see its other side. Without

further inspection I see only roughly half of the tomato's surface. Am
I entitled to say 'I saw a tomato'? Well, of course I am since I frequently say such things without misleading anybody. Indeed, if in
these circumstances I said 'I saw half a tomato' that would be really
misleading since I would be taken to have seen only one of the pieces
of a tomato which had been cut in half. Now people say such things
as 'You wouldn't say you had seen Lloyd George if you had merely
seen a foot even if you were told, on good authority, that it was
Lloyd George's foot.' Of course, but this is different and of doubtful
relevance to my theme. It gains its effect by the way it is put. We
can see this if we try to make the suspect inference fit the inference-
pattern in question. It becomes

> I saw a foot;
> that foot was Lloyd George's foot;
> so I saw Lloyd George.

This is clearly invalid; but it is also clearly not of the pattern

> I saw x;
> x is y;
> so I saw y,

since 'y' has been substituted at its first appearance by 'Lloyd
George's foot' and at its second appearance by 'Lloyd George'. On
the other hand, an inference which does fit the pattern is

> I saw a foot;
> that foot was Lloyd George's foot;
> so I saw Lloyd George's foot

and that is valid if 'saw' in the conclusion means 'simply saw'.

4. SOME DIFFERENT INFERENCE-PATTERNS

I now wish to return to the possible complexity of the inference-
pattern

> I saw x; x is y; so I saw y.

If we allow that 'saw' may be used in the different ways I have
mentioned we can see that this pattern is ambiguous and may be
regarded as concealing a number of different inference-patterns,
some valid and some invalid. If so, it is misleading to say that this
pattern is shown to be invalid by the examples I have considered.
What their consideration can help us to see is that we have here not

one but several patterns, or several ways of understanding this pattern, which amounts to much the same thing.

Nevertheless, as we have seen, one of the ways of understanding this pattern is not shown to be invalid by any of the alleged counter-instances since they turn out to be valid when they are understood in such a way that they fit this interpretation of the pattern. Inferences of the pattern

$$\text{I saw } x; \; x \text{ is } y; \text{ so I saw } y$$

work if 'saw' in both occurrences means 'simply saw'; but they also work if 'saw' in its first occurrence means 'saw that something was' and in its second occurrence means 'simply saw'. That is, the following more explicit patterns (or sub-patterns) are valid:

> I simply saw x; x is y; so I simply saw y.
> I saw that something was x; x is y; so I simply saw y.

The second of these is valid because seeing that something is x entails simply seeing x. On the other hand, simply seeing x does not entail seeing that something is x, so the pattern (or sub-pattern)

$$\text{I simply saw } x; \; x \text{ is } y; \text{ so I saw that } x \text{ was } y$$

is invalid. Just as obviously invalid is the pattern

I saw that something was x; x is y; so I saw that something was y

because seeing that something is x does not entail seeing that it is everything that x is.

The following patterns (or sub-patterns) using *seeing as* are valid.

> I saw x as y; x is y; so I simply saw y.
> I saw x as y; x is not y; so I did not simply see y.

The second premiss is needed in each because seeing x as y does not alone entail either seeing y or not seeing y, whether simply or otherwise. Similarly, the patterns (or sub-patterns)

$$\text{I saw } x \text{ as } y; \; x \text{ is } y; \text{ so I saw that } x \text{ was } y$$

and

$$\text{I saw } x \text{ as } y; \; x \text{ is not } y; \text{ so I did not see that } x \text{ is } y$$

are also valid, and the second premiss is necessary because seeing x as y does not alone entail either seeing that x is y or not seeing that x is y. In order that I may see that x is y, x must be y.

If I am right about this, it is not a necessary condition of the validity of the general inference-pattern

$$\text{I saw } x; \; x \text{ is } y; \text{ so I saw } y$$

that 'saw' be used in the same way in both its occurrences. Clearly it may mean anything in the second occurrence which is entailed by its meaning in the first occurrence, and validity will be preserved. What is true is that using various combinations of the various possible uses of 'saw' produces different inference-patterns. Thus, it is a necessary condition of an inference's being of a certain pattern that in the pattern and in the inference the use of 'saw' in corresponding positions be the same. Thus the inference

> I saw an animal as a buffalo;
> that animal was a buffalo;
> so I simply saw a buffalo

is an instance of the pattern

> I saw x as y; x is y; so I simply saw y

whereas the inference

> I saw a man;
> that man was my father;
> so I simply saw my father

is an instance of the pattern

> I saw x; x is y; so I simply saw y.

Austin in *Sense and Sensibilia*[1] suggests that we do not *normally* see things *as they really are* and this has been taken to mean that it does not make sense to talk of seeing x as y if x is y or if we know that x is y, that is, that it makes sense only if we are in some way doubtful about x's being y. I think this is not what Austin meant and, more relevantly, I think that this conclusion is false. I may know that x is yellow and, if I am colour-blind, not see it as yellow: that is, I may not see it as different from something I know to be green. If I suddenly see them as different I can surely say 'I now see it as yellow'. This is, as Austin says, a special case, but it is not special because I am doubtful about how things are; it is special because I move from knowing that I am not seeing something as it really is to knowing that I am seeing it as it really is.

In the light of all I have said I am inclined to think that to say merely that our general inference-pattern is invalid is to draw attention in an excessively dramatic way to the necessity for sorting our various uses of 'to see' and at the same time to discourage attempts to proceed with this task. The fact that in normal discourse 'to see' may be used to report sometimes *simple seeing*,

---

[1] Austin, *Sense and Sensibilia*, p. 100 ff.

sometimes *seeing as* and sometimes *seeing that* does not show the inference-pattern to be invalid for every one of these uses or for every combination of them. I am content to say, here, that the pattern is valid for at least one familiar use of 'saw' and that where it appears to be invalid we are covertly understanding a different use and would be well-advised to use a different pattern to represent the inferences in question.

I can perhaps summarise the basis of my conclusions thus:

  (i) there is a use of 'saw' such that 'I saw x' and 'x is y' together imply 'I saw y';
 (ii) there are other uses of 'saw' such that 'I saw x' and 'x is y' do not together imply 'I saw y';
(iii) this situation is likely to arise for any valid inference-pattern and no more makes our general pattern invalid than does equivocation about the constants of any other inference-pattern make that pattern invalid. (Here, 'equivocation about the constants' means 'taking the constants used in one way as if they were used in another way'.)

In other words, I am suggesting that because there are different, and not explicitly distinguished, uses of 'to see' in everyday discourse the general inference-pattern, which is valid when understood in one way, may be mistaken for other patterns which are invalid or for the same pattern understood in a different way. One way of making, and obscuring, this mistake is to say flatly that the general pattern is invalid. We must not confuse the problem of what is to count as a substitution-instance with the problem of the validity of the pattern. Deciding which are the substitution-instances involves investigating various uses of 'to see'.

It may be wondered why I have not used the fashionable word 'intentionality' in discussing this matter. The alleged invalidity of some of these inferences is said to show that 'to see' is an intentional verb. That is, it is the basis of one criterion of intentionality. The statement that 'to see' is an intentional verb has the air of explaining something. It is also thought to have certain consequences for some philosophical approaches to epistemology, such as those of sense-datum theorists and 'ordinary language' philosophers.[1] It seems to me that, on its own, it does not explain anything because there is a great deal more to be said about the criterion itself, that is, about the alleged invalidity of the inference-pattern. When this is said it may be that the alleged consequences for epistemology will not be as clear or as telling as they seem, but I cannot pursue that here.

[1] See, for example, Anscombe, *Analytical Philosophy*, p. 171.

5

PERCEPTION AND ACTION

M. R. Ayers

THERE is an ancient and ambiguous philosophical doctrine that perception is passive. This can mean that the mind contributes nothing to the content of our sensory experience: its power of perception is a mere receptivity. In this sense the principle has often been questioned, and is indeed doubtful on empirical grounds, given one reasonable interpretation of what it would be for the mind to make such a contribution.

The principle that perception is passive can also mean something less controversial and, I think, initially less obscure: that perception is not a voluntary activity. As Locke puts it, 'The objects of our senses do obtrude their particular ideas upon our minds whether we will or no.' I shall be concerned with the principle only in this second sense, and in connection with one problem to which Locke brings it, the problem of our knowledge of physical reality.

Locke's answer to the sceptic of the senses is not accorded any great prominence in the *Essay*, and he seems to intend some sort of snub to the Cartesian method of doubt; for he represents the doubt whether anything exists behind the so-called 'idea' given in sensation not only as a doubt that no one could seriously induce in himself, but also as a doubt that, if it did arise, could not be allayed by the kind of proof that Descartes tries to provide. Locke starts by conceding that we cannot, merely from the presence in our mind of an idea of something, conclude that it actually exists. But in sensation we are aware not only of an idea, but that it is being *caused* in us by something external to us. We may not know *how* the idea is caused by the object, and this is a limitation on how much we can conclude about the actual nature of the object; but at least we know that an object exists capable of producing this idea in us.

If the quality *white* is defined, as Locke recommends, as the power to produce an idea of white through the senses, then from a sensation of white we can with confidence, although not with logical certainty, infer the actual existence of something white, possessing such a power.

What could justify, against the sceptic, Locke's claim that sensation involves an awareness of an external cause? One of Locke's arguments is an appeal to the 'given' nature of sensation:

> Sometimes I find that I cannot avoid the having those ideas produced in my mind. For though, when my eyes are shut, or windows fast, I can at pleasure recall to my mind the ideas of light, or the sun, which former sensations had lodged in the memory: so I can at pleasure lay by that idea, and take into my view that of the smell of a rose, or taste of sugar. But, if I turn my eyes at noon towards the sun, I cannot avoid the ideas which the light or sun then produces in me. So that there is a manifest difference between the ideas laid up in my memory . . . and those which force themselves upon me and I cannot avoid having. And therefore it must needs be some exterior cause and the brisk acting of some objects without me, whose efficacy I cannot resist, that produces those ideas in my mind, whether I will or no.

In interpreting this passage it should be borne in mind that for Locke memory includes imagination, since all our simple ideas are supposed to have been sensations originally, and so to be lodged in the memory.

It might seem invalid to draw the categorical conclusion that there are sensations or ideas that I cannot avoid having, from the hypothetical premiss that *if* I turn my eyes towards the sun, I cannot avoid the sensation of light. For this looks like concluding that there are crashes I cannot avoid, from the premiss that *if* I drive on the wrong side of the road, I cannot avoid hitting the oncoming traffic. The Lockean reaction to this objection can only be that perception is intrinsically involuntary precisely in the sense that it occurs only as a necessary consequence of something other than an act of will. I may very often be able voluntarily to prevent this sufficient condition, and so by this means indirectly prevent the occurrence of the sensation, but I cannot voluntarily and directly refrain from having the sensation as, in principle at least, I can refrain 'at pleasure', as Locke would say, from having or conjuring up a mental picture in imagination.

This account must be supposed to cover, not merely the sensation of an object that I get when I look at it, touch it, smell it and so on, but any sensation of the action itself, such as the sensation of turning my eyes. Although I turn my eyes voluntarily, and could refrain from doing so, I do not, at the same time and in the same way, voluntarily have the sensation of turning my eyes. Locke's own example most relevant here, although not exactly parallel, is that of writing: the act is voluntary, but the perception of the letters formed is not. I cannot continue writing before my open eyes, and yet choose not to have the appropriate sensations. This shows that these sensations are the effects of the changes that I am making in the real world, and are not 'the sport and play of my own imagination'.

Now although this reply succeeds in rebutting the objection to the principle that perception, as opposed to imagination, is essentially out of a person's control, it does so at the cost of seriously diminishing the value of the principle for Locke's anti-sceptical purposes.

First, is it not odd that he agrees with the sceptic that, if we do have knowledge of a physical world, it can only be by inference from our sensations, and yet he presupposes that we can act directly in the physical world? So where our knowledge is direct, at the level of ideas, our action is indirect, i.e. our ends must be achieved by means of action at the different level of physical reality. But where our action is direct, our knowledge is only indirect and inferential. Given the nature of intention, I am strongly inclined to conclude that this account must be wrong, and I do not think that it can be saved by the unattractive theory that all physical action is really indirect, as being a consequence of a mental act of will or volition. Even a volition would need an object, and on Locke's account volitions to do such things as turning my eyes must be performed, presumably, *before* the observed necessary consequences of such acts have given me reason to believe in the existence of eyes or of any other physical object.

Locke says of the act of writing, that 'whilst I write this, I can change the appearance of the paper and, by designing the letters, tell beforehand what new idea it shall exhibit the very next moment, barely by drawing my pen over it'. Now the objects of my designs, i.e. what I aim to produce, are the physical letters; but the form of the argument suggests that it is only by observing the perceptual by-product of success in these designs that I can have any reason for believing that such objects as letters, pens and hands exist at all.

The circularity of any anti-sceptical argument based on the principle of the involuntariness or 'given' character of sensations can be expressed even more simply. We have seen that the principle can only be defended and interpreted if we recognise a distinction between, on the one hand, voluntarily effecting a change, or acting, in the physical world, which in turn causes an alteration in our sensations, and, on the other hand, directly, as Locke would say, 'operating on' our ideas in imagination. But this is to presuppose precisely what the sceptic doubts, that there is a physical world.

Let 'us turn to Berkeley's immaterialism. Berkeley thought that what is wrong with Locke's response to scepticism is his concession that our knowledge of the physical world is only as secure as an inference from our sensations to whatever causes them. Berkeley himself avoids making such a concession as a consequence of his famous denial of any distinction between the given idea or sensation, which like Locke he treats as the immediate object of perception, and the physical quality or object of which it is the idea. He himself anticipates the objection to his thesis that, if there were nothing over and above ideas, there would be no ground for the distinction between reality and illusion, or the chimeras of the imagination. His answer is, roughly speaking, to take what Locke gives as reasons for our belief in an external physical reality as constituting a *definition* of the concept of reality. Locke puts before us a number of characteristics of some of our ideas which, he says, give grounds for supposing that they have external causes: not only their involuntariness, but also their distinctness, their connection with physical pain and pleasure, which cannot be summoned up at will, their coherence one with another, so that our senses bear one another out, and the constancy and regularity with which they recur. Berkeley, on the other hand, claims that we simply call the ideas having these features 'real' by definition, and consequently there can be no doubt that, when we perceive such an idea or set of ideas, we are perceiving a real thing. Physical reality is itself constituted by such ideas.

The structure of this brilliantly ingenious move, and the parasitic character of his doctrine of reality, is made quite explicit in a passage in the *Third Dialogue between Hylas and Philonous*. Philonous concludes his response to the objection that he cannot account for the difference between dreams and waking life with the following remark: 'In short, by whatever method you distinguish *things* from *chimeras* on your own scheme, the same, it is evident, will hold also upon mine. For it must be, I presume, upon some perceived difference, and I am not for depriving you of any one thing you can perceive.'

Nevertheless, most of the features of ideas specifically mentioned by Locke figure positively in Berkeley's own system, and he does offer us an explanation of why we have this concept of reality, defined as he says we define it. The involuntariness of so-called 'real' ideas is indeed, as Locke thought, a sign that they have an external cause, namely God, who produces them in us by an act of his will.

They occur in an orderly and coherent fashion because God acts in accordance with his own laws of nature. This he does so that we can have some foresight, and can know that 'to obtain such and such ends, such and such means are conducive'. Pleasure and pain are associated with these dependable sequences of involuntary ideas, it seems, in order to give some point to our activities and to make morality possible, which is essentially concerned with means and ends, pleasures and pains.

This résumé of a relatively small part of Berkeley's magnificent theocentric metaphysical system will allow us to see that what gives rise, for Locke, to a difficulty in his account of intentional physical action, and a circularity in his argument against the sceptic, re-appears, for Berkeley, as the source of a direct contradiction in his theory.

It is clear that involuntariness must be a necessary condition of the reality of Berkeley's 'real' ideas. That it is not a sufficient condition Berkeley admits by implication in his discussion of dreams, just as Locke must concede that involuntariness is not by itself sufficient ground for a belief in the existence of an external object. In the last resort, dreams are to be distinguished from reality, Berkeley claims, not by their voluntariness, for they are not characteristically voluntary, but by their incoherence and lack of connection with preceding and subsequent events. But neither philosopher questions the intuitive principle that ideas having reality are necessarily involuntary: if I am inducing my own states of mind at will, I may be picturing or imagining, but I cannot be perceiving. For Berkeley there is, moreover, an intrinsic connection between involuntariness and the other criteria of coherence, regularity and association with pleasure and pain: for all these criteria derive from the causal dependence of 'real' ideas on God.

The contradiction in his argument arises because he allows, and must allow, the possibility of human action at the level of reality. Consequently some ideas must be both voluntary and involuntary. There are reasons within Berkeley's system, apart from common sense and his own proper predilection for free will, why voluntary physical action must be possible. Firstly, as we have seen, the only plausible interpretation of the criterion of involuntariness depends upon this assumption: as Berkeley himself has to propose it, '*When in broad daylight I open my eyes*, it is not in my power to . . . determine what particular objects present themselves to my view.' Secondly, he tells us that the reason why God acts in accordance with the laws of nature that impart regularity and coherence to our experience is to enable us to regulate our actions for the benefit of life, by adopting set means to the ends of pleasure and avoidance of pain. It follows that some so-called 'real' ideas are voluntary: for otherwise we could never adopt means, let alone achieve ends.

Another place in which the possibility of physical action is assumed is in his account of motion, in which he tries to reconcile its relativity with an intuitive conception of absolute motion: 'For to denominate a body *moved*', he writes, 'it is requisite, first, that it change its distance or situation with regard to some other body: and secondly, that the force or action occasioning that change be applied to it.' This force, according to Berkeley, is always volition, and in the case of the human body, the volition is commonly that of its owner. That is why, as a man walks along the street, he knows that it is his feet that are moving, and not the stones they pass over.

Yet another interesting and relevant passage is Berkeley's discussion of our knowledge of other minds. We know of their existence because we perceive changes in our sensations or ideas that are convincing proof that, as he says, 'human agents are concerned in producing them', or that 'agents like myself . . . concur in their production'. These careful phrases are explained when he says, soon after, 'that it is evident that in affecting other persons, the will of man hath no other object than barely the motion of the limbs of his body; but that such a motion should be attended by, or excite any idea in the mind of another, depends wholly on the will of the Creator. He alone . . . maintains that intercourse between spirits, whereby they are able to perceive the existence of each other.' Hence, Berkeley holds the curious view that, in physical action, I voluntarily operate on my own idea of my body, while God kindly affects other people's ideas of my body in appropriate ways. One possible view that he evidently rejects is that it is God who affects even my own idea of my body, and that a volition to perform a physical action functions only as a kind of prayer to God to move my limbs for me. Berkeley wrote in his notebooks, 'We move our legs ourselves, 'tis we that will their movement. Herein I differ from Malebranche.' His motive here is doubtless a combination of common sense and theology.

Thus in all that Berkeley says about action, whether odd or commonsensical, he fails to remark the contradiction of an event that is both involuntary and voluntary, or to offer any coherent account of the difference between the willing an idea that is a kind of imagination, and the willing an idea that is, according to him, physical action. The will 'excites', 'produces' and otherwise 'operates on' ideas, but these expressions have to cover its function both as the principle of voluntary imagination and as the principle of motion.

The opening that there is for Locke to distinguish the two in terms of the different *objects* of the will – although with awkward consequences for his own argument – is quite non-existent for Berkeley.

Berkeley's system is an ancestor of the phenomenalism adopted, for example, by A. J. Ayer and some positivists. Its inconsistencies are hereditary. The modern phenomenalist does not say that physical things *are* ideas, nor even, perhaps, need he tell us, as Russell does, that things are 'constructed' out of the data of sense. Avoiding such talk as too crude, he may speak instead of a logical relationship between statements about sense-data and statements about physical objects such that the latter are reducible to the former by however complex or, indeed, elastic a principle of logical translation. To talk of physical objects, so we are told, is to use language at a higher and less basic level than the language of sense-data. The concept of objectivity and the concepts of physical space and time are said to function as part of a conceptual system within which the orderliness and dependability of sensory experience can be briefly expressed. They function, so it is claimed, in something like the way in which, according to Operationalists, the concept of an electron or of a light wave functions in the theories that introduce order into a mass of multifarious experimental results and low-level generalisations. But this neo-Berkeleyan view that physical objects are merely theoretical entities has no peculiar answer to Berkeley's dilemma. To stress the complexity and length of the sense-datum statement to which the statement that my hand moves is supposed to be more or less loosely equivalent, is merely to attribute, even less plausibly, a similar complexity to whatever 'operation on my ideas' it is that constitutes my voluntarily moving my hand. There is nothing to distinguish this from a similarly complex and similarly orderly bit of imagining. There also remains the problem of how, by operating on my own ideas, I succeed at the same time in operating on the ideas of indefinitely many witnesses of my act and its consequences, the correlation that Berkeley assigned to God's grace. And it is difficult to see how my intention in any physical action can have as its object a merely theoretical entity, or logical construct from my own given sensations.

Some phenomenalists might react by insisting that voluntary physical action must be defined entirely at the level of physical object language, i.e. behaviouristically. Hence the problem of how an intentional physical action is possible is 'dissolved'. This ostrich-like but, I think, foreseeable reaction, which would pretend to deal with the awkward subjective aspect of intentional actions simply by ignoring it, could also be said to come strangely from those who are obsessed by the subjective aspect of perceptual events. Moreover, if involuntariness is *retained* as a criterion of perception as opposed to voluntary picturing, then it would follow that physical actions that are, on a behaviouristic definition, 'voluntary', are like all other physical events, logical constructs from sensory states that are, in an entirely different sense, not 'voluntary'. To propose such a story would be a desperate manœuvre.

Could the criterion of involuntariness be dropped altogether without loss to phenomenalism? After all, some states of mind analogous to sensory states, e.g. dreams, must be distinguished from perception by other means. There is in fact a strong tendency in modern phenomenalism to concentrate on the factor of coherence, partly perhaps because of the influence of Hume, who carefully refrains from mentioning involuntariness. There is also the obsession with the co-called 'argument from illusion', which may lead one to suppose that the only important line of distinction lies between perception and hallucination. It is ironical that in spite of this neglect the criterion of involuntariness should have become enshrined in Russell's term 'sense-datum'. Its importance can be illustrated by what is a logical, although not a psychological, possibility. It is no doubt true that in picturing or calling to mind an image of something, however vividly, one does not really induce in oneself anything more than a pale and partial shadow of a perceptual state. But it is not *logically* impossible that a man should be capable of putting himself at will into mental states just like perceptual states, and of doing so for indefinitely long periods in a thoroughly orderly manner. To such a man any definition of the perception of reality that did not include involuntariness would read like a recipe for creation. Yet, of course, he could tell – or would not need to tell – that his quasi-perceptual states lacked real objects, simply because they were self-induced. Thus the phenomenalist cannot escape the requirement that he should explain the difference between voluntary mental activity and voluntary physical actions, and how it is that the latter are possible: a requirement that I do not think he can convincingly fulfil.

I have criticised answers to scepticism, but I am not a sceptic. My criticisms are concordant with the view that scepticism, the causal theory as it appears in arguments against scepticism, and phenomenalism all suffer from the same defect. All assume that it could be objectively doubtful, from the point of view of a sentient being, whether anything physical exists. But it is at least a philosophical possibility, and by no means contrary to common sense or to science, that any experience is necessarily the experience of an animal, that is, a physical object, a denizen of space. If this is a necessary truth, then scepticism about physical reality is incoherent, and can be met with a very general answer: 'I think, therefore a physical object exists.'

I can now only touch on what seem to me convincing, if abstract, reasons for the view that all experience is necessarily the experience of an animal. They chiefly have to do with the nature of the distinction between particulars and universals, real things and abstractions, and with demonstrable logical flaws in the doctrine that the identity of a particular consciousness is intrinsically independent of any physical existence or continuity in space and time. The ancient characterisations of universals such as whiteness or humanity either as changelessly existing outside space and time, or else as capable of existing at indefinitely many places at the same time, point to the only intelligible way of conceiving of a particular, such as a particular white man: as an occupant of a determinate position in space-time, or at least as a function of such a being. My thoughts, like every other existent, are particular, and are modifications of me, who occupy space, and am spatio-temporally related to every other particular.

This very general argument offers no guarantee that one's sensory experience is not deceptive on some occasion, but then neither can Locke or Berkeley offer such security against illusion. The difference from their arguments is in their concession to the sceptic that the existence of the physical world is not implicit in the mere *fact* of experience. Hence they conceive of our belief in it as the conclusion of a sweeping inference, causal or deductive, from the *nature* or *structure* of experience. I believe that such a conception is incoherent, in that any characterisation of those features of experience that can plausibly be held to be the basis of a belief in, or concept of, physical reality will itself presuppose the existence of that reality. My argument has been limited to the criterion of involuntariness, which presupposes reality as a possible sphere of voluntary action. Here epistemology can be related attractively to the theory of action; for it is only on the reasonable view that an agent is a conscious animal, rather than a theoretically independent consciousness, that the concept of an intentional physical action appears in the least perspicuous.

Such an approach to epistemology has, in its emphasis on the requirements of particular existence and on the essentially physical nature of persons, a certain amount in common with that of Professor Strawson, as propounded in his important book *Individuals*. But underlying some of his arguments there seems to be the traditional presupposition that experience might have been insufficiently orderly and coherent to give ground for a concept of physical or objective reality. Such a line of argument I shall now examine.

In our conceptual scheme as it is, Strawson says, material things are, in some sense, the basic particulars. The identification of particulars of other kinds, e.g. events or states, is parasitic on the identification of appropriately related bodies in space, to which in the end we can simply point. Now Strawson asks the question whether this *must* be so for every conceivable conceptual scheme that, like our own, 'provides for a system of objective and identifiable particulars' to serve as the objects of perceptual states, from which they are distinct. In explanation of this notion of an objective particular, it is said that a pain is not an objective particular, since it is a state of an observer's mind: whereas the knife entering his flesh is such a particular.

Strawson's response to this question is his hypothesis of what he variously calls 'a purely auditory experience', 'a no-space world in which experience is purely auditory', 'a sound-world', and even 'a purely auditory universe'. He asks the question: 'Could a being whose experience was purely auditory make use of the distinction between himself and his states on the one hand, and something not himself, or a state of himself, of which he had experience on the other?' Strawson then tries to give a sense, within such a limited experience, to the notion, not only of a particular sound which lasts as long as it is heard, nor of a reidentifiable *kind* of sound, but of a reidentifiable *particular* sound, a sound that could be thought of as surviving interruptions in the observation of it, and as different from other sounds qualitatively identical. To be objective it must be capable of unperceived existence, even though, *ex hypothesi*, it cannot be supposed to derive such continued existence from the continued existence of something other than a sound, as, for example, 'the visible but inaudible scrapings of the street violinist as the street band marches by'. We need, Strawson says, a non-temporal dimension in which to house the objects that are held to exist continuously though unobserved.

He claims to supply the requisite auditory analogy of space by the hypothesis of a continuously heard master-sound of a distinctive and constant timbre and loudness, but varying in pitch by a smooth progression. This smooth variation gives us the concepts of movement and position, of returning to the same position, and of observing sound-sequences other than the master-sound at particular positions. For as the master-sound changes, other sound-sequences can be supposed to fade in and out. If qualitatively identifiable sound-sequences are observed always at the same pitch-position, or change position only in regular ways, then we have the possibility of reidentifiable sound-sequences, and therefore of unobserved existence and the concurrent existence of indefinitely many qualitatively identical sound-sequences at different positions. Strawson conceives of his sound-world as 'containing many particulars unheard at any moment, but audible at other positions than the one occupied at that moment'. He uses the radio as an analogy for his own analogy of space: 'One can tune out a station', he writes, 'and tune it in again while the same piece is being played; or, instead, one might tune in a different station where the same piece is being simultaneously played by a different orchestra.' For the auditory experience, of course, the analogy for tuning in is also auditory, i.e. change of pitch level: and it is solely this pitch-position, rather than the independent criterion of numerically different sources of sound such as orchestras, that differentiates particular sounds in the no-space world.

At this point Strawson argues that the conceptual scheme allowing for reidentifiable particulars that is applicable to his imaginary experience, as so far described, would *not* have to allow for any distinction between the observer and his states on the one hand and the objects of his observation on the other, since the concept of the Self would have no use. The personal pronoun, even the verb 'to hear' is superfluous. Now, however, Strawson introduces the concept of action, supposing that the being with the purely auditory experience can sometimes initiate change of pitch-position, although sometimes such change merely occurs. A conceptual distinction between initiated and non-initiated change of viewpoint, and between intentions and other predictions, would now be necessary for its thought. But even so the concept of the Self is unnecessary, and would only become necessary, Strawson goes on to argue, if there were an auditory analogy for our own physical characteristics, physical bodies and physical activity: thus *ipso facto* opening up the possibility of meeting and communicating with other people in auditory space. Hence the observer must be capable not only of initiating a change of position for the purposes of observation of sound-sequences, but also of initiating some sound sequences themselves, 'endowing him, so to speak, with a voice'. A persistent audible body might be provided by postulating a different timbre for each individual's master-sound, 'though no one hears another's except when it is at the same pitch-level or nearly the same pitch-level as his own'.

The tendency of this argument is borne out, Strawson claims, by the fact that, in our actual conceptual scheme, one thinks of oneself as a being with both mental and physical characteristics and states, such that whatever can be attributed to oneself can meaningfully be attributed to others. Strawson's purpose is anti-sceptical. He claims to have shown that the possibility of a concept of oneself and one's own mental states presupposes, first, the acceptability of a concept of reidentifiable objects that can exist unperceived, and secondly, the acceptability of a concept of a person having both mental and objectively observable characteristics. Thus any conceivable language in which it is possible to describe and identify oneself must reflect a conceptual scheme in which material or quasi-material objects, among them persons, are basic particulars. The sceptic, therefore, in postulating that he himself, or rather his own purely *mental* history, is or might be the only existent, is using a conceptual scheme to think what, given the acceptability of that scheme, must be false.

Now I am chiefly concerned with the claim that, appropriately structured, the so-called 'sound-world' can supply an adequate formal analogy of space: sufficient, that is to say, to allow for real objects, the *esse* of which is not *percipi*, and for observers who have a place and can act in the world they observe. I believe that the formal analogy that Strawson has contrived is quite inadequate for this purpose, and that ultimately it cannot even account for individual or particular existence. The reason for this should be familiar to philosophers, since Strawson is attempting a part of precisely the task at which Leibniz failed, the postulation of a qualitative manifold, or system of qualitative relationships, that is capable of replacing the quantitative manifold, or system of spatio-temporal relationships. Leibniz, of course, tried to solve his problem by the doctrine of the identity of indiscernibles, i.e. he was prepared to accept that a particular thing is individuated by purely general properties that it possesses, so that no two things *could* be qualitatively the same, or occupy the same place on the qualitative manifold. This doctrine is unacceptable just because any universal comprising however complex a set of qualities is intrinsically capable of being reproduced in indefinitely many places at once. Qualitatively identical candlesticks can be numerically different just because they occupy different positions on the mantlepiece: a thing's position is not one of its qualities.

The analogy with Strawson's system is clear, for in it position is defined qualitatively, by the pitch of the master-sound. But awareness of one's position in real space is necessarily an awareness of one's relationships with identifiable particular things. In a sense it may be the character of one's experience that enables one to locate oneself as, say, somewhere in Egypt; but this is because it enables one to identify particular things, such as the pyramids, or at least kinds of things known to be locally restricted, such as the desert flora. In Strawson's world the observer does not have to learn his location from his relationship to identifiable landmarks, but rather he can identify particulars because of his awareness of the quality of his experience, which is what *defines* his position. It is as if, *per impossibile*, we could directly perceive our position in absolute space.

Strawson discusses the related objection that awareness of the spatial is an awareness of 'a system of relations over and above those which arise from the definite character of each element', whereas position and movement in his auditory system turn on qualitative change. He dismisses the objection, suggesting that this difference is contingent on the peculiar nature of *visual* experience in which we are directly presented with a spatial manifold. This response, how-ever, has the unacceptable implication that it is only from the peculiar *quality* of a pain in his left foot that a blind man could know that it is in his left foot. Awareness of the spatial, visual or otherwise, is awareness of a system of relationships, not because of the peculiar-ities of any mode of awareness, but because that is what spatiality is. This is true even for the sense of hearing: to hear a sound as coming from the left is not to be aware of any qualitative peculiarity of the sound, since a qualitatively indiscernible sound could equally well be heard as coming from the right.

In a later chapter Strawson actually opposes his auditory world to the system of Leibniz, arguing that, although points in the auditory space-analogue could be determined descriptively as different pitch-levels, yet the necessity of demonstratives of time, e.g. 'now', is implied by such un-Leibnizian distinctions, possible in the sound-world, as that between qualitatively identical sounds occurring at the same pitch-position, but at different times. Thus he admits that only Time saves his system from the fate of that of Leibniz: a failure ever to descend from the abstract world of universals and concern itself with concrete reality, with this and with that. But this is tacitly to confess that he has not achieved the aim that he earlier set himself, of endowing the sound-world with, in his own words, 'a non-temporal dimension in which unperceived particulars may be housed'. What Strawson has done is not the philosophically exciting and significantly unprecedented feat of describing a possible non-temporal and non-spatial dimension, but that of subtly disguising the inadequacy of Time to serve alone as the basis for individuation, rather as a painter may disguise the fact that a plane does not *really* allow for one thing's passing behind another. Strawson's world may not be that abstract world in which the identity of indiscernibles is true, but it embodies a sawn-off version of the doctrine. The same uneasiness is engendered that logical necessities are being explained as consequences of cosmic contingencies. In order to parallel the necessary fact that whatever has experience exists *somewhere*, Strawson adopts the plainly contingent hypothesis of an ever-present sound with varying pitch. As an analogy for the necessity that people have bodies and are themselves perceptible, he suggests, not indeed Leibniz's divinely ordained harmony between monads, but the device of an individually peculiar timbre, which seems to require the assumption that no one has a twin, or, at least, ever meets him. The danger of Strawson's story is in its implication that the validity of our own conceptual scheme, centred as it is on things and persons, depends equally on natural facts: the fact that experience follows a specific orderly course. But it is the concept of particular identity that is at issue: it strikes me as an entirely implausible assumption that the distinction between particulars and universals, like some especially subtle bit of biological classification, reflects some natural feature of the world.

Another distinction that can only be misrepresented if it is supposed to rest on the contingent character of experience is surely the distinction between oneself and other things. It is in trying to answer the question: 'What are the conditions of our making this distinction, and how are they fulfilled?' that Strawson considers what conceivable features in the purely auditory experience would make it, as he says, useful or convenient or necessary to advert to the distinction in any description of that experience. The argument *seems*, at least, to rest on the assumption that, if some simplified kind of thought about a simplified kind of experience is conceivable without overtly using a particular conceptual distinction, then to conceive of a world in which experience is of this simplified kind is to conceive of a world to which this distinction has no application. Yet that a being of limited experience might have no reason, in terms of what is convenient or useful or necessary, for drawing the self–other distinction, is of course no ground for the conclusion that we who imagine him are entitled to deny that the distinction has application to his world. To put the point another way, to imagine such a limited creature is not the same as to imagine a limited world. The earthworm, the new-born baby, the blind man, inhabit the same world as the rest of us; if we sometimes *talk* of their peculiar worlds, we do not *mean* it. Yet Strawson passes without comment from a description of a purely auditory experience to talk of a no-space world.

Strawson describes a system of sounds, but what is he describing? Is his subject merely how things sound to an observer, so that Strawson is mentioning only sensory states; or are they real sounds, i.e. physical events and processes? The reply implicit in the argument is, of course, that until an appropriate structure is postulated for the sound-world, this distinction has no application; even if the vague word 'experience' is used, it must be purged as far as possible of its connotation of mental states. But this response, so reminiscent of Russell's extraordinary theory of sense-data as a neutral world-stuff, neither mental nor physical, is like a refusal to discuss the history of dogs, on the ground that dogs have no use for the concept of the past.

Now, at last, I return to the concept of action. The question whether Strawson's sounds are real is both like, and connected with, another: are they voluntarily induced or not? It is very possible that, until the point at which Strawson introduces into his story the distinction between changes that are voluntarily initiated and changes that simply occur, his creature will have no use or need for such a distinction. But this will be true whether, in the story so far, no changes were voluntary or all were. Given that voluntary change is logically possible, one answer or the other must be given. And only in so far as events were involuntary could they rightly be said to be perceptions of an independent reality, however orderly or coherent they may otherwise be: only on that condition could there be anything appropriate in the use of the concept of objectivity 'to do justice to' the structure of the sound-system. Yet, as I have argued, this concept of involuntariness can only be explained in a way that presupposes the existence of a real physical world, and the possibility of physical action.

Moreover, when eventually Strawson admits the voluntary/non-voluntary distinction into his system, he must be prepared to tell us whether voluntary change is initiated in the way in which a mental state might be self-induced, or in the way in which a physical action is performed. If the latter, then the presupposition of a self-other distinction has been recognised with a vengeance, so that it is even possible to initiate sounds that are never heard; and Strawson is stranded on the sands of Lockean circularity. If the former, then he runs up against the Berkeleyan contradiction of the self-induced perception, or imaginary reality. There is no third way, and scepticism cannot be refuted from its own premises.

The reason why something must be 'given' in perception is not mysterious. As every psychologist knows, the study of perception is by definition the study of how objects causally affect animals in such a way that the animal learns something about the object. This precludes the purely voluntary production of perceptual states. So much of the causal theory is impeccably true. What primarily is pernicious about the philosophical theory with this name is that it presents itself as an answer to scepticism. Another and related shortcoming is that it presents the causal relationship as holding, not between physical things in general on the one hand, and states of animals on the other, but between Matter on the one hand and Mind on the other. These two mistakes are connected because, as Descartes explicitly and rightly argued, as soon as the possibility is admitted of a coherent, even merely methodological, doubt about the existence of the physical world, it is also admitted that minds are substances theoretically capable of existing on their own. I have tried to indicate reasons for thinking that Descartes was arguing from an incoherent premise.

6

THINKING AND PERFORMANCE

A. Palmer

THE explanation of change or movement has always been a central concern of philosophers. Some, like Aristotle, have taken the movement of living things as their paradigm, and tried to explain all movement or change in that way. Others, after the fashion of Descartes, concentrate on the movement of inanimate things and generalise explanations of this to encompass all movement or change. For Aristotle, things have a principle of growth, organisation and movement in their own right. The movement or change of a natural thing is explained by its tendency to move in that way. The line he draws is not, as the line which we would perhaps like to draw is, between organic and inorganic things, but between these grouped together as subject to the same kind of explanation and, on the other hand, artificial things. A problem that results from this division is that while it might seem plausible to explain changes which occur in a baby when it grows into a man by saying that babies naturally tend to grow into men, and if they do not then something has interfered with their natural development, it seems odd to treat inorganic things in this way. Restricted to the contrast between the natural and the artificial, the explanation of stones falling when unsupported is clearly going to provide some difficulty. Although it is true that Aristotle does not think that because in the case of man the form with which matter is formed to make that substance is called a soul, that therefore any kind of form joined with matter to make a substance is called a soul, nevertheless the explanation of things which are a combination, a natural combination, of form and matter is the same for both man and other substances. Confronted with the explanation of falling bodies in this way, it first of all seems implausible and then suggests that things should happen which in fact do not. If it is assumed that the principle of movement is in the stone, ought it not to be assumed that the principle of stopping is in it too? Babies grow into men because it is in their nature to do so perhaps, but that stones fall downwards because it is in their nature to do so has, as Molière noticed in the case of a similar explanation of why opium puts you to sleep, a hollow ring.

There is evidence to support the view that it was from a consideration of the difficulties involved in the Aristotelian explanation of physical phenomena that Descartes was led to his own view that the explanation of all movement, with the sole exception of human beings, should be based on a model that could handle these without difficulty. Present-day psychologists have gone even further in extending this form of explanation to the behaviour of human beings. The difficulties they encounter are no less than those which the Aristotelian explanation of falling bodies encountered. For some time now arguments have been current in philosophical literature which have the result of showing that human behaviour, in any respectable sense of the word, cannot be reduced to or explained in terms of movements, no matter how complex these movements and no matter what they are movements of. Making a signal, giving a gift, or writing a cheque, all need movement to be performed, but they are not mere movement. Because of this the ideal of explaining behaviour in terms of 'colourless movements' has, as a glance at any text in behavioural psychology will reveal, remained unrealised.

Each of the paradigms adopted by Aristotle and Descartes does an injustice to the central feature of the other. It should be clear that the lesson to be drawn from history is that it is a mistake to look for one paradigm for the explanation of all change or movement. My aim in this lecture is to draw some of what I consider to be the epistemological implications of this lesson from history. Explanation is simply the other side of the coin from knowing and understanding, so the historical moral is that a single paradigm of knowledge or understanding is not to be sought. If that is what epistemology seeks, then epistemology should be given up. My attention will largely be concentrated on the empiricist line that I have sketched as coming from Descartes, so that in part what I am after is a rationale for the failure of the behaviour-to-movement reduction. But this reduction only makes sense in the background of a particular epistemological outlook, and so can be used as a test case for it. My general argument is that such a reduction commits the fallacy of analysing the necessary condition for a state of affairs in terms of the state of affairs that has this necessary condition. If A is a necessary condition of B, then A cannot be analysed in terms of B. To take a well-worn example from the history of philosophy, if a necessary condition of 'X knows that Y' is that Y is the case, then Y's being the case cannot be analysed in terms of X's knowledge. A failure to realise this led philosophers, from Descartes onwards, on a long and unprofitable route.

Now clearly I am not going to argue that behaviour is a necessary condition of movement. If this were the case it would presumably be clear that an analysis of behaviour in terms of movement would be absurd. But behaviour is not such a necessary condition. On the contrary, the relationship is *prima facie* the other way round – omitting acts of omission, doing something by doing nothing – and there is no corresponding difficulty in analysing something in terms of its necessary conditions. But I shall try to show that behaviour is a necessary condition for thinking about movement. If one could not do things like signing a cheque or building a house then one could have no idea of change or movement. But this is sufficient to rule out the reduction of behaviour to movement since such a reductive endeavour is at least the attempt to conceive of behaviour without straying beyond our ideas of movement, and as such commits the fallacy I outlined a moment ago.

II

One necessary condition for thinking of movement or change is the possibility of having the idea of something being other than it is. The book is on the shelf but it could be on the floor, and if it were impossible to think of it in that position then the idea of it falling to the floor would be unintelligible. In this case, the book remains, but its position has changed. It is possible to think of all sorts of other things about the book being different, and in the limiting case, the change would be such that it would be true to say that the book no longer exists. Thinking of things as other than they are, and thinking of things that do not exist, differ only in degree and not in category. A world in which things popped in and out of existence, without their changing in any other way, would be queer just because one limit of this continuum is maintained while the rest is discarded. Thinking of unicorns, when there are no unicorns, is logically on the same level as thinking of things moving or changing. One is the limiting case of the other. Once this is recognised, difficulties in a variety of philosophical positions become clear. It shows, for example, the problem which lies behind Descartes's otherwise confusing Fourth Meditation. For if the ground for knowledge is solely the presentation of particular things in perception, then, by this fact, the possibility of error is removed, and knowledge has no grounds at all. When perception is treated in this way, as the passive reception of particulars, the world is always as it is seen, and the fact that it is manifestly not always as it is thought to be cannot, from the starting-point of perception, be explained. Thought has to have some generality for it to be possible to think of things as other than they are, and this generates, given the Cartesian perceptual starting-point, the difficulty of moving from the particularity of perception to the generality of thought. When perception is treated as the passive reception of particular impressions, the generality of thought, the possibility of error, and hence the possibility of knowledge, needs a doctrine of abstraction to support it. There is no need now to argue that such a doctrine cannot be maintained.[1] Seeing Descartes's difficulties is one way of coming to realise that (*a*) being mistaken, (*b*) the generality of thought, and (*c*) thinking of things moving or changing, are not things that can be understood independently of each other. It is not by accident that two of Parmenides' doctrines can go hand in hand, viz. that the world is a plenum in which nothing moves, and that the order of thought is the order of reality. Given that we can think of things other than they are, it follows that the Cartesian view must be wrong. While it may be true that perception is of particulars, it cannot be a reception of particulars, otherwise the generality of thought is unintelligible. In what way, then, can the generality of thought be made intelligible?

III

One of the points that I have just raised about the characteristics thought must have, in order for thought about movement or change to be possible, could be expressed grammatically by saying that the object of the verb 'to think' need not be any existing thing. Along with this characteristic go others. If different descriptions of the object are substituted, the truth value of the proposition expressed by the sentence may change: if I am thinking of John, and John is the tallest man in the room, it does not follow that I am thinking of the tallest man in the room. There are other verbs of which this is not true, e.g. 'to kick' and 'to see'. Moreover the object of 'to think', un-

---

[1] See P. T. Geach, *Mental Acts* (London, 1957).

like the objects taken by these other verbs, may be indeterminate; if I kick the table it is a determinate particular table that I kick, but I can think about a table without there being a determinate particular table that I am thinking about. If we call those verbs which share these characteristics with the verb 'to think' intentional verbs, then we could call those characteristics of thought necessary for thought about movement or change to be possible intentional characteristics. This would merely be to provide a label. But if it is true that the activities which can be intended have characteristics parallel to those of the objects of thought,[1] then the label might seem apt. And if the background of intentional activity renders these characteristics intelligible, i.e. if no problems with regard to intentional activity arise, comparable to those created by setting thought in the background of the passive reception of particulars, then the way will be left open for the consideration of intentional activity as a necessary condition for the intelligibility of thinking about movement or change. To put this to the test it is necessary to show what limits can be set to what can be intended. I have so far used the vague word 'activity'. This must now be made more specific.

The verb 'to intend' needs to be followed, in general though not always, by some other verb. Is it possible to delimit the verbs which can be found in that position? Recent philosophical literature contains various discussions of verbs, mainly centring round distinctions made by Aristotle. The two main overlapping writings are a paper by Zeno Vendler entitled 'Verbs and Times' in *The Philosophical Review* (1957), and a chapter in Anthony Kenny's book *Action, Emotion and Will* entitled 'States, Performances and Activities'. Both distinguish between verbs which have, and those which do not have, continuous tenses. Vendler then makes a distinction within both of these classes, while Kenny only makes a distinction within the class of continuous tense verbs. It is pretty clear that 'to know' does not have a continuous tense, while 'to run' has: 'I am knowing' does not make sense, while 'I am running' does. Like 'to know' in this respect are 'to reach', 'to love', 'to win' and 'to believe'. Does it make sense to say that one intends to do the things signified by these verbs? It is pretty clear that these are all poor candidates for intending. 'To win' might have some *prima facie* plausibility, but this does not survive close inspection. If someone said that he intended to win the game, this would be interpreted not as telling us that winning was his intended action, but that he was determined to do everything in his power to ensure his winning, i.e. that he intended

---

[1] See G. E. M. Anscombe, 'The Intentionality of Sensation: A Grammatical Feature', in *Analytical Philosophy, Second Series*, ed. R. J. Butler.

to try tremendously hard. Strictly speaking winning is not, and could not be, what is intended. I can think of no verb lacking a continuous tense that can follow 'intend', so there remain those verbs with continuous tenses. It is clear off-hand that many of these fill the bill. This does not mean that any such verb is suitable, but only that having such a tense does not rule out the verb from being used in such a way. So on to the subdivision of this class.

Kenny makes the distinction as follows: 'Where "A is ϕing" implies "A has not ϕd" I shall call the verb a "performance verb" and say that it stands for a performance; where "A is ϕing" implies rather "A has ϕd" I shall call the verb an "activity verb" and say that it stands for an activity.'[1] I find many of Kenny's examples difficult at this point, although the principle of distinction seems clear enough. His example of 'to kill' as a performance verb seems to lack the basic qualification for this, namely a continuous tense. To use one of Ryle's criteria, could 'killing Tom Jones' be something I was doing all morning, was interrupted while doing and then recommenced after the interruption? Unlike 'trying to kill': compare 'find' and 'trying to find'. Nor is 'killing Xs' in any better position, since this means killing one, and then another, and then another, and so on. It is something that I could do continually, but not continuously. However, I do not wish to quarrel with examples, so let us take an example of a performance with which everyone would agree, e.g. 'building a house'. It is clear that this is something that can be intended.

On the other hand, more difficulty is presented by verbs which signify activities. 'To build' is an example of an activity verb. 'He is building' implies that he has built, although not that there is any specific thing that he has built. But while 'he intends to build a house' is perfectly intelligible as it stands, 'he intends to build' has an air of incompletion about it, and is dependent upon the context in which it is said for it to be comprehensible. So if we considered this example alone, we would be tempted to say that only performances can be intended.

But the situation is not so straightforward as this. It is possible to take any verb which you have reason to suppose is, on Kenny's criterion, an activity verb, and find yourself debating whether or not it can be intended. The debate will proceed via a series of imagined contextual circumstances, in some of which it would be possible to see what a person might mean when he said that that activity could be intended. But the contexts thus necessary would be just those that

<hr />

[1] Kenny, ibid., pp. 172–3.

should make one doubt whether the verb in question was correctly placed in the class of activity verbs. In other words there is something wrong with the procedure I have adopted so far of supposing that verbs with continuous tenses can be divided into two groups, of which it then makes sense to ask, as a distinct question, whether intention is at home with one group and not the other. This leads me to suspect that the distinction between activity and performance is not as clear as it first seemed, which may account for the trouble originally experienced with Kenny's examples.

Perhaps the difficulty is that Kenny is attempting to distinguish by means of grammar things which are in fact not grammatical. The criterion he suggests for making the distinction between activity and performance is not self-applying, so let us ask how we decide whether '*A* is ϕing' implies or does not imply that '*A* has ϕd'. The obvious, and I think the only, answer is that if ϕ can be construed as something which has a destination, an aim, or a point, then the possibility opens up that the destination has not been reached, the aim not realised, or the point not attained, and it is just the question as to whether this possibility is open that is being sought in asking whether or not '*A* is ϕing' implies that '*A* has not ϕd'. If ϕing cannot be construed in this way then it will be classed as an activity verb. Now clearly there will be some verbs which are obviously to be construed as performance verbs, and others equally obviously not to be so construed. But for many verbs it will not be obvious how they are to be taken, and there the decision will depend heavily on the context. Whether a verb signifies an activity or a performance is not – as whether it is in the perfect tense is – a grammatical quality of that verb. Consider, for example, the verb 'to walk'. On the face of it '*A* is walking' does seem to imply that '*A* has walked', and so we would allocate it to the class of activity verbs, as opposed to 'walking to the university', which certainly does not imply 'has walked to the university', and which in contrast would be allocated to the class of performance verbs. But now, if we ask whether it makes sense to talk about an intention to walk, it is clear that situations could be envisaged in which this would make sense. Imagine someone recovering from the paralysing effects of an accident. He could express his determination by saying that he intended to walk. Now one could handle this in two ways. One could say that the envisaged situation is one in which walking refers to an achievement, in which case it needs to be treated in the way in which 'winning' and 'finding' were treated; or we can take walking to be what he in his attempts is doing, which leaves open the possibility of failure, in which case it is being treated as a performance, and there can be no inference from present to perfect tense. Hence the distinction between activity and performance needs concepts associated with intention for its application, concepts like 'aim', 'point' and 'destination'. The distinction is not, of course, just that between what can be and what cannot be intended, as an example like 'flowing to the sea' shows. But in making the distinction we need to employ those very concepts we need to employ when deciding whether intention is present.

To ask whether a verb signifies something which can be intended, and to ask whether it is a performance verb, is not then to ask two unrelated questions. Further characteristics attributed to performances reiterate this point. What a performance verb signifies goes on for a time, but it has a logically definite finishing-point, and would not be finished just at any moment when it stopped.[1] This means that it is possible to begin them, and not succeed in them. In this they differ from activities which, once begun, are – if the concept of success can be applied to them at all – necessarily successful. One cannot begin to build without doing some building, just as one cannot begin to walk without doing some walking. This possible lack of success indicates the possible application of the notion of intention. One can only intend to do those things which it is possible to fail to do. Hence, in so far as a verb signifies something which it is difficult to think of someone beginning and not accomplishing, it is absurd to think of him as intending to do what the verb signifies.

IV

The reason for being particular about what can be intended was the hope that intentional activity could provide the background in which the characteristics of thought necessary for the conception of movement or change would be intelligible. The intelligibility of these characteristics had been called into question by the recognition of the inadequacies of the theory of abstraction demanded by a particular epistemological outlook. But if activities could be intended, the idea of intention would be as problematic as that of abstraction, *vis-à-vis* the intelligibility of the characteristics of thought, simply because in the case of activities characteristics parallel to those of thinking are not evident. With performances one can produce parallel characteristics. Take as an example 'walking to the university'. The parallel to the possible non-existence of the object of thought is found by noticing that the correct description of what a

[1] See C. C. W. Taylor, 'States, Activities and Performances', in *Proc. Arist. Soc.*, Suppl. vol. (1965).

person is intentionally doing may still be 'walking to the university' even if, perhaps because of a recent fire, the university no longer exists. Again, substituting different descriptions may alter the truth value. If, for example, the university is correctly characterised as the most bureaucratic institution in England, it may not be true that what I am intentionally doing is walking to the most bureaucratic institution in England, even when it is true that I am walking to the university. An activity, in contrast to a performance, is defined in terms of what is going on at a particular moment; it does not have changes built into it by virtue of anything that is in the future, and consequently does not carry with it the intentional characteristics of future reference. Its progress is not mapped out for it; it can continue or it can stop, but it has no destination. Performances are not like this. The difference between the two is like that between a line drawn at random on a graph, and one drawn in accordance with a particular formula. The formula tells you how to go on drawing the line: it gives you its direction. An intention is concerned with the direction of our doings, which is why activities cannot be intended.

Now when a person is doing something intentionally it follows that he knows what he is doing. So we can use this implication to explain how it is that thought possesses the characteristics it does, which in turn helps us to explain how it is possible to think of movement or change. The characteristics of thought are the characteristics of action when thought and action are wedded in performance. If thinking is considered without the background of performance its characteristics will inevitably seem baffling. When, in the chapter on self-knowledge in the *Concept of Mind*, Ryle is making the point that you can know things about yourself, namely what you are doing or thinking, without having to inspect your actions or introspect your thoughts, he employs the notion of a serial operation or a non-sudden task. (This is the equivalent of performance.) He argues that you can know what you are doing because you are doing whatever it is with your mind on your job:

> Now if the agent is carrying out such a serial operation with any degree of heed, he must at any given stage in it have in mind, in some sense, what is to be done next and what has already been done; he must have kept track of where he had got to and he must be expecting, or even intending, to be getting on to the stages after the present stage.

What such a person will do in certain contingencies is dictated by what it is in fact that he is doing. All that he does has reference to

anticipated future doings. The graph of his behaviour is circum-
scribed by the formula of the serial operation in which he is engaged.
There is nothing mysterious about future reference here. Yet Ryle in
another place ('A Puzzling Element in the Notion of Thinking',
Lecture to the British Academy, 1958) confesses that he finds
puzzling the inceptive quality of thinking. What he there highlights
and finds puzzling strikingly resembles that feature which is introduced as non-puzzling, or at least not puzzling in the same way,
in *The Concept of Mind*. This is clear in the examples he gives:

> A rowing enthusiast says that he had been thinking about the
> Oxford University crew; and if asked bluntly, would deny that at
> that moment he had been thinking about the Cambridge crew.
> Yet it might transpire that his thought about the Oxford crew was,
> or included, the thought that though it was progressing, it was not
> progressing fast enough. 'Not fast enough for what?' we ask. 'Not
> fast enough to beat Cambridge next Saturday.' So he had been
> thinking about the Cambridge crew, only thinking about it in a
> sort of threshold way.

The same is the case of the man who thinks, 'How lovely your roses
are', and whose thought is an incipient thought of his wife. It is
noticeable that a further example which Ryle gives is that of a child
indulging in a serial operation, namely that of multiplying £9 17s 4d
by 8. Inceptivity only becomes a puzzling element in the notion of
thinking if thinking is considered in isolation from performance. For
certain purposes it may be necessary to treat the two as separate, but
they can never be divorced.

It must be stressed at this point that the argument is not intended
to show, what seems to be manifestly false, that thinking is a performance; we can talk of 'thinking about' which is activity, as contrasted with 'thinking out', which is performance. All thinking is
not a sort of problem solving, it need not necessarily have any point
or be conducted towards some end. It is one thing to remove some of
the puzzles about thinking by stressing the concept of thought as it
operates in intelligent and attentive performance, bringing out what
Ryle calls its polymorphous character (i.e. that it does not consist in
some uniform activity process or operation). But it is quite a different
matter to say that this is so because all thinking is in fact a sort of
attentive and intelligent performance. Concepts such as 'musing' and
'daydreaming' seem specifically designed to introduce thinking
which is not any sort of performance. Nor is it an improvement to
think of it (as Stuart Hampshire does) as the beginning of a performance when the rest is cut off, a shadow of something that never

was but which, but for restraint, might have been. What is at stake in the argument is not the existence of thought as a part, detachable or non-detachable, of some whole, which could be pointed out by pointing out the whole of which it is such a part; it is not a case of discovering a new phenomenon, or rediscovering something which is lost, but rather that certain ingrained views about the way in which knowledge is gained make the characteristics of thought, and consequently knowledge, problematic. In the notion of thinking there are, if you like, no elements which by themselves are puzzling, only certain theories make them so.

v

I have argued, then, that the characteristics of thought that appear baffling in empiricist epistemology are not found to be so when seen in the background of intentional activity. The possibility of failure introduced by the application of notions such as 'aim', 'point' and 'destination', which allows the concept of intention to get a grip, brings with it also the intentional characteristics of thought without which thought about movements or change which have no aim, point or destination would not be possible. Hence an attempt to account for intentional activity in terms of such movements or change is self-stultifying.

If activities (in the Kenny sense) could be intended, the original bafflement about the characteristics of thought would still be with us. For while it would still be true that the notion of intentional activity brings with it the requisite characteristics of thought, it would be by virtue of the addition of intention to activity that this is so. We would then be in the position of trying to make the characteristics of thought less baffling by referring to the coincidence of intention and activity, when in fact it is just this coincidence that is baffling. The worry about how an intention can join with an activity to produce an intentional activity, reflects the same views on the relation of mind and body which generate the difficulties in empiricist epistemology over how thought could be about movement or change. What the discussion of the relation of intention to activities and performances showed was that, in the case of activities, the question of the coincidence of intention and activity does not arise, since activities cannot be intended, while the fact that the question of whether something is a performance is not distinct from the question of whether it can be intended also implies that there can be no problem of coincidence, since there are not two things to coincide.

The view of mind and body reflected in empiricist epistemology could be questioned in detail by extending the discussion of the characteristics of thought into the treatment of other psychological concepts, e.g. 'to believe' and 'to imagine', etc. It would be a mistake, however, to press this extension, as is sometimes suggested, as a way of using intentional characteristics to distinguish the mental from the non-mental. Such an attempt could not fail to bring with it problems akin to those about the characteristics of thought that I have been discussing. The general moral for the philosophy of mind that emerges is that it is a mistake to divide a person's mental history into segments; what he thought about, imagined, dreamed, etc., on the one hand, and on the other, what he did. When we describe a man as walking to the university, or building a house, we are saying more than that certain movements occurred with certain consequences. We are saying something about him which could not be true unless other things which could be described by intentional verbs were also true of him, and conversely what is signified by intentional verbs could not be the case without the background of performance. Deprived of this background the characteristics of these concepts would be unintelligible. We can only think about the world as we do because we behave in the ways we do. It is because thought and movement are unified in performance that thought about movement which is not performance is possible. Philosophers have sought to understand the world; they can only do so because they change it.

7

PHILOSOPHICAL
BEHAVIOURISM

C. W. K. Mundle

Professor C. A. Mace, the psychologist, once wrote: 'It is difficult
. . . to present and defend any sort of behaviourism whatever
without committing oneself to nonsense.'[1] I shall illustrate this thesis.
I shall comment on the writings of some psychologists. This is
relevant to my topic; for psychologists' expositions of behaviourism
contain much more philosophy than science, and the inconsistencies
which permeate their versions of behaviourism reappear in the works
of eminent philosophers. My quotation from Mace comes from a
paper defending what he calls 'analytical behaviourism'; which he
distinguishes from 'methodological behaviourism' and 'metaphysical
behaviourism'. According to Mace, analytical behaviourism does not
question the truth of our everyday statements about a person's
mind or states of consciousness; what it claims is that such statements 'turn out to be, on analysis, statements about the behaviour
of material things', that is, about a person's 'bodily acts, bodily
states, bodily dispositions, bodily "states of readiness" to act
in various ways'.[2] The father of behaviourism, J. B. Watson,
rarely says anything suggesting *this* doctrine. As he presents it, behaviourism is both a methodological principle and a metaphysical
theory.

Watson was proposing a method for scientific psychology when
he wrote in 1925: 'Let us limit ourselves to things that can be observed, and formulate laws concerning only those things. Now what
can be observed? Well, we can observe behaviour . . . .'[3] His reasons
for making this proposal are made clear. In his first manifesto in

[1] 'Some Implications of Analytical Behaviourism', in *Proc. Arist. Soc.* (1948–9) 4.
[2] Ibid., pp. 2 and 4.
[3] *Behaviourism*, p. 6.

1913,[1] he explains that he wants to discard completely the methodology practised by Wundt and his many pupils, according to which introspection is the primary source of data, and experiments and the natural history of mankind are auxiliary methods. Watson says sarcastically: 'If you fail to reproduce my findings . . . it is due to the fact that your introspection is untrained. . . . If . . . a feeling seems reasonably clear to you, your introspection is again faulty. You are seeing too much. Feelings are never clear.' And he concludes that 'psychology must discard all reference to consciousness' (p. 163); and that 'there is no reason why . . . introspective data should ever be sought during the experimentation, or published in the results' (p. 170). In 1925 he asserts that 'instead of self-observation being the easiest and most natural way of studying psychology, it is an impossible one' (p. 10).

Watson also commits himself to a metaphysical thesis – rejection of mind-body dualism in favour of physicalism. This is not stressed in his first manifesto, where he recommends that psychologists should ignore the 'time-honoured relics of philosophical speculation' (p. 166). But in his books, he says things implying that he is not only asserting physicalism but is also denying the occurrence of conscious states and processes; he even speaks of 'the fiction that there is such a thing as mental life'.[2] He urges psychologists to stop using not only words like 'consciousness', 'mental states' and 'mind'[3] but also 'all subjective terms such as sensation, perception, image, desire, purpose. . . .'[4] His reason appears to be that he thinks that there *are* no states of consciousness to which such words can be applied.

In his first manifesto Watson writes: 'I must confess to a deep bias . . . I have devoted nearly twelve years to experimentation on animals' (p. 175). Watson later became professionally interested in people, and profitably so. But in applying his methodology to the study of people he introduced inconsistencies which have been embraced by generations of psychologists, and by distinguished philosophers. I shall describe two of the most important inconsistencies and Watson's way of trying to camouflage them. The first concerns introspection. As we have seen, Watson asserts that introspection is impossible and that psychologists should never seek or publish 'introspective data'. But he did not practise what he preached. In his first manifesto he says, concerning 'what psychologists call imagery', that 'closer examination leads me to deny in my

---

[1] 'Psychology As The Behaviourist Views It', in *Psychological Review*, xx. (Hereafter referred to as 'PBV'.)

[2] *Behaviourism*, p. 180.   [3] 'PBV', p. 166.   [3] *Behaviourism*, p. 6; cf. p. 193.

own case the presence of imagery in the Galtonian sense' (p. 173). On the evidence of his own introspection, Watson inferred, despite the evidence of Galton, that everyone is like himself in this respect; he dismissed mental images as fictitious.[1] He adopted his notorious hypothesis of identifying thinking with muscular movements involved in sub-vocal speech. This, he says, 'makes reflective processes as mechanical as habit'.[2] But this hypothesis owes any plausibility it ever had to introspective data – to the fact that most people find, on introspection, that when they are thinking they are usually talking to themselves. Indeed Watson himself supports his hypothesis by appealing to the evidence of introspection. He says that the movements in the speech-organs 'rarely come to consciousness in any person who has not groped for imagery in the psychological laboratory'.[3]

Claims by behaviourist psychologists to dispense with introspective data have continued to be a kind of make-believe. They have gone on asking their subjects to report their experiences, to make what were formerly *called* 'introspective reports', and have rechristened these 'verbal behaviour', as if this made objective and scientific what was previously subjective and unscientific! Following Watson's advice, psychologists have tried to make experiments with people as similar as possible to experiments on rats. The method was described in principle by Watson in 1913. The experimenter is to ask the human subject to adjust the apparatus until, as he puts it, 'a standard control offered no basis for a differential response' (p. 171). He denies that this method involves 'using introspection'. This seems naïve. Watson's proposed method requires the experimenter to say to his subject something like this: 'Turn the knob until, or tell me when, this disc looks to you the same colour as that one.' In such a context, if the subject is co-operating, his response, stopping turning the knob, or saying 'Now', functions as a *statement*; a statement describing the subject's private experience. Watson and most of his followers ignore the fact that the recommended method of experimenting presupposes that the subject understands his instructions as a request for information about his own conscious experience, about something *not* observable by the experimenter.

Mr B. A. Farrell, a philosopher, also overlooks this point. He is endorsing a claim commonly made by psychologists when he says: 'It is not necessary for the psychologist to make [a human subject] talk to him. *In principle*, everything he wants to know can be discovered by

---

[1] See *Behaviourism*, p. 213.
[2] 'PBV', p. 174; cf. *Behaviourism*, pp. 191 ff.   [3] 'PBV', p. 174.

making [the subject] behave like a dog and depress keys or open lids. . . .'[1] This is false. Some psychologists are still curious about our states of consciousness and the light these throw on the workings of our sense-organs and central nervous system. Does anyone think that Wilder Penfield's important discoveries of the experiential effects of electrical stimulation of the brain are of no concern to psychology?[2] These discoveries could only have been made by relying on introspective reports. And how else could anyone discover the different effects on different people of the same psychedelic drugs? And so on. It is more than time that everyone recognised the double-think incapsulated in many psychologists' use of 'verbal behaviour' – pretending to treat an utterance merely as a conditioned muscular response, while in fact treating it as a *statement* about something to which the speaker has privileged access.

I turn to another influential inconsistency, misuse of the word 'behaviour'. We have no right to complain because psychologists have changed the meaning of an everyday word. Scientists, like philosophers, need to introduce and define technical terms. My complaint that Watson and others have *mis*used 'behaviour' is because they have used it in ways that are incompatible with their stated purpose, i.e. that the data of a scientific psychology should comprise only what *has* been observed and is *publicly* observable. Watson extended 'behaviour' to include what is not publicly observable, what he called 'internal' or 'implicit behaviour'.[3] Watson defined 'behaviour' as a response to a stimulus, but he oscillated between two very different ways of using 'response'. On the one hand he says: 'The response the behaviourist is interested in is the common-sense answer to the question "what is he doing and why is he doing it?" ';[4] and this is how Watson is thinking in his account of emotions. On the other hand he claims to be using 'response' as the physiologist does, to refer to muscular and glandular reactions;[5] and this is how he is thinking in his account of thinking. Watson asserts that 'speaking . . . to ourselves (thinking) is just as objective a type of behaviour as baseball'.[6] He does not notice the inconsistency between this and his admission that the muscular processes with which he identifies thinking are rarely noticed

[1] 'Experience', in *Mind* (1950).
[2] See Penfield and Roberts, *Speech and Brain Mechanism* (1959).
[3] See e.g. *Behaviourism*, p. 15.
[4] *Psychology from the Standpoint of a Behaviourist* (1919) p. 15.
[5] 'We should mean by response the total striped and unstriped muscular and glandular changes which follow upon a given stimulus.' (Ibid., p. 14.)
[6] *Behaviourism*, p. 6.

by anyone who has not 'groped for imagery', i.e. by introspection[1].

Some psychologists who call themselves 'behaviourists' have even stretched 'behaviour' to cover *all* the physical and chemical changes occurring inside the body, including hypothetical, not yet understood processes which, they assume, must determine how a person behaves, in the normal sense of 'behaves'. They have evidently forgotten the motive of Watson's methodology – that the data of scientific psychology should be *facts* which have been *observed*. How odd to classify hypothetical, not yet understood, brain-changes responsible for my recollecting something as '(observable) behaviour', while denying that my recollecting it is an introspectible datum!

'Behaviourism' is a term of approval among psychologists, especially in America; so psychologists tend to apply this word to their own theories, whatever these may be. Thus Mace appropriates 'analytical behaviourism' for his own theory, *although he rejects Watson's central proposal*, for he acknowledges introspection as an indispensable source of data, and does not even substitute a synonym for 'introspection'.[2] And Mace is one of those who stretch 'behaviour' to cover all 'bodily states', that is, apparently, everything that goes on inside an organism. Professor B. F. Skinner, however, has not forgotten the motive of the behaviourist methodology. He does not stretch 'behaviour' to cover processes in the central nervous system. For him an organism's behaviour is what you and I can observe, and the psychologists' task is to establish laws connecting such behaviour with environmental changes.[3] Yet Skinner, whether consistently or not,[4] acknowledges what he calls 'private events' or 'unemitted behaviour', including the experience of seeing what isn't there (imaging, dreaming, etc.). Skinner readmits introspective reports, and though he *calls* them 'verbal behaviour', he comes close to admitting that they are *statements*. He says: 'The verbal report is a response to a private event, and may be used as a source of information about it' (p. 282).

That is enough to show that psychologists use 'behaviourism' in very different ways. This should warn philosophers against using this name without explanation. Those philosophers who assert or deny that Ryle or Wittgenstein was a behaviourist, without any attempt

---

[1] Watson and others, by attaching instruments to their subjects' throats, tried, unsuccessfully, to confirm that thinking is always accompanied by muscle-movements. But this enterprise presupposed that the experimenters had an independent way of knowing when (and what) their subjects were thinking, i.e. their introspective reports!

[2] Op. cit., pp. 8–9.   [3] See *Science and Human Behaviour*, ch. III.

[4] I think not, in view of what he says about 'psychic inner causes'; ibid., pp. 29–31.

to explain their own use of this term, have not learnt Socrates' first lesson. I shall now show that the inconsistencies and camouflage-operations common in psychologists' writings reappear in philosophers' theories which are in some sense behaviouristic.

Since philosophy became, for many of its practitioners, a study of everyday language, philosophical behaviourism has usually taken the form of analytical behaviourism *à la* Mace; though it is often presented in jargon like 'discovering the logic of mental-conduct concepts'. This is a way of saying 'describing the uses of the words with which we describe a person's mind'. I shall distinguish two species of linguistic philosophy: *a priori* linguistics and pseudo-empirical linguistics. By the latter I mean practising *a priori* linguistics while professing to do empirical linguistics.

Professor Ayer's *Language, Truth and Logic* is a paradigm case of *a priori* linguistics. Ayer, though professing empiricism, propounds a rule in chapter 1 which he treats as *a priori*, i.e. the verification principle; and he deduces from it that we cannot significantly say things that we do significantly say, or that we don't mean by them what we do mean by them. One of Ayer's deductions is of a thesis which he describes as 'behaviouristic';[1] namely that if you say 'John is in pain', you are talking about *your own* sense-data – what *you* experience when you do what you'd normally describe as watching John wince, hearing him groan, etc. Ayer's reasoning is that John's pain would be a 'metaphysical object', if it were something 'completely inaccessible to *my* observation' (p. 129: my italics). He concludes that other people's experiences must be 'reduced' to his own (p. 130). As Ayer's use of it reveals, his verification principle asserts that a statement is meaningful for me if and only if it is verifiable *by me*.

Professor Carnap had made a very different deduction from the verification principle. He too had inferred that 'John is in pain' is 'a metaphysical pseudo-sentence' if it is about something unobservable by himself.[2] Carnap's solution is to *define* words like 'pain' or 'excitement' in terms of 'the physical structure (microstructure) of [the] body (especially of [the] central nervous system) . . .' (p. 172). How odd that Carnap should commit this inconsistency common among psychologists. For Carnap explicitly starts with the epistemological question: 'How can I verify that another person is in pain or excited?' Obviously he defeats his own purpose by defining 'pain', etc., in terms of the microstructure of the CNS; for none of us can

---

[1] *Language, Truth and Logic* (1946) p. 20. (Hereafter referred to as *LTL*: references are to the revised edition.)

[2] 'Psychology in Physical Language' (1932); reprinted in *Logical Positivism*, ed. Ayer, p. 174.

yet complete, and few of us can even begin, a description of the microstructure which Carnap decided to identify with pain.

In 1936 Professor Ryle offered Ayer a way of escaping from some of his paradoxes by amending the verification principle so that 'verifiable-by-me' is replaced by 'verifiable-by-someone-or-other'.[1] Twenty years later Ayer adopted Ryle's suggestion,[2] but only after making desperate attempts to defend his verifiable-by-me principle; by saying, for example, that it is logically possible that I should have one of your sense-data.[3] Unfortunately Ryle did not himself adhere to his 1936 version of the verification principle, and seems to have applied a different version in his post-war writings.

I shall now consider the pseudo-empirical linguistics which have been inspired by Wittgenstein's later remarks. I shall limit my attention to three examples: Ryle's *The Concept of Mind (C of M)*, Wittgenstein's *Philosophical Investigation (PI)* and Malcolm's *Dreaming*. In each of these books a version of the verification principle is a suppressed premiss, i.e. is needed to support the arguments, but is never formulated or acknowledged; presumably because Wittgenstein had laid it down that philosophers 'may not advance any kind of theory'.[4] Each of these books makes assertions which imply analytical behaviourism *à la* Mace. What is most remarkable is that each author presents such claims as a description of the grammar of everyday language, as reminders about how people talk when not corrupted by philosophy. Naturally this curious programme creates conflicts, for the beliefs built into the grammar of English and other Indo-European languages are not behaviourist but dualist. (Not that *that* settles any philosophical problems.)

Ryle's *C of M* is full of false statements of the form 'we cannot or may not, properly or significantly, say so and so', where 'so and so' is something we *do* say: like 'he is healthy in mind and body' or 'his behaviour had both mental and physical causes'. Ryle qualifies this thesis at one point by saying that such sentences could only be used to make a joke.[5] Plato, Descartes and the average Englishman have failed to see the joke. Ryle sometimes does *a priori* linguistics, deducing from rules of his own invention that we cannot say things that we do say.[6] Presumably Ryle's *intention* was not to reform the English

---

[1] 'Unverifiability by Me', in *Analysis*, IV.

[2] *The Problem of Knowledge*, pp. 199, 238–9 and 246.

[3] *Foundations of Empirical Knowledge* (1940) p. 169.

[4] *PI*, § 109.   [5] *C of M*, pp. 22–3.

[6] For example, he makes up rules for distinguishing 'achievement verbs', and deduces from them that we cannot say 'he hit the target successfully' or 'he saw the nest rapidly' (p. 151), and that inferring something cannot be described as a slow or quick process (p. 301).

language. His false statements about the rules of English grammar are the result of his attempting to justify some kind of behaviourism by appealing to ordinary language. Ryle makes many sweeping claims implying that his thesis is behaviourism, analytical or metaphysical. For example:

> The sorts of things that I can find out about myself are the same as the sorts of things that I can find out about other people, and the methods of finding them out are much the same [p. 155].
> The radical objection to the theory that minds must know what they are about, because mental happenings are by definition conscious . . . is that there are no such happenings [p. 161].

And, referring to 'cognitive processes', like 'making judgements or passing from premises to conclusions', he says:

> The imputed episodes seemed impenetrably 'internal' because they were genuinely unwitnessable. But they were genuinely unwitnessable because they were mythical [p. 318].

But the facts which Ryle ostentatiously kicks out of the front door are quietly readmitted by the back door, but without acknowledging that the bold initial claims then need to be modified. Ryle uses the simple device invented by Watson, extending 'behaviour' to include 'internal' or 'implicit behaviour'. Ryle's term is 'covert (as opposed to "overt") behaviour'. I shall illustrate Ryle's way of having it both ways. He writes that when we describe people as exercising qualities of mind, we are referring to their 'overt acts and utterances themselves' (p. 25). Yet later in this chapter he writes: 'Knowing how is a disposition . . . its exercises may be overt *or covert*, deeds performed *or deeds imagined* . . .' (pp. 46–7: my italics). Many similar examples could be given.

The psychologists' way of camouflaging the other inconsistency in behaviourism was to rechristen introspective reports. This is what Ryle does too. Officially, Ryle's hostility to introspection is as implacable as Watson's. One of his chief targets is what he calls 'the doctrine of privileged access', defined as the view that 'direct access to the workings of a mind is the privilege of that mind' (p. 14). In chapter VI this becomes 'the theory of twofold privileged access' (p. 155). Ryle presents the traditional view of self-knowledge as involving two kinds of privileged access: constant awareness of one's own states of mind and the occasional deliberate scrutiny of such states (p. 154). (Though no one would say that we have two kinds of access to tables because we may be conscious of them with or without scrutinising them!) Ryle asserts that 'consciousness and introspection cannot be what they are officially described as being since their supposed objects are myths' (p. 155), having just indicated that the supposed objects include 'feelings, volitions, emotions and thinkings'. As usual, Ryle's bold behaviourist beginning is cancelled out as the argument proceeds. A person's constant awareness of what he is doing and thinking is unobtrusively admitted with the help of Romely expressions like 'is *au fait* with'. Ryle tells us that a person acting intelligently is '*au fait* both with what he has completed and with what remains to do' (p. 178) and he says that we 'eavesdrop on our own unvoiced utterances' (p. 184). The deliberate scrutiny of private experiences is likewise readmitted, provided only that we rechristen it and call it 'retrospection' instead of 'introspection' (pp. 167–8). Ryle's way of disposing of self-consciousness and introspection is word-play of the same kind as that of the psychologists who rechristened introspective reports as 'verbal behaviour'. Psychologists are not paid to do metaphysics. Watson may be excused for arguing as if rejecting Cartesian dualism requires one to dispense with, and even to deny the possibility of, introspection. It is a different matter when professors of metaphysics endorse such arguments.

Regarding Wittgenstein, several hundred books and articles have already been written trying to interpret his enigmatic and disconnected remarks, and the commentators disagree widely, especially those most confident that they can read between his lines. Wittgenstein denies at one point that he is a behaviourist, but what he says here shows that he is equating 'behaviourism' with what Mace called 'metaphysical behaviourism', i.e. denying the occurrence of mental processes (§§ 308–9). Wittgenstein is sometimes interpreted, and with justification, as advocating a sophisticated kind of behaviourism; namely denying that we can talk about private experiences. Consider what he says when he offers us his conclusion (something he rarely does). He makes his imaginary critic say: 'You again and again reach the conclusion that the sensation itself is a nothing'; to which Wittgenstein replies: 'Not at all. It is not a *something* but not a *nothing* either. The conclusion was only that a nothing would serve just as well as a something about which nothing could be said' (§ 304). I assume that Wittgenstein meant what he said here, for this conclusion would follow from the conclusions of arguments that he used earlier, notably the diary argument (§§ 258–65) and the beetles argument (§ 293). The kind of sensation which Wittgenstein discusses in all these passages is pain. His conclusion that nothing can be said about 'the sensation itself' requires him to explain what we *are* doing, when we do what we normally describe as 'talking about our sensations'. He recognised this and offers an account according to which the function of a sentence like 'I have a pain' is purely expressive; that is, it has the same function as groaning or weeping (§ 244).

I shall now describe a few of the most influential inconsistencies in Wittgenstein's remarks. He prescribes, as the correct way of doing philosophy, that we should shun theories and attempts to explain anything, confine ourselves to describing, assembling reminders about, everyday uses of language, and 'leave everything as it is'.[1] He says: 'Grammar tells what kind of object anything is' (§ 373). But he does not practise what he preaches. We find very few remarks which appear to be reminders about everyday usage, and these are usually false.[2] What he does more frequently is to telescope two very different questions: 'How *do* we use a certain word?' and 'How did we *learn* to use it?' He treats his incomplete answers to questions about learning as if they answered his questions about our actual usage. Thus, he raises the question: 'How do words *refer* to sensations?' and immediately substitutes the question: 'How is the connection between the name and the thing set up?' (§ 244). His answer is that adults teach a child to utter sentences like 'I'm in pain' as a *substitute* for natural expressions of pain, like weeping. 'They teach the child new pain-behaviour.' Here we have Wittgenstein's version of our now familiar device – rechristening reports about private experiences and pretending that they are not statements.

If anyone practised what Wittgenstein preached, described the grammar of everyday talk, and treated it as the test of philosophical truth, he would be obliged to reject any kind of behaviourism. In everyday talk we distinguish the following statements:

   (i) John is in pain;
   (ii) John is behaving as if he is in pain;
   (iii) John is pretending to be in pain;
   (iv) John is concealing his pain;
   (v) John is expressing his pain.

It is an elementary fact of English grammar that the fifth statement ('John is expressing . . .') is a way of asserting both the first two ('John is in pain' and 'John is behaving as if in pain'). It is an elementary fact of English grammar that the first and second statements are logically independent; for the third ('John is pretending...') implies that the first is false and the second true, and the fourth ('John is concealing . . .') implies that the first is true and the second false. Wittgenstein exploits statements of type (v); exploits them because he does not acknowledge that they assert two independent claims,

---

[1] See *PI* §§ 109, 116, 124, 126–8 and 654–5.
[2] See *PI* § 246 and p. 222.

through ignoring their relationship to the other four types of statement.

Wittgenstein has reintroduced what has been called 'the genetic fallacy'; i.e. the assumption that we can discover the correct analysis of an idea, or use of a word, by considering how it is acquired, or learnt. Presumably philosophy teachers when discussing the history of philosophy still point out that Locke, Berkeley and Hume made this mistake. No one seems to have noticed that Wittgenstein has reintroduced it, and that his followers have been following suit, with the help of jargon-words like 'concept' and 'criterion'.

A suppressed premiss in Wittgenstein's *Investigations* is a version of the verification principle, but one which has very different implications from those proposed in 1936 by either Ayer or Ryle. Wittgenstein's version may be formulated thus: the ascription of any predicate to any person is meaningful for anyone including that person if and only if the overt behaviour of that person provides *other* people with 'criteria' by which they could verify it. More briefly, a statement is meaningful if and only if it is publicly verifiable. All readers of the *Investigations* will have noticed that when he discusses the meanings of expressions like 'I understand . . .', 'I said to myself . . .' or 'I dreamt . . .', he neglects the meaning for the speaker, and asks what justifies *us others* in accepting such a statement, by what 'criteria' can *we others* verify it? In Part I of his book he follows a maxim which he formulates in Part II; 'Do not ask yourself "How does it work with me?" – Ask "What do I know about someone else?" ' (p. 206). In so far as he was deriving his conclusions about our use of language from a verification principle, Wittgenstein was doing *a priori* linguistics – in a book where his description of philosophy would make it a branch of empirical linguistics.[1]

I shall illustrate how Wittgenstein's example has been followed in Malcolm's book *Dreaming*. Wittgenstein's *Investigations* contains two short and cryptic passages about dreaming (pp. 184 and 222–3). Malcolm apparently wrote his book to explain these texts. Malcolm's message *seems* to be that we do not dream, but only wake up with delusive memories of experiences we never had – as Ayer has put it.[2] Malcolm rejected this interpretation.[3] But though he wishes to avoid this paradox, he has, in his book, embraced many others. For example, 'that in the familiar concept of dreaming there is not provision for the duration of dreams in physical time' (p. 79). This is plainly false. The premises of Malcolm's *a priori* linguistics

---

[1] My potted polemic concerning Wittgenstein is much in need of elaboration, and qualifications.

[2] 'Professor Malcolm on Dreams', in *J. of Phil.* (1961).

[3] 'Professor Ayer on *Dreaming*', in *J. of Phil.* (1961).

are less concealed than they were in Wittgenstein's remarks. They are: (i) A verification principle, as shown by Malcolm's statement: 'I have stressed the senselessness, in the sense of the impossibility of verification, of the notion of a dream as an occurrence "in its own right" ' (p. 83); (ii) the genetic fallacy as practised by Wittgenstein – deducing a false answer to the question 'How *do* we use "dream"?' from his own, very inadequate, answer to the question 'How did we *learn* to use "dream"?' Malcolm's answer to the latter question is: 'The concept of dreaming is derived, not from dreaming, but from the description of dreams, i.e. from the familiar phenomenon that we call "telling a dream" ' (p. 55); or as he sometimes puts it: 'The [*the*!] criterion of someone's having a dream . . . is that upon wakening he tells the dream' (p. 49). (The latter sentence is ambiguous because Malcolm makes no clear choice between the incompatible senses in which Wittgenstein used 'criterion'.)

How odd that a philosophical exponent of ordinary language should so define 'dreaming' that dogs, deaf-mutes, and as yet speechless infants cannot significantly be said to dream. And odder still that anyone should not just ignore, but deny, the fact that one's own experience of dreaming may play a part in one's 'forming the concept of dreaming'!

Whereas 'behaviourism' is a fair name among psychologists, it is a somewhat pejorative term among philosophers, at least in Britain. The last three philosophers I have discussed would not welcome this label.[1] But if we do not apply it to them, we shall need another name for philosophical theories which claim that the meanings of mind-predicates must be explained solely in terms of the behaviour which provides one's evidence for ascribing them to *another* person.[2] The motive for advancing such theses disappears, however, as soon as empiricists recognise that 'empiricism' can and should be defined without accepting *any* version of the verification principle. As we have seen, 'the' verification principle has been variously interpreted. According to Ayer's earlier version, a non-analytic sentence is meaningful *for oneself* if and only if it is verifiable *by oneself*. According to Ryle's 1936 proposal (adopted by Ayer in 1956), a non-analytic sentence is meaningful if and only if it is verifiable *by someone, living, dead or yet unborn*. ('Meaningful for whom?' we should then ask. If the answer is 'for someone', this version of the verification principle is an

---

[1] See *C of M*, pp. 327–8.

[2] This statement is unclear, for 'explained in terms of' is here ambiguous. I do not wish to question the thesis that the meanings of mind-predicates must be *taught by reference to* overt behaviour, but to question the inference that statements containing such predicates must be analysed solely in terms of overt behaviour.

uninteresting tautology. If the answer is 'for anyone' or 'for oneself', this version is false.) The principle implicit in the later writings of Wittgenstein, Ryle and Malcolm is that a sentence used to make a statement about a person, P, is meaningful *for anyone*, including P, if and only if it is verifiable *by people other than P*. Each of these principles generates unacceptable paradoxes. But why should anyone accept or apply, overtly or covertly, any such rule?

The traditional conception of empiricism is something like this: that all of a person's 'ideas' are derived from *his own* experience; and that the evidence for the truth or falsity of any non-analytic statement consists of the data of *some*one's observation or self-awareness. Why should anyone wish to replace these claims with a rule designed solely to distinguish meaningless from meaningful sentences? In so far as empiricists want a rule for eliminating meaningless sentences, they may adopt the rule implicit in the arguments of earlier empiricists; namely that a sentence is meaningful for a person only if he can interpret each of the linguistic expressions which it contains in terms of what he himself has observed or experienced. This principle is implicit in Russell's kind of empiricism; and also in Hume's first principle, if this is interpreted as not being a psychological generalisation.

Ayer misrepresented Russell's kind of empiricism in the 1946 introduction to *Language, Truth and Logic* (p. 14). By quoting only half of a statement by Russell, and ignoring the context, Ayer made it appear that Russell's principle would not permit us to use words designating unobservables like the particles of physics. This is astonishing, for Russell stresses in this very passage that the importance of his principle is 'that it enables us to pass beyond the limits of our private experience'.[1] That is, it enables us to do what Ayer's verifiability-by-me principle precluded Ayer from doing, and led Ayer to conclude that another person's pain is a 'metaphysical object'!

I hope I have shown how right Mace was in the statement I started by quoting.

---

[1] *Problems of Philosophy* (Home University Library) pp. 91–2; (Oxford Paperback) p. 32.

8

FREEDOM, KNOWLEDGE, BELIEF AND CAUSALITY

David Wiggins

WHEN we try to think about the causal nexus and the physical nature of the world as a whole we may be struck by two quite different difficulties in finding room in it to accommodate together (a) knowledge or reasoned belief and (b) causal determinism. (a) may seem to us to exclude (b) and (b) may seem to us to exclude (a). Taking it as a fact that there is knowledge and that knowledge seems to be indefinitely extensible, it has been felt by some philosophers that we can disprove total determinism by showing that if there were laws of nature which purported to govern all movements of matter in the universe there would still be something which even an 'all-knowing' predicter could not predict, viz. his own predictions or his own actions; and that given enough knowledge any agent could refute anybody else's predictions of his actions. So it has been thought that the phenomenon of knowledge somehow shows there cannot be laws to govern all movements of matter in the universe. This comfortably anodyne reflection is examined in the second part of the lecture. It elevates human minds and even confers a sort of cosmic importance on them. The other difficulty in making room for both (a) and (b) is in some loose sense the dual of this. Instead of taking knowledge for granted and questioning total determinism, it merely takes causality for granted but then deduces the total impossibility of knowledge. It simply asks: 'How can we take a belief seriously, or consider it seriously as a candidate to be knowledge,

---

Addendum to note 2, page 140. The criteria of soundness in an argument (a) take in considerations which are special to the relevant subject matter, (b) do not in general preserve the principle of *monoticity*. If P justifies Q it does not follow that (P & R) does. Soundness is 'defeasible' by adding extra considerations, e.g. 'NN is not going to lecture today'.

if it is no better than a simple physical effect?' This is a more pessimistic reflection and I shall begin with it.

I

If we suppose that mind is just one part of nature and that it does not there enjoy any special autonomy or metaphysical insulation from ordinary causality, then it may be said that we must see that our believing what we believe and think we know is as much the creature of causality, and as much at the mercy of the brute impact of not specifically intellectual or rational determinants, as are our physical make-up, our genes, the colour of our hair, our physical maturity or senility, or our reaction to the aspirin we were given last night. People may *say* that they have 'made up' their minds about some question. But it can begin to look as if this figure of speech only incapsulates an illusion. No doubt some account could be given of the circumstances under which it is proper, and the circumstances under which it is improper, to claim sufficient intellectual autonomy to have made up one's own mind and not (as we sometimes say) had one's mind made up *for* one on some question or other. But in the face of an unanswered challenge from the causal argument this typology could count at best as a mere catalogue of linguistic proprieties. It is no good just to list the kind of circumstances under which we do or do not *say* we have made up our own minds. The catalogue could do nothing to provide any point for this distinction between two ways of ending up with a belief about the world. Still less would it serve to connect the favoured case of purported intellectual autonomy with our interest in the *truth* of our own and other people's beliefs.

This anxiety is more a perplexity of common-sense philosophising than any concern of professional philosophers.[1] They do not seem to find it as interesting as I believe it to be, and their present dealings with it add up to two:

(a) There is the excessively summary dismissal usually accorded to one interesting but special case of the anxiety – the so-called causal argument for scepticism about perception. This argument, which it is rare to see sympathetically treated, finds reason in the complicated mechanical genesis of perception to question the

---

[1] But see G. E. M. Anscombe's critique in *Socratic Digest*, IV (Oxford, 1946) of ch. 3 of C. S. Lewis's *Miracles*.

veracity or real representativeness of the end-state of the process
of coming to see something. (How could it reveal the object seen
for what it really is?)[1]

(*b*) There is the uncomprehending and excessively *ad hominem*
reply given to marxists who seek to undermine the political beliefs
of their capitalist opponents by ascribing their beliefs to social
conditioning and the operation of the bourgeois consciousness.

I shall begin by saying a little about (*b*). The habitual riposte to it
has been to say that the marxist's beliefs must be socially determined
too. He can no more step outside than his opponent can, and so his
beliefs are no less tainted by causality. But where does this leave us?
The reply is no better than *ad hominem* because it leaves perfectly
open the possibility that beliefs, capitalist, marxist, and all others,
are *uniformly* tainted by the causality which determines them. It
cannot tell against this that if it were so then nobody would have the
knowledge of this fact but at best an accidental true belief. Perhaps
that is how things are.

The reply at (*b*) is not only *ad hominem*; it is uncomprehending.
For, although the reply gives no respectable or satisfying answer to
the scepticism I have described as resulting from the causation of
beliefs, it insists on treating the marxist argument as a mere variant
on that general sceptical position, which surely it cannot be. The
general scepticism rests on a fear or distrust of causality *in general*, a
causality which (on the picture offered by the sceptic) no intellectual
feat before or after the demise of capitalism could possibly surmount
or transcend or fight free from. But the alleged disability of the
bourgeois consciousness is its amenability to a particular form of
causal determination. And if so, then any argument about Marx's
position should really turn on a much more special question, the
question 'What is particularly and specially pernicious about this
particular (bourgeois) sort of social conditioning?' To understand
how there could be relevant or interesting differences in the causal
histories of beliefs, how some histories are acceptable and some not,
may certainly involve a consideration of the general scepticism. And
it is this which I shall undertake. But consideration of Marx would
involve something else as well – an appraisal of the relative trans-
parence and murkiness of the different forms of social consciousness.
What distinguishes the consciousness of the proletariat? (The
insights of suffering?) That question I shall not attempt.[2]

---

[1] Something is said about this on pp. 140–1, n. 3.

[2] But I do feel constrained to make about these questions a single (long) remark.
If we could get the general problem sufficiently well under control to undertake

We may start by making one thing clear. 'Causality corrupts' cannot mean that whatever belief is causally determined is *ipso facto* false. For even if the law of excluded middle fails, we cannot both deny the belief that P and deny the belief that not-P. It means that a causally determined belief is an altogether suspect source, that nothing it says can be taken at its face value, even if something could be 'read' off it; that some rational creature's entertaining a belief that P is not even the most minimal reason to suppose P is true. Why? The most recent statement I can find of the thesis I want to examine is to be found in John Lucas's article 'Freedom and Prediction':[1]

> Truth is a perpetual possibility of being wrong. We cannot therefore explain our holding a belief by seeking to show that it is true at the same time as giving a complete causal explanation

---

the marxist question then the *tu quoque* argument might certainly come into its own again. But not in a way calculated to cheer either side in the controversy. It might, for instance, take the form of suggesting that capitalism and marxism are precisely alike in one important, special and causal respect – that both ideologies are formed and vitiated throughout by a special obsession, an obsession with a concept of *work*, or more specifically *production*, which capitalism communicated to marxism even as marxism reacted to it. It is this common aetiology which is anthropologically special, and philosophically and imaginatively so impoverished, in both positions. In a world where some Gresham's law propagates the cultures of the more powerful and industrialised nations it may come to take more imagination than it takes now to see that it is not logically *constitutive* of human rationality to delegate decisions of ends and their components to economists or cost accountants, or to find it a matter of surprise if the result disappoints. But even now the result of the preoccupation with economically quantifiable *output* has been to degrade, or sentimentalise (which is worse), the evaluation of absolutely everything which cannot be described or accounted for properly in such terms. (Witness our now etiolated and apologetic notions of 'leisure', 'amenity', and even 'welfare'.) That is the remark. In this use of the causal argument, however, *tu quoque* discredits both positions and both the capitalistic and communistic forms of consciousness. But adjudication must really wait on the answer to the question which directly concerns me – why does not the causal determination of a belief *as such* corrupt it?

[1] *Proc. Arist. Soc.*, suppl. vol, XLI (1967). I might also have cited an article in *The Times* newspaper (25 Jan 1969, p. 9) 'Why the brain is more than a mere computer' by Professor W. H. Thorpe, F.R.S.: 'Even assuming the pre-Heisenberg conception of a physically determined brain, we cannot from the very nature of the case thereby "explain" our acquisition of knowledge of the external world or explain away our ability to make a personal choice. Whatever the direction in which future advancement of knowledge concerning the action of the brain may go, it cannot have this consequence; for if it were true none of our knowledge on any subject could be valid and so it is self-destructive.'

of it that leaves no room for our having held any other [belief].

It is for this reason we feel, although often obscurely, that determinism, if true, would preclude our rationally discussing its truth . . . nor is there any point in making true views public if their acceptance by men is determined by physical factors only, and not by the rational appeal of truth. . . . Voltaire's successors today find their intellectual attitudes belying their determinist beliefs. They are committed to the view that whether or not determinism is true, they will believe that it is, as a result of certain physical variables' having had certain values at a certain antecedent time. Even if determinism is false, they will, according to them, still say that it is true, and therefore their saying that it is true affords us no reason whatever for supposing that it really is true, but is to be construed solely as the end-product of some physical process.

I think that Lucas is wrong about this, and that to see why he is wrong is to make it easier to see all the more clearly what is actually right about the rest of his eloquent insistence on the incompatibility of determinism and the authentic fully-fledged concept of freedom which men still operate to appraise themselves and one another. I want to try to show what is questionable in Lucas's contentions without attacking directly (what my approach might at the end enable one to attack indirectly) his apparently rather question-begging contrast between physical variables or factors or processes and non-physical ones.

Neither Lucas nor I think human beings are very like thermometers, but it is worth starting with the observation that in the case of thermometers the truth is quite the reverse of what Lucas says it is for us. One can only trust what a thermometer reads if one has reason to suppose that its state of reading what it reads *is* brought about by causal factors which leave no room for another reading. They have to be the right sort of causal factors, of course; but if they are, and if one thinks the thermometer has been correctly calibrated, then one accepts the thermometer's reading. One even accepts it, if you like, 'at its face value', not as a mere symptom for further interpretation.

This is all very well. It starts a doubt whether causality corrupts, but in itself it leaves 'genuinely' propositional attitudes – the propositional attitudes of men and sentient creatures – quite innocent of causality. So I shall begin by pointing out that a large and important class of them are for the most part not innocent of it. The class is one which one might call 'epistemic' and it comprises those propositional attitudes expressed by verb-concepts V such that $(Vx(P)\rightarrow P)$ or $(Vx(a)\rightarrow(\exists y)(y=a))$. Which is to say that for it to be true that person x has V to proposition P is for it to be true that P; and that for person x to have V to object a is for there to be such a thing as a. 'See', 'hear', 'smell' are (in their primary uses) such verbs. So are 'perceive', 'remember', and, of course, 'know'.

At one time it was fashionable to try to expel causality (which was held to belong to a quite different sort of talk) from any part of the account or definition of such states as these, and from almost any other philosophically interesting mental state. But this has not always worn very well,[1] and there is a now increasingly familiar argument for the involvement of these concepts with causality, which can be extended from the cases of 'see' and 'remember' to most of the other verbs just enumerated. Except to 'know', it is very straightforwardly extended. The argument is this. To make a correct and adequate report of what is in front of me, and do so on the strength of what I seem to see, is not in itself a sufficient condition of seeing what is before me. I may, for instance, be seeing a mere *trompe l'œil* picture which, it so happens, depicts the very scene it obstructs. Or someone may be by-passing my eyes and retina altogether and passing electrical impulses to my optic centres directly by stimulating my optic nerve in a way which again simply happens (at least at that moment) to result in a correct perceptual claim.[2]

For there to be *perception* of it, the scene I report must itself figure in the explanation and causal ancestry of my visual state. Deutscher and Martin[3] have extended this argument to 'remembering X-ing'. Here again the true report that one X-ed, made on the strength of a memory claim, is insufficient for remembering X-ing. One might for instance have been informed of the X-ing and filled in the details imaginatively but, it so happened, fortuitously correctly. It is important to see that as they stand these are conceptual claims, that they need not *specify* the causal mechanism, and that for present purposes the claim is only that they are necessary conditions. The extension of these points to 'hear', 'smell', etc., is immediate.

With 'know', epistemic concept *par excellence*, matters are much less straightforward, and there is nothing to point to in the philosophical literature which enjoys the finality of Grice's argument

---

[1] See Donald Davidson's 'Actions, Reasons, and Causes', in *Journal of Philosophy* (1963).

[2] Cf. H. P. Grice, 'The Causal Theory of Perception', in *Proc. Arist. Soc.*, suppl. vol. xxxv (1961).

[3] 'Remembering', in *Philosophical Review*, lxxv (1966).

about perception. But here I think that any progress one makes will do much to explain why causality *must* figure in the analysis of *any* interesting epistemic concept.

One starting point is a family of puzzles which E. Gettier has proposed.[1] The general account I should give of the difficulty is this. A man may truly believe something P on the strength of evidence represented by the true proposition Q, where Q is the kind of evidence which justifies propositions of the same kind as P; and he may still not rank as knowing P. For though Q-type evidence may justify P-type beliefs, still, wherever (as standardly) Q does not logically imply P, Q *can* always be true without P. The connection between them cannot be logically guaranteed. That is the price of empirical knowledge. But sometimes it may happen both that the connection fails and that, by what is relative to Q an accident, P still turns out to be true. For example, suppose that I believe that today, Tuesday, at 10.30 a.m., my colleague NN. is in his office (P), and that I believe this on the strength of my knowledge (Q) that NN. is down to lecture on Tuesdays at 11.00 a.m. and habitually composes his mind to do so in his office from 9.00 a.m. to 11.00 a.m. of the same morning. Q is true, we may suppose, and NN. being a creature of routine, it certainly justifies me in believing P. But now it so happens that NN. is indeed in his office, but not because he is going to lecture. He has a temperature of 100°, but having cancelled the lecture he has dragged himself into the building for a moment because he has forgotten to post a letter of vital importance – a testimonial, say. Relative to Q, his presence there is a pure accident. One needs good fortune to employ a principle like Q and not come unstuck, but NN.'s presence in the building cannot count as good *enough* fortune to constitute my *knowing* he is in his office. It is a pure accident that I am right.

In the face of this sort of example we can join forces with the sceptic about empirical knowledge; or we can try to amend the traditional account of knowledge. Many specifics have been proposed but I myself am convinced[2] that no remedy can succeed which does not require that for genuine knowledge the Q which gives the putative knower's title to know and justifies his belief must be one and the same as something in virtue of which one can argue that P must be true. And Q must be that in virtue of which this thinker, *x*, *is* justified in believing, not merely that in virtue of which

---

[1] 'Is Justified True Belief Knowledge?', in *Analysis*, XXIII 6 (June 1963).

[2] Lack of space precludes a fuller expansion of the argument here, but I hope to do so elsewhere. It proceeds by letting the principle of sufficient reason push every kind of alternative proposal to its unsatisfactory conclusion.

he *would* be justified. Applying this to my present example, what was wrong was that what made me think NN. was in the building had nothing to do with what really accounted for his presence.

The requirement just sketched is a little more complicated, I fear, than it looks. Q must not only bear the right relation to P; it must also be what is *operative* on *x* and is *responsible* for *x*'s propositional attitude. It is not enough that he simply happens to believe Q, for instance. Very much more needs to be said about what the *in virtue of* Q connection comes to in relation with the knower's belief. The sort of account with which I should attempt to link the requirements on its relationship with P to the requirements on its relationship to him who believes P is this: person *x* knows that P only if there is some sound argument via some Q from his believing P to the truth of P. Q mediates the sound argument and it will have two roles, one of them always causal, the other sometimes causal. On the one hand it explains *x*'s propositional attitude (belief or whatever), and it accounts for it causally. On the other hand, it provides a link in a sound argument from *x*'s belief in P (and an argument which may be of less than deductive strength, and in the case of empirical knowledge will usually be a causal or inductive argument) to the conclusion that P must be true.[1] Suppose that NN. had been in his office and about his normal Tuesday morning business. We must be able to argue in this sort of way about me if I am to rate as knowing NN. is there: Wiggins must have a reason to think NN. is in his office and since he has not seen NN. this morning it must be based on NN.'s habits, which in NN.'s case are regular enough to base an inference on. So if Wiggins believes that NN. is in his office then NN. must be in his office.

Now the way in which causality has, according to my account, to be involved in knowledge is rather different from the special way in which it has to be involved in perception or personal memory. In seeing *a* or remembering X-ing, the thing or event operates to produce an effect (short or long term respectively) which is the seeing itself or the remembering itself. I have not made this a general requirement on knowledge. But the three theories I have committed myself to are compatible with one another, and some seeings and

[1] A causal or nomological *necessitas consequentiae*, not *consequentis*. It is true that nothing like these requirements applies to such concepts as *believes fortuitously correctly*, which qualifies with 'know' and 'see' by my definition of an epistemic concept. But the definition could be delimited further and in any case there are obvious limits to the usefulness or importance of such fortuitous concepts. What we plainly could not dispense with are the ones which are framed to exclude accidental correctness. And of the latter such as 'know' and 'see' I hope to make it seem credible that they all are and must be partly causal.

rememberings do turn out to be species of knowing.[1] My visual state
of its being as if I see that P may under the right circumstances, and
with the right supplementation, yield a sound causal or inductive
argument to the truth of P. In the case where it does, where Q takes
the value *it is as if I see that P*, and Q also provides an argument to the
conclusion that it is true that P, there is perceptual knowledge.
The peculiarity of this sort of case, and of perceptual knowledge, is
the intimacy of the link between the values of P and Q, and the fact
that the inductive argument required for knowledge assumes the
quite special form of an effect-to-cause argument. Similarly, seeming
to remember X-ing at *t* does sometimes provide a sound argument
to the conclusion that one X-ed at *t*. What else, we may be able
to say, could account for the apparent memory? Unless we can say
something like this I maintain that no memory-*knowledge* is present.[2]

The relevance of these claims both to scepticism and to the concept of a sense is obvious.[3] But what concerns me here is only the status

[1] A thorough examination would bring into prominence what could have been
said apropos of knowledge itself, that it is really too strong to specify *belief* in the
necessary condition. Limitations of space prevent me from importing the qualifications and amendments I should wish here.

[2] It is important to emphasise that the kind of definition of knowledge I have
been defending works out in quite different ways for different sorts of case. A belief
constitutive of knowledge of some future fact P, for instance, could hardly be the
effect of P. What the definition suggests that we should look for is a linkage
between some Q which prompts the belief that P and P. Nor could the mathematical knowledge that there is no greatest prime be the causal effect of the
structure of the number system. Here my definition of knowledge suggests that we
look and see why the knower believes this. If the relevant Q is the fact that he has
been told so, then we must see whether his source was good enough for us to accept
the proposition on the strength of this. (It is neither here nor there that this gives a
very derivative sort of knowledge.) If Q be the fact that he has reasoned about the
matter, then is the fact that this particular man has reasoned good grounds to
accept his conclusion? (Again this is all beside the point so far as mathematical
truth is concerned. But I am talking about *knowledge* of mathematical truth, not
mathematical truth.) To defend it against trivialisation and to get a fully satisfactory definition of knowledge of P it is necessary, for reasons into which I shall not
enter, to add conditions (iv) and (v) as follows: Where *x* believes that P, *x* knows
that P if and only if (i) *x* believes P, (ii) there is a Q such that *x* believes P because
of Q, (iii) Q and *x* *believes* P together yield a sound (not necessarily deductive)
argument to the truth of P, (iv) this argument needs the premiss *x* believes P, (v) no
subset of this argument's premises can be made to yield the conclusion that P. (A
sound argument requires true premises.) But *believes* is too strong. *v*. note 1 and p. 132.

[3] Only amplification along such lines can begin to complement the standard
quick answer to the causal argument for perceptual scepticism (see page 134). It is
not enough to say that the concepts by which we describe the perceived object
(which the sceptic doubts is truly revealed in perception) are themselves formed
around the human senses and may only thus gain their place in thought and speech.

(*continued p. 141*)

of knowledge as an effect. And before I can go any further there is an objection I must answer. Granting that an inductive and indirectly causal argument (but not necessarily an effect-to-cause or cause-to-effect argument) must link the propositional attitude that P with the truth of P if the propositional attitude is to constitute knowledge, it will be said that it still does not follow, at least from this requirement, that the knowledge that P must itself be an effect. In the case of perceptual or memory-knowledge it has to be, but this follows from the nature of seeing and remembering, not from the nature of knowing.

To meet this point I must revert to the requirement that the right thing, the common element Q should be *operative in producing* and *account for* the propositional attitude in question. There would seem to be two sorts of case – the case where x's title to knowledge of a certain kind requires x's citing or having an articulable and separable reason, and the case where x's title to knowledge does not require this. Now knowledge by memory or the senses is what mainly comprises the latter kind, so if I am right about their causal nature, then what principally remains to be considered is the former kind of knowledge. I maintain that the operativeness of Q is causal in these cases as well. And I begin by remarking that what my opponent who would deny this faces is the problem of giving a non-causal account of the *because* in, for example, 'He believes that the sun will rise tomorrow *because* he believes that it rose yesterday.' Such an account must meet the following requirement of adequacy. It must distinguish between this statement about x's belief and, for example, 'He believes that the sun will rise tomorrow and *when* he thinks the sun will rise tomorrow he also thinks it has risen in the past.' This is obviously *not* a sufficient condition of the first statement. Past performance of the sun must be not only a reason but *his* reason. It must be the one which operates.

It is a little difficult to say much more until the opponent replies, and I really do not know what it is open to him to say (compare Davidson's discussion of 'acting because', ibid.). But one matter which must be touched upon is the logical grammar of x *believes P because Q*. We must find a way to confine attention to cases where Q gives something which x might e.g. *cite* as *his* reason. It is no objection to a causal account that there are causal values of Q which obviously fail this requirement; for example, 'She believes in God

---

We can only block the sceptic's attempt to get behind the way in which meanings are fixed for descriptions of objects if we show why a human sense *must* have a causal relation to its object. But even this is not enough without a decent account of the relevant distinctions between primary and secondary qualities and their respective titles to be real properties of objects.

because she needs a father-figure.' There are different species of
(Humean) causality and this is obviously a wrong one. I maintain
that we can distinguish between them as two species of causality.
But the example has the virtue of forcing me into one explicit
contention about reason-giving statements. As I think is indicated
in Latin by the need in all such cases to put Q in the subjunctive,[1]
the thesis I shall defend requires me to regard statements of the form
'He believes that P because Q' as shortened versions of the fuller
form 'He believes that P because he believes that Q.' The causation
in question in this sort of reason-giving statement is a relation between propositional attitudes. If I am asked what distinguishes this
causation from the causation which is at work in the case of the
person who believes in God because she has need of a father-figure, I
shall reply that the distinction depends on what must interest everyone on every side equally – the general account of what 'good
grounds' are, and the correct description of how a man's having
what he *regards* as good grounds Q 'leads into' his coming to believe
that P. What I am insisting on here is the requirement of operativeness. What makes the reason *his* reason? Pending the production of a
non-causal account of 'believing P because Q' or of Q's 'leading into'
the belief that P, I think that this is quite enough to create an initial
presumption in favour of the idea that knowledge both is and must
be an effect.

At the beginning I said that we attach much importance to the
idiom 'making up our own minds'. Now I think this idiom is

---

[1] Even with 'quod', which can take the indicative in Latin, the subjunctive
would have to be used to phrase Q in 'Credit P quod Q'. For the form we are
considering involves indirect speech, Q being a reason the man himself could cite
as *his* reason for believing. The question arises: what about the Latin for my
canonical form 'He believes P because he believes Q?' On my view 'Credit P quod
credit Q' is compatible with 'Credit P quod (subjunctive) Q' and leaves it quite
open whether or not Q is something *x* could give or could not give as a reason for
believing P. It is undetermined whether or not the causality is of the relevant
(Humean) species. 'Credit P quod credat Q', on the other hand, means that he
could *cite* his *believing* Q as his reason for believing P. Unless he were psycho-
analysing himself Q would have to be some sort of *grounds* of his for believing P. I
am not here or anywhere advancing a causal account of the evidence-conclusion
relation itself. I am only attempting to show that a causal theory of what it is to
believe on grounds Q is not necessarily involved in various simple-mindednesses of
which it will otherwise be accused. The subjunctivity of Q in 'Credit P quod Q'
might suggest the hypothesis that what is believed is rather the proposition 'P quod
Q' (the subjunctive being that of a dependent clause within existing oratio
obliqua). But it seems to me that a man can believe (be willing to assent to, etc.)
'P quod Q' without Q being *his* reason for believing P. Thus if, as seems likely,
'Credit P quod Q' (with subjunctive Q) is really a form for his giving *his* reason, the
suggested analysis is wrong. It certainly seems very unlikely.

sufficiently counterbalanced in any case by such idioms as being 'led by an argument' or 'struck by a truth' (or in Latin *compelled* by one – 'quasi ab ipsa veritate coactus') to temper any optimism we may feel about the significance of unargued reliance on the active–passive distinction which we find in the idiom of natural languages. But even if it were not counterbalanced, it seems obvious that there are limits within which we think it important to make up our own minds. It will not help much to cut down the volume of error in the world if we all exercise our supposed right to make up our own minds about the general theory of relativity. And I think it is equally manifest that, when we are required to exercise some such right (in perceptual matters and other matters where we are not disqualified), there are stringent limitations on our autonomy. I shall now try to show that these derive from the nature of the concept of belief itself.

It is up to me to make up my mind. But how far is this from the platitude that if it is my mind then only I *can* make it up, or the truistic interpretation of 'you must believe what you think true'? It does not seem to follow from any 'duty' I may have to do these things that I am exempted from thinking what *is* true, or that it is up to me *what* to think true. And it cannot be up to me if belief is to retain its connection with the world. And this connection must, from the nature of belief and its onus to match the world, be subjection. If belief does not retain this connection and subjection it could not be belief. For unless I am God or Reality myself – unless my knowledge is not human knowledge at all – reality is most of it precisely what is *independent* of me and my will. Its arrangement is precisely what is *not* up to me – a point which impressed thinkers as diverse as Berkeley and Hobbes. From which it would seem to follow that if my beliefs are to relate to the world at all, I simply have to lay myself open to the world in order to let the phenomena put their print upon me. How otherwise can my beliefs even aim at a correct account of the world? If my state is one which seals itself off from the outside, this surely enfeebles its claim to be a state of *belief*. For there is subtracted everything which distinguishes belief from fantasy and the state of the sane man who can tell the difference of belief and fantasy from the state of a lunatic who by his inability to distinguish them approaches the point where he can hardly be credited with belief at all.

The right way to put the constraint thesis I am advancing with respect to belief is not that belief is constrained where every other state of mind is unconstrained. For, although idle wish and fantasy may be logically unconstrained, wanting, to which I shall argue that belief is asymmetrical, or the practically oriented kind of wanting which can be a partial determinant in decision and the conception and execution of plans,[1] is not so clearly logically unconstrained. If someone properly wants something, there is room for the question 'Why does he want?', and not just anything can count as a reason. There are limits, and perhaps (I do not feel sure about this) there are even limits to how far he can get by insisting that he just wants it 'and that is the end of the matter'. So the difference I want to argue for between believing and wanting is a more subtle difference than that between logical constraint and logical unconstraint. It arises from the *kind* of limitations set on belief and desire, and from the way in which these limitations are enforced. In both cases the reason must admittedly 'match' the mental state it justifies, whether belief or desire, just as a practical reason must 'match' or rationalise the action it determines. But the difference between belief and desire is to be found in a difference in the nature and direction of the requirement of 'match'.

Suppose a man gives as his reason for believing that British public schools give the best education to be had in Britain, 'I find I do not really feel comfortable with people who do not believe in private schooling'; or gives a games-theoretical argument, the stake being eternal damnation, for getting to believe the tenets of the Catholic faith (if necessary by stupefying himself, cf. Pascal, *Pensée* 233); or urges in defence of his beliefs that 'those who do not believe in private property do not get offered jobs at such-and-such State college' (such-and-such being where he lives and wants to teach); or suppose that in reply to the question why he believes P, a man says that he is a road engineer (lawyer, professor, copy-writer) and P is 'our line' on so-and-so. And suppose this turns out to be all he can say, and that he admits it is all he can say. As Williams has pointed out in similar connections, this begins to undermine his title to believe. In some cases it may even be weak evidence of a sort that he either *dis*believes or *does not* believe the proposition at all. Now why do these considerations not count as reasons for believing? And why does their production even count against belief? The answer is obviously that they have no tendency to show that the putative beliefs are *true*, and that they are not even supposed by the thinker to have this tendency. Their only relevance to the matter in hand is that they relate to settled choices of the thinker. All they could do would be to make certain actions appropriate for him and at very best make him desire to believe various things.

But, it may be insisted, why does it matter that they do not relate

[1] Cf. Aristotle, *De Motu Animalium*, 701, and, for a committedly causal interpretation of this determination, see Davidson, in *Journal of Philosophy* (1963).

to truth? The only answer I think there can be at this point is that believing P is precisely that state for which a certain kind of sensitivity to evidence for or against the truth of P is *criterial*.[1] But evidence relates to and must have its source in a reality which is distinct from the choices of the thinker. For its arrangement does not in general depend on him at all. And here we reach bedrock.

I labour this point and it seems fundamental. But, as so often happens, all that emerges is a collage of truisms. Well, perhaps one could make what I have said seem better worth saying by seeing whether there is any other arrangement in which to place the truisms of the subject. Consider these platitudes: that in a belief, to be false is a defect; that it is in a way the only defect a belief can have; that the only good argument there can be for or against a belief is an argument for its respective truth or falsity; that the point of gathering evidence for a belief, and the reason why this is called for, is that it increases the belief's chances of being *right*. It is surely such platitudes which make our distinction between belief and fantasy. But they seem to generate a demand for truth in our beliefs which is *exceptionless*.[2] It has the mark of something criterial. If we tried to displace the notion of truth from its radial position here and tried to allow that just as a belief can be part of the reason for a desire so a desire can be part of the grounds for a belief, this would all over again destroy the distinction between belief and fantasy. It would certainly render these platitudes unintelligible. Could there still remain any distinctive state to which they pertained?

All this leads, I believe, to a point of some importance for determinism. As an agent, the only picture of myself which is available to me is a picture of one whose actions proceed not at the dictate of an external agency but from within, from my desires and appraisals and preferences for this or that sort of existence. If my beliefs are *true*, the fact that they interact with my desires to produce action cannot detract from my autonomy. And if they are false through some fault of my own, that cannot detract either. What then constitutes my autonomy? If my desires causally determine my actions,[3] then surely

---

[1] This is not a behaviourist account of belief. This sensitivity is a disposition. Not everything which is sensitive always reacts to its proper irritant, and we cannot in general define dispositions by any set of observation statements or 'if . . . then . . .' statements. Properly construed, dispositions are rather inscrutable – even straightforward ones such as brittleness or flexibility – and their inscrutability well matches the inscrutability of belief.

[2] My debts here will escape no reader who knows M. A. E. Dummett's 'Truth', in *Proc. Arist. Soc.* (1959) or B. A. O. Williams's further development of a similar theme in 'Consistency and Realism', in *Proc. Arist. Soc.* suppl. vol. xl (1966).

[3] And this in *one* coherent account of the difference between doing X, which it so

my autonomy can only depend on my powers of self-determination at the level of conceiving wishes and desires and settling on a view of life. There is also my invention perhaps. My invention can prompt hypotheses and courses of action which may even issue in beliefs. So in one way invention can help determine the set of my beliefs. But, by the earlier argument, these beliefs are not unconstrained or 'up to me' in the way that invention, desires and will themselves are conceived to be unconstrained. At his pleasure a man's conceptual daring can carry him to places nothing else could. Once arrived at a place, what he finds there is not at his pleasure.

Now I sympathise with Lucas in supposing that total causal determination of desire is incompatible with the concept of an agent. It must be up to me what to will. But what concerns me here are Lucas' contentions as they bear on the notion of belief. The libertarian conception of an agent simply cannot make the same demands of causal unconstraint for belief as it makes for desire and the will, unless it fuses belief with fantasy. And this asymmetry in the requirements for freedom reflects the fundamental distinction which Miss Anscombe's *Intention* brought into prominence, between thoughts for which the required direction of fit is from the world to the words and thoughts (characteristically couched in the subjunctive, imperative or optative mood) for which the required direction of fit is the other way about, from the words to the world. Freedom of thought is a rather special freedom. The principal point of making the demand is not to think true whatever you like – though no doubt it happens that acceptance of some slogan vulgarly so put is politically required to secure the principal point – but freedom to think or get into a position to think whatever really *is* true. And it is simply not clear how determinism or causality affects *this* freedom.

I have indicated a general agreement with Lucas and singled out, in order to disagree with him, a point on which he says little. A number of questions might still be asked on his behalf and in a number of ways I am conscious that I have not done full justice to him. In some cases my answer to the questions is incomplete.

(i) If knowledge and belief are effects, as I say they can be, how are the good and bad reasons which I am prepared to think of alike and equally as causes to be distinguished from one another as good

---

happens you want to do, and doing X because you want to (see Davidson, in *Journal of Philosophy* (1963)). The philosophy of action so far lacks a proof that this is the only *conceivable* account, it must be admitted, but it is at least one account of this difficult difference.

and bad reasons? To this my reply is that though they are causes
it is not *as causes* that they are distinguished in evidential discussion.
This need be no more mysterious (and import nothing logically
more occult) than the fact that a distinction of good and bad *players*
in an orchestra cuts across and necessarily ignores the alternative
classification of good and bad *men* which can also be made within
the same body of men. Just as the distinction between good and bad
and indifferent musical aptitudes cannot be recovered from moral
or other information about the members of the orchestra, so
evidential distinctions need not be recoverable from radically
different kinds of information about the working and efficacy of the
various causes which create belief. Nor need the possibility of the
one classification undermine the other.

(ii) I confess that it may be failure of imagination which makes
me so certain that the only correct account of 'He believes P because
(he believes) Q' necessarily imports causality. What might nag a
questioner here, and I sympathise, is something to do with Lucas'
requirement that the causal explanation of a belief should not be so
complete as to 'leave no room for our having held any other
[belief]'. 'What about the sophisticated kinds of knowledge where
evidence has to be *weighed* and it seems that choices do have to be
made? These are areas in which the realistic view of truth is vulnerable to certain kinds of important misunderstanding, but guarding
against them, surely there must be real choices if we are to take
people seriously or (where they are right) ascribe knowledge to them?'

This objection could be combined with the question whether,
if determinism is really true, and the volitional requirements of
libertarianism mutually agreed by Lucas and myself are unsatisfied,
that can really leave unscathed what is, according to me, 'the other
half' of the picture, viz. knowledge and reasoned belief. If willing,
wanting, investigating, thinking and choosing are *alike* causally
determined, then does not knowledge degenerate into a mere effect
after all, as Lucas said it did?

To answer this fully would lead into a long examination of the
whole issue of determinism and the impact of causal determinism on
the concept of agency which Lucas and I largely share. Now I think
(or I should think if I could get clear about one very difficult logical
point in the alleged argument from physical determinism to *he
could not do otherwise*)[1] that causal determinism does undermine the
whole point of almost all the distinctions of self and not-self, control

[1] It is not enough for the argument to move from 'necessarily if P, *x* does A' and
P to '*x* necessarily did A, and therefore had no real choice'. For this apparently

and lack of control, on which our notion of an agent depends, and on which the whole possibility of retribution and resentment depends. And it is not in my opinion a condition of this incompatibility mattering or being a genuine incompatibility that Lucas's and my notion of an agent, or the notion of a causal undeterminedness, should survive conceptual scrutiny. I suspect that it is enough for the point – and quite enough to subject present practices of blame and resentment to criticism – that it should be conceivable that these notions should have been coherently conceivable. This is enough for them to be *our* notions. But it seems to me to make all the difference exactly *how* determinism undermines the distinction between the cases where I can and the case where I cannot do otherwise. Although a philosophical proof that one can never do otherwise than one does – the paradoxical denial of something we all believe on the level of common sense – will not remove the possibility of continuing to draw our habitual everyday distinctions between cases of control and cases of non-control, it does seem completely to remove their principal point. At least so far as the will is concerned I am certain that it removes their point. But I have tried to show in expounding the fundamental asymmetry of belief and desire that the notions 'choice' and 'up to me' and 'freedom' have really quite different points in the realm of desire and in the realm of *belief*. If the demand for truth in beliefs had the form 'for each P, if P is true believe P' then perhaps we could rail against our impotence to satisfy it. But rationality is not the same as omniscience, and does not even require that we decide every question which actually confronts us. At most it enjoins 'For any P see to it that you do not believe P unless P is true'. But if the distinctive aspiration of belief is not to shape the world, but to contrive to match or represent it as it is, then I can surely honour this enjoinder in an autonomy of belief untrammelled by the absence of the genuine open alternatives which my freedom requires when I come to deliberate how to *act* upon the world. The world must not dictate how a man should deliberate to *change* the world; but on any view the world must dictate how the world *is*.

II

I come now to the other incompatibility which I began by mentioning – that between knowledge and total determinism. I arrive at it

apes the patently invalid argument $\Box(P \rightarrow Q)$, P, $\vdash \Box Q$. I believe that another argument and some supplementary premises will do justice to what worries the libertarian. But this is not easy to construct.

with little time left to me, and quite unelated by the tentative conclusion of the first part. Knowledge may, and perhaps must, be the effect of a causal transaction, and in spite of this it can still count as everything we think it to be; but any reassurance this provides is strictly conditional on the autonomy and freedom we think we have being there to be discovered in the province of volition. If what we seem to want in that province is as seriously confused as I fear it may be, then there are no grounds whatever for optimism about the human condition. If the conceptual confusion surrounding our idea of agency were removed, should we still have anything we could still accept as the idea itself? I do not think we can honestly fortify our determination to regard our notion of an agent as coherent by subscribing to the idea, which I shall now rather cursorily examine, that *knowledge* can somehow push back the causal determination of actions. There are bewilderingly many forms which this argument could take, however – not all of them even consistent with one another – and I can only deal with some of them.

Suppose that every event and every conjunction of events has a cause and that every cause together with the conditions which obtain at the time nomologically implies its effect. Let the laws of nature be $L_1, L_2, \ldots L_n$ and suppose they are finite in number. Determinism then says something like this: there is a vocabulary of causally adequate total world descriptions $D_1, D_2, D_3, \ldots D_n$ (each finite in length even if there be an infinite number of such descriptions), such that for every world state there is a description D_j which, together with one or more laws L_j, L_k, logically implies the next world state under another causally adequate description D_{j+1}; and that these laws, and the composite rule for predicting one total state from the last total state, hold eternally and exceptionlessly. Every situation can perhaps be indefinitely elaborately described but, according to this determinism, it is possible to hit on an interesting, partial, but causally adequate, description which is adequate for predicting all movements of matter and whatever else the laws L mention.

About such a determinism two arguments, (i) and (ii) below, which I have in mind say this: If there existed such laws $L_1, L_2, \ldots$ and descriptions $D_1, D_2, D_3, \ldots$ then it would have to be theoretically possible for them to be *known*. At any rate it would have to be possible for them to be exploited and put onto a computer programme or whatever. But then sentient creatures could come to foresee their own future. But now (i) suppose they did. Then surely sentient creatures could always, if they chose, refute the laws or discredit the adequacy of the descriptions. They could simply do the opposite of what was predicted for them. But then a certain possibility of knowledge, it will be said, refutes and pushes out total determinism. That is one argument. Again, it is said (ii) that in order to predict my own actions, performed at time t_k, I should need first at t_i to predict the outcome of my own prediction made at the intermediate time t_j. But this I surely could not do. And now it is said that the possibility of a certain sort of knowledge, a possibility allegedly logically implied by total determinism if it were true, actually refutes determinism.

These are very different arguments. There is yet a third argument which says this. (iii) A mind M which comes to know a fact $\langle x, y, z \rangle$ must somehow in some part of it take on a structure which mirrors $\langle x, y, z \rangle$ by means of an internal array $\langle t, u, v \rangle$, with a matching multiplicity of elements with analogous mutual relationships. Now a mind M could hardly within itself, M, both represent a total world state D_i and represent itself, M, *within* that world state, knowing both the state of the rest of the world and the state of M itself. So either the notion of total state or the notion of total knowability is discredited. But of these the former is the more suspect. For what we mean here by the determinism we are considering is precisely the theoretical availability of a finite set of laws which together with finite descriptions calculate other finite descriptions of world states. And if they existed what could be unknowable in principle about such rules for calculating? So if the universe had this structure it would have to be knowable. But it could not be knowable. Therefore the universe could not have this structure.

I will take (iii) first, and shall not here comment on this representational theory of knowing, or say much about the suspect and difficult idea of states of affairs having a determinate multiplicity. To examine the latter carefully might suffice to refute the argument but it would be a long business and involve extended discussion of the intensionality or extensionality of reference to states of affairs.

In the barber's shop in the village where I once went to school there were two enormous Victorian mirrors covering the upper half of two opposite walls. While one was having one's hair cut it was possible from the barber's chair to see in one of these mirrors an image of oneself in front of the other mirror. In this other mirror, as depicted within the first, there was an image of the other side of oneself obstructing a view of the first mirror, which first mirror depicted. . . . The mirrors were old, and to my disappointment the images of images and images of images of images rapidly got too dark to make anything out. But there is no mathematical difficulty, and the situation can even be given a rather simple abstract representation in the system of the natural numbers. If we accept argument (iii)'s view of knowledge, however, and do not disturb anything else, we do seem to need to invoke the idea that the world contains a denumerable infinity of elements. But even this can be avoided if we point out that one and the same world state may be identifiable under different descriptions of different complexities. One of the less fine-grained descriptions may be causally adequate. (Argument (iii) is not well placed to dismiss this possibility because the argument seems from the start to be committed to a non-intentional view of reference to the states of affairs.) Suppose we have a world which contains a mind M and one fact C which it knows – that the cat is on the mat, for example. Then, using this idea, we need not describe M as knowing 'there is a world and in it there is a cat on the mat and a mind M which knows "there is a world and in it there is a cat on the mat and a mind which knows ..." ', or find embarrassment in the awkward fact that unfortunately no sentence is longer than the length it is. M is simply a mind which knows 'there is a world and in it there is a cat on the mat and a mind which knows of the situation the last word of one of whose sentential expressions is THIS.'

Finally, argument (iii) casts understandable doubt on the idea of total world states. I believe it can be shown that talk of these is replaceable by talk of the sequence of larger and larger chunks of the world and laws by which states of these chunks can be mapped onto succeeding states of them.[1]

I shall now go back to argument (i). It has been given a number of uses but in all of them I think it begs the question.

Given laws yielding a uniform prediction function, a vocabulary of causally adequate descriptions, and the means of ascertaining a world state's satisfaction of any one of them, a predicter should indeed be able to predict his own movements. These would be described simply as, or by reference to, movements of matter.[2]

[1] A final point about (iii). Even if it showed that a man could not be in a position to predict all events or every component of a world state it could not show that there was any one event or component which he was unable to predict. $\sim\Diamond(x)$ (A predicts x) $\supset (x) \sim\Diamond$ (A predicts x) is not a logical truth.

[2] It is sometimes said that he could not predict them himself though another predicter could predict them. But his movements are no less the values of variables than anyone else's are. Given the assumptions just mentioned, what conceivable difference could it make who did the computations? And even if it did make a difference it is not clear why two predicters could not use one another as predictive devices. If there is alleged to be an interference problem that is dealt with below under argument (ii). If it is alleged that this would not count as knowledge, does the objector have an account of knowledge which does not lead to a regress of reasons? As will be evident from my discussion of knowledge in Part 1, I do not believe any theory of knowing can define 'knowing' in the traditional rationalistic

Now argument (i) says that if the predicter dislikes what he predicts for himself he can try to do otherwise. My answer to this is that if he tries and always fails the option to try is quite empty. And if he does do otherwise he will simply refute the laws he had accepted before and will have to reconstruct his predictive apparatus. This is not however to say that it could not be reconstructed. And in any case the question is being begged. For to assert that he would succeed in doing otherwise than was predicted is precisely to deny the truth of determinism. And how does the champion of (i) know determinism is false? That was what was at issue, and he was trying to bring an independent argument against it. It is also worth remembering that it ought in any case to have been predicted by the self-predicter, if he had complete laws and descriptions, that he would certainly entertain objections to doing what he was in due course to do.

There are two general possibilities in the hypothetical case of a man who predicts by the route of a physical law an action which at the time of prediction he dislikes. It might often simply happen that a self-predicter gradually changed his mind and was usually sufficiently reconciled to the act by the time when the moment should come for it. This should incline us to accept determinism. Or it might be that no such change was inevitable and that usually when the time came for the act the man felt quite unable to help himself; that physics, as it were, took over and did the act for him. In this case he would come nearer than any human being yet has to knowing what it must be like to be a railway locomotive. Again we should accept determinism. We do not know this feeling perhaps – but then we have not a prediction function. And it is our ignorance of what that would be like and how we should then behave which vitiates the whole argument. No empirical facts about our present conviction of choice can really be brought to bear on what it *would* be like if we had a prediction function.

If this is right I think it suffices to break all known variants on argument (i). It is no good, for instance, to make our freedom reside in the opportunity which knowledge would give us to acquiesce in the action and thus make it ours (Hampshire) or understand our situation and play our part with the cool precision and unflurried style of a well-trained actor (Schopenhauer). This would only be a real freedom if there had been a real alternative to our doing exactly the thing we did do in exactly the manner we did do it. But there was not.

Argument (ii) remains. It hardly needs to be remarked that it would be difficult to subscribe simultaneously to both (i) and (ii).

manner and exempt the notion from all dependence on the external fact that the knower is simply (but non-accidentally) *right*.

And, given a choice, (ii) is surely to be preferred. But it is under-determined, I am afraid. Is it alleged to be logically necessary, or is it alleged to be empirically necessary, for the predicter to take account of his own state at the time of issuing or making the prediction? Adherents of the argument do not always say. Nor do they say whether the impossibility of the predicter's ascertaining his own present or future state is a logical impossibility or something imported by the actual laws of physics.

I think that what some adherents of argument (ii) have had in mind is a difficulty which is as simple as this. The predicter at t_j is aiming at a prediction for that world state D which will obtain at t_{j+2}. (From now on I will write this as D_{j+2}, and similarly for the other total world states holding at the times to be indicated by the subscript.) In order to get D_{j+2} he has to know world state D_{j+1} which includes his own act of prediction P_{j+1} for D_{j+2}. (I will write this $P_{j+1} [D_{j+2}]$.) And he cannot know D_{j+1} unless he knows P_{j+1} $[D_{j+2}]$. But he cannot know P_{j+1} until he has already completed the prediction. But it is this very prediction he is at present working on. So he cannot work it out until he has already completed it!

Whatever the merit of other variants of argument (ii), this and a number like it are not convincing. There is nothing in logic, or so far as I can tell in physics or physical determinism, to show that there is only one route to the prediction of the total state D_{j+2}, or that all alternative routes must proceed through a calculation of the state D_{j+1}, or (even if they had to do that) that all such routes through D_{j+1} would necessarily require the *prior and separate* calculation of its component $P_{j+1}[D_{j+2}]$. Why suppose any of these things?

There is however one sort of case which we do have to take seriously – where the prediction $P_{j+1}[D_{j+2}]$ has a causal effect on D_{j+2}. Such cases abound in real life, for example, newspaper predictions of a fall in share price levels, traffic engineers' predictions of private car ownership leading to the creation of road space which stimulates car use and undermines the economics of public transport, etc. It is philosophically important (and in some cases politically important if specialists are not to defraud us of our freedom) to recognise them. But only confusion of the plausible proposition that every event has a cause with the different and quite implausible proposition that every event has an effect could make one suppose that all predictions actually enjoyed this status. They do not.

Still, it will be asked, what about predictions which do have an effect on the states of affairs to which they relate? There are at least two things we can say about these. First, there may still be a different route to the prediction $P_{j+1}[D_{j+2}]$, direct from an earlier total state D_j, for example, or through D_{j+1} without the separate calculation or identification of its component $P_{j+1}[D_{j+2}]$. It all depends on the simplicity and strength of the physical laws L_1, L_2, ... L_n. Second, even if the prediction had to go through P_{j+1} there would be nothing to prevent the calculator hitting on it by a method of gradual approximation.

Suppose that a financial journalist were in a position to pair his predictions of the price of gilt-edged securities at 3 p.m. the next day with the resulting price, taking into account the normal factors *plus* the prediction of his newspaper column. There is no *a priori* reason why he should not find at least one prediction which he could make and which would influence the market in such a way that it turned out to be exactly true. Physical determinism would assert that this could always be done (though not necessarily within the theoretical vocabulary and laws of micro-economics); and that the act of prediction itself would be determined in any case. If there are good objections to this contention, they cannot be any logical objections to the idea that in an enumeration of possible predictions mapped onto their causal outcomes no pair could take the same values.

I suspect that what a successful variant of the general sort of argument I have been examining would have to do would be to question the assumption that a predicter could *ever* have the means to obtain the causally adequate descriptions D of the world states he needed to make his predictions. Since it would seem that the predicter could always go arbitrarily far back in time (to times before his own existence if there really is, which I doubt, a problem about ascertaining his own states), the difficulty would have to be a general one, but not a purely logical one, about the effect of the knower on what is known. This would involve a discussion of an issue in quantum mechanics which it was not my purpose to discuss,[1] my only objective being to show that it is at least dubious that there is a general difficulty in accommodating together (*a*) indefinitely extensible knowledge and (*b*) any conceivable total determinism. The difficulty is not, I think, a systematic or logical one. And contrary to the tenor of arguments (i), (ii) and (iii) I gloomily doubt that determinism would be the losing partner if there really were such a difficulty of accommodation.

---

[1] Unless to make one remark. Some people say (1) that quantum mechanics are ultimate and reflect *ultimate reality*; electrons simply cannot have both determinate velocities and determinate mass – they are not that sort of thing; and (2) that quantum mechanics show the limits of knowledge; for the act of getting to know interferes with what is known. Can one really have it *both* of these ways? And see again note 2, page 151.

9

PHYSICAL DETERMINISM

R. G. Swinburne

THE object of this paper is to examine what evidence we can have for or against the truth of determinism, a doctrine often set forward by the proposition 'every event has a cause'. I understand in this context by the cause of an event a set of prior conditions jointly sufficient for the occurrence of the event. Since the determinist is concerned with all physical states and not merely with changes of states, which are most naturally termed events, we may phrase this claim more precisely as follows: There is for every physical state at some earlier instant a set of conditions jointly sufficient for its occurrence.

By a physical state I understand an arrangement and condition of constituents of the universe, that is, physical objects, in some part of the universe at some instant. The determinist asserts that however precisely we describe any of the characteristics of the universe at any instant, they can be explained by characteristics of the universe at an earlier instant.

I will begin by distinguishing this thesis, which seems to me the thesis most naturally described as the thesis of determinism, from other theses which are often confused with it. Firstly, there is the stronger thesis that there is for every physical state at *every* earlier instant a set of conditions jointly sufficient for its occurrence. This thesis involves the denial of the occurrence of what Russell termed 'mnemic causation',[1] states producing effects at later instants without doing so by producing effects at intermediate instants; it affirms, on the contrary, the continuity of the causal process. However, determinism as such would seem to be simply the claim that there is for every physical state at *some* earlier instant a set of conditions jointly

[1] B. Russell, *The Analysis of Mind* (London, 1921) p. 78.

sufficient for its occurrence. Secondly, determinism must be distinguished from the thesis that there is for every physical state at some *later* instant a set of conditions jointly sufficient for its occurrence. Determinism does not claim that with sufficient knowledge of present and future physical states and of the laws of nature we can successfully *retro*dict all or any past states[1] – for determinism is the thesis that all events are caused, and causes precede, do not follow, their effects. Thirdly, the determinist's thesis, as I have set it forward, must be distinguished from the thesis that man does not have free will. For, even if the issue of determinism in my sense were settled, it would be open to philosophical dispute whether man has free will. Some philosophers claim that determinism in my sense is compatible with free will, and some that it is not. Because determinism is sometimes used as a name for the thesis that man does not have free will, I have used as the title of my paper the phrase 'physical determinism' to show that I am discussing only the thesis about events in the physical world.

Because of the difficulty of showing what would confirm or disconfirm 'every event has a cause', philosophers have sometimes wanted to say that this sentence, while appearing to make a statement, did not do so, but merely gave a piece of advice – to scientists to go on looking for causes – or expressed a hope – that persistent scientists would always find causes.[2] This analysis does not however do justice to the way in which the sentence or its equivalent in other languages have functioned during the last two and a half thousand years. If it is used to give advice or express hope, its form suggests that it does so by making a claim. ('The treasure is somewhere on the island' may be used to give advice, but it does so by making a claim.) That men have expressed by the sentence a claim about events, both those of which the causes have been found and those of which the causes have not been found, can be seen by the fact that the vast success of science from the seventeenth to nineteenth centuries in dis-

---

[1] Laplace, of course, made this larger claim in the famous remark: 'Une intelligence qui, pour un instant donné, connaitraît toutes les forces dont la nature est animée, et la situation respective des êtres qui la composent, si d'ailleurs elle était assez vaste pour soumettre ces données à l'analyse, embrasserait dans la même formule les mouvements des plus grands corps de l'univers et ceux du plus léger atome: rien ne serait incertain pour elle, et l'avenir comme le passé serait présent à ses yeux. L'esprit humain offre dans la perfection qu'il a su donner à l'astronomie une faible esquisse de cette intelligence.' P. S. de Laplace, *Theorie Analytique des Probabilités, Introduction. Œuvres Complètes* (Paris, 1847) VII, p. vi.

[2] See, for example, A. Pap, *An Introduction to the Philosophy of Science* (New York, 1962) p. 311, where he is in doubt whether to treat the sentence as making a claim or giving a piece of advice.

covering causes was seen as confirming it and the discovery of Quantum Theory in the twentieth century has been seen as disconfirming it.[1] Evidence of observation was always considered relevant. The object of this paper is to show in what ways such evidence is relevant.

Some philosophers of the past, including of course Kant, while agreeing that the statement made an assertion about the world, have argued that it could be known to be true *a priori*. There is no space here for general discussion of their arguments nor great need, since most of them do not have much appeal today. But it would be appropriate to say a *very few* words about Kant's claim[2] that it is a necessary condition of thought about an objective world that we suppose that all physical states have causes. Kant's argument is that we can only infer from the states which we perceive to states which we do not perceive if we suppose causal relations to hold between them, and unless we do make such inferences, we will not be thinking of the states which we perceive as states of an objective world. Hence, he claimed, we must suppose that 'all alterations take place in conformity with the law of the connection of cause and effect'. Now Kant is indeed right to claim that we must use many states which we perceive to infer to other states, which we do by supposing causal relations to hold between them, if we are to think of states as states of an objective world. But Kant's arguments are completely inadequate for showing that we must think of *all* the states which we perceive, as well as those to which we make inference, as having causes. If we can often make inferences to unperceived states, that suffices for us to be thinking of the states which we perceive as states of an objective world.

If *a priori* arguments in favour of determinism fail, what empirical arguments could be produced? Surely, if we could identify for each of many physical states chosen at random a prior sufficient condition thereof, viz. a cause, and did not know of any physical state for which

---

[1] Warnock has argued in favour of the view that the sentence makes a statement, but claims that the statement is vacuous, because nothing could count against it. There could never, he writes, 'occur any event which it would be necessary or even natural to describe as an uncaused event'. (G. J. Warnock, 'Every event has a cause', in *Logic and Language*, Second Series, ed. A. G. N. Flew (Oxford, 1953) p. 106.) Men have been mistaken, Warnock claims, in considering the scientific evidence which they have adduced to be relevant to the cited claim. I hope to show this view to be mistaken by analysing in detail what would count for or against the claim.

[2] I. Kant, *Critique of Pure Reason, Second Analogy*. For detailed criticism of Kant's arguments, see J. F. Bennett, *Kant's Analytic* (Cambridge, 1966) ch. 15, and P. F. Strawson, *The Bounds of Sense* (London, 1966) Part II, Section 3.

this could not be done, we would be justified in inferring by induction that every physical state has a prior sufficient condition. The inductive argument would be more strongly justified in so far as the states examined were of different kinds, and occurred in different parts of the universe and at different *temporal* instants. Such an inductive argument is surely the strongest argument which could be given for the truth of determinism. The inductive argument, it should be noted, would show not merely that physical laws predict with perfect accuracy, but that no physical states occur except those which can be predicted.

Now at any stage of the history of science, scientists will give different accounts of what physical states there are – a hundred years ago men did not recognise protons and electrons as constituents of the universe and so would not have included descriptions of their states and arrangements among physical states. Determination of what physical states there are is partly a scientific and partly a philosophical matter. Arrangements and conditions of objects which we can all perceive and recognise are paradigm cases of physical states. Examples are arrows pointing to figures on a dial, tubes being illuminated and so on. The scientist then constructs his theories to explain some of these obvious physical states. He explains them in terms of certain unobservables – photons, genes, electrons and their properties – velocity, spin, etc. Now whether that which he postulates to explain the clearly observable is itself a physical state, that is, an arrangement of physical objects with certain properties, or whether it is merely a complicated way of describing and predicting how the clearly observable things behave, is a question for philosophical analysis. It is a question to which the answer is sometimes pretty clear. When men postulated viruses to account for the transmission of smallpox, they were postulating the existence of unobserved physical objects. In so far as their observations supported their theory, men had good reason to believe that among physical states were the positions and properties of viruses. On the other hand, when a nineteenth-century scientist accounted for the motion of a planet by the strength of the gravitational field in its vicinity, he was not postulating the existence of an unobserved physical object. Gravitational fields are not physical objects, and a full description of what there is in the universe need make no reference to them. But there are more difficult cases which require careful philosophical analysis – are Minkowski's curved 'space-time' or some of the latest postulated 'fundamental particles' postulated physical objects or not?

Philosophical analysis will consider whether these postulated entities are sufficiently similar in their properties to obvious cases of physical objects to justify our calling them physical objects. It is a scientific question which theory with which entities explains phenomena; it is a philosophical question whether we are to characterise the entities in the theory as physical objects. By the co-operation of scientist and philosopher we may hope to reach reasonable conclusions about what physical states there are in the universe.

Also, at any stage of the history of technology scientists will only be able to describe states to a certain accuracy. With whatever instruments we have there are limits to accuracy of measurement. The strongest possible evidence for determinism that could be obtained at any time would thus be that for each of many states chosen at random among those recognised at that time, described as accurately as was possible at that time, a cause could be identified, and there was no known state for which a cause could not be identified.

In order to show some physical state to be the cause of another state, we must first show good reasons for claiming that a certain set of lawlike statements which together form a scientific theory $L_1 \ldots L_n$, are the laws of nature, fundamental laws governing the occurrence of physical processes. The reasons will be that these lawlike statements are well confirmed on the basis of observations made and better confirmed than any rival set of lawlike statements. What the criteria are for a scientific theory to be well confirmed on the basis of observations is a problem which has exercised philosophers of science for many years, and one to which they are providing increasingly complicated technical answers. I shall not go into the details of these, but simply remark that for a scientific theory to be well confirmed on the basis of observations it is necessary that it should be consistent and be expressible as a relatively simple set of simple lawlike statements which predict many observations to a high degree of accuracy. The awkward problems, which I shall not discuss, are what are the criteria for simplicity and for accuracy and how the various criteria are to be weighed against each other, e.g. if a theory T_1 predicts more and is more accurate but less simple than another theory T_2 which is better confirmed by the observations?

Lawlike statements are general statements about all members of some class and may be either universal (viz. of the form 'All A's are B' or 'Any A is B') or statistical (viz. of the form 'n% A's are B' or 'There is an n% probability that an A will be B'). In his attempt to find as many connections in nature as possible, the scientist will always postulate a universal law unless he has strong reasons for not doing so. A universal law by its very form predicts more fully than a statistical law and hence is to be preferred even if a statistical one is somewhat more accurate. But if a statistical law be significantly more accurate in its predictions than any universal law, that will be grounds for adopting it. However, an isolated statistical law would not fit well into a scientific theory consisting otherwise of universal laws. The theory would become very much more complicated and so highly unacceptable both because one of its laws was statistical and also because one of its laws was of a different type from the others. Yet if a theory consisting exclusively of statistical laws were to give far more accurate predictions than any rival theory consisting of universal laws, there would be strong grounds for adopting it.

Now we can identify the cause of any state E_1 if we can show a state C_1 to have occurred previously, E_1 being an event of type E and C_1 being an event of type C, and if we can show it to be a law or a consequence of laws of nature that every event of type C is followed by an event of type E, which law or laws predict, as far as men can measure, with perfect accuracy. The laws used to show this will thus have to be universal laws, and the cited evidence will then show C_1 to have been the cause or prior sufficient condition of E_1.

What will be our ground for believing a past state C_1 to have occurred? It will be either that observers observed C_1 or that there are contemporary traces of its previous occurrence. Thus suppose that a car has a crash (E_1) and we wish to identify its cause. We can account for the crash if we suppose that one of the car's wheels fell off (C_1), because it is a consequence of well-established laws of mechanics that a car crashes if a wheel falls off. What is the evidence that one of the wheels did fall off? Evidence would be provided if someone had seen it fall off. But if no one saw it fall off, we would have to rely on present traces to establish that it fell off. We would have to show the present existence of a state or combination of states S_1 which would very probably only have occurred if C_1 had occurred. The evidence for this might be simply that whenever states of type S had been observed to occur, then whenever observers would have seen a state C had it occurred, they almost invariably did see a state C. The evidence would thus be the observed correlation of S's and prior C's. Alternatively the evidence could be, and normally is, more indirect. We show from our knowledge of the laws of nature that C_1, if it occurred, would very probably have been followed by a combination of states S_1, one of which is E_1, and that no other known state (apart from states which would themselves very probably be followed by C_1 or would very probably follow C_1) would have been followed with high probability by just that combination of states. Thus, suppose the car's wheel is found in a ditch at a distance from the rest of the car, two of the bolts which normally hold the wheel in place are found undamaged, the axle previously joined to the wheel is found bent, and various other states are observed, all of which together (S_1) would very probably have followed a wheel falling off the car (C_1). Yet there is no other known state which would have been followed with high probability by just those states. For other states than C_1, had they been followed by one or more of the states S_1, would also, it is highly probable, have been followed by other states which are not observed. Thus someone could have bent the axle in a vice; but, had he done so, there would very probably have been marks on either side of the axle where the vice had gripped it – but there are no such marks. Thus the evidence that C_1 occurred is that it is the only known state which with high probability would have been followed by S_1 (apart, that is, from states which would themselves very probably be followed by C_1 or would very probably follow C_1).

If the retrodiction that C_1 preceded by E_1 is to support the supposition that C_1 was the cause of E_1, it must be shown that events of type C are followed by events of type E in accordance with laws of nature which predict as accurately as men can measure. There must be no detectable error in the predictions given by the relevant laws of nature. We have seen earlier that lawlike statements are taken to be laws of nature in so far as they are simpler in form and give more accurate predictions of observations than other lawlike statements consistent with observed data. Now, in view of the immense mathematical and physical difficulties involved, lawlike statements are often tested in isolation from each other – other laws are presumed to have only a small effect in the field in question. Thus when quantum theory is tested, the laws of relativity theory are often ignored, and conversely. Further, initial conditions are never described in full – only the components judged to be most important are delineated. A lawlike statement, if it belongs to a simple theory, other laws of which are equally well confirmed, is taken as a true law if the predictions which it gives, tested in this imprecise way, are fairly accurate. The determinist's claim is that if we took into account all the relevant laws and all the relevant initial conditions, all predictions of well-established scientific theories would be accurate to the degree which men can measure. To show this of a particular law we would have to show that whenever other relevant laws and initial conditions are taken into account perfect prediction results; to show, that is, that all discrepancies between observation and prediction can be eliminated by taking into account all relevant laws and conditions.

It does not in any way seem necessary for the truth of determinism that we be able to predict any effect before it happens. Popper has argued[1] that, even if classical mechanics be true, it is in an important sense not a deterministic theory, because while it claims that physical states are followed by other states in accord with universal laws, for some types of cause it is physically impossible to find out whether the cause C_1 occurred, from which we could predict an effect E_1, until E_1 has itself occurred. In that case, given classical mechanics, E_1 would not in the strictly literal sense be *pre*dictable. But such impossibility does not seem to be relevant to determinism in the normal sense of the term with which I am concerned. Determinism is the claim that every event has a prior sufficient condition. Whether we can find out completely which events are going to occur before they do occur is an entirely different issue.

Now clearly at the moment the strong proof of determinism cannot be given, nor has there ever been a stage of history at which it could have been given. We have never been able to deduce to as much accuracy as we can measure from the occurrence of previous states and well-confirmed lawlike statements the occurrence of each of many physical states chosen at random. We have always known of physical states for which we have been unable to find causes. Predictions have always been far from being accurate to the degree of accuracy that men can measure. The determinist claims that this is because we have not taken into account all the relevant laws of nature or all the relevant initial conditions, or we have wrongly retrodicted past states. If the determinist can show that his inability to find prior sufficient conditions has one of these sources, he will have a less direct argument for determinism. He will have shown that although he cannot identify for each state a sufficient condition for its occurrence, a being with more powerful detectors and calculating machines could do so. How could the determinist show that the inaccuracy of his predictions has this source? I know of only one argument which – given certain empirical facts – determinists could use to show this, and it seems to me that it would have some force, but not very great force, in support of the claim.

The circumstances are that, for any given physical state, the scientist knows of or is able to infer the occurrence of a past state from which he can predict, albeit inaccurately, the occurrence of the present state. Further, he has a set of well-confirmed universal lawlike statements, and he finds that the more of such statements he takes into account and the wider and more precise are the initial conditions which he takes into account, the better are his predictions. The

[1] K. R. Popper, 'Indeterminism in Quantum Physics and Classical Physics', in *British Journal of the Philosophy of Science*, 1 (1950), 117–33 and 173–95.

argument then goes on that since accuracy increases with the number of well-confirmed lawlike statements and initial conditions taken into account, perfect accuracy will be achieved when all well-confirmed lawlike statements and initial conditions are taken into account. In that case, since all events could have been predicted with perfect accuracy, every event would have a cause. Now certainly if we find from our limited study that the more lawlike statements and initial conditions are taken into account, the more accurate are our predictions, we are right to argue by induction that this process will go on as we take into account more lawlike statements and initial conditions. But it does not immediately follow from this that perfect predictions will ever be reached. The difference between observations and predictions will get less, but may or may not converge to zero, when more and more well-confirmed lawlike statements and initial conditions are taken into account. It may be urged that it is simpler to suppose that the difference does converge to zero, but that seems only moderately plausible. Nevertheless, if more universal lawlike statements and initial conditions taken into account did increase accuracy of prediction, the determinist *would* have a less direct, though *weaker*, argument than the strong argument previously considered for the truth of his claim. So evidence of observation could support the determinist's claim, either through the stronger or the weaker argument.

What next of evidence for indeterminism – could it be shown that determinism is false? Clearly we would have first to show that even if we took into account all well-confirmed lawlike statements and initial conditions (as well as the evidence about what happened at earlier instants), we could not find prior sufficient conditions for some physical states. We could show this *either* by taking into detailed account all well-confirmed lawlike statements and initial conditions (as well as the evidence about what happened at earlier instants) and showing that we could not find prior conditions for some states *or* by showing that the lawlike statements were of such a form that whatever the initial conditions, sufficient conditions could not be found for states of certain types. Thus it might be shown that the lawlike statements simply did not make any predictions about states of certain types. Or it could be shown that all the lawlike statements in some field are statistical in form, for in that case they will only predict overall patterns of physical states, not the characteristics of individual states.

But showing that on our current theory we cannot assign causes to some states is not showing that these states do not have causes; it is only showing that if they do have causes, we do not know what these causes are. However, the observations from which we have constructed our current theory T_1 are evidence against any rival theory T_2, rival in the sense of making predictions conflicting with those of T_1. For the evidence in favour of T_1 is evidence in favour of the predictions of T_1 and hence evidence against the predictions of T_2 and hence evidence against T_2. They are therefore evidence against the constructability of any rival theory which might assign causes to all states. The observations however are not evidence for or against the constructability of a more fundamental theory T_3, from which – perhaps, given also certain empirical circumstances which in fact hold – all the predictions of T_1 would be a deductive consequence. T_3 would not be a rival to T_1, for it would predict whatever T_1 predicted, but it would predict more than T_1. It thus might predict with perfect accuracy the characteristics of individual states, while T_1 only predicted overall patterns. T_3, being a more fundamental theory, would need more evidence to support it than was needed to support T_1, but it would be evidence as to the occurrence of which in general T_1 would be indifferent. Hence if we are to show that causes for all physical states have not merely not been found, but do not even exist, we would have to produce evidence that an overall theory T_3 from which perfect predictions of all states could be made could never be confirmed; that is, could never have evidence produced in its favour which was not simply evidence for T_1 but evidence which would give grounds for going beyond T_1 and adopting T_3. The evidence of observations from which T_1 was constructed would have in this case to be evidence that no more fundamental theory than T_1 with universal laws could be confirmed. Then we would have evidence that T_1 (or another more fundamental theory with statistical laws) provided the most fundamental explanation of observations. For if a certain theory in some field is supported by observations better than any other theory, we normally take its laws as the fundamental laws governing phenomena in the field, the laws which ultimately determine how phenomena occur. If we are hesitant to do this, it can only be because we suspect that one day some more fundamental theory will be established. We may have strong or weak reasons for the latter belief – e.g. that our theory was established merely on the basis of data of some peculiar kind. But if we have evidence that in some respect no more fundamental theory will ever be established, we must surely take the laws of the theory which we have in that respect as the fundamental laws governing phenomena. Evidence that a theory with statistical laws provides the most fundamental explanation of phenomena would be evidence that some states do not have causes.

What kind of evidence could show that no fundamental theory T_3 with universal laws could ever be confirmed as an explanation of T_1? Clearly it would always be logically possible to *construct* a theory T_3 from which – for certain postulated empirical circumstances – all the predictions of T_1 could be derived, T_1 having merely statistical laws and T_3 having universal laws which predict all states with perfect accuracy. Thus suppose that the current theory T_1 is statistical and includes such laws as that 90% A's turn into B's. We then postulate that 90% A's have an unobservable characteristic C, while 10% A's lack this characteristic. We then propose the theory T_3 which includes the laws that all A's which are C turn into B's, and no A's which are not C turn into B's. The predictions of T_1 are then a deductive consequence of T_3 for the postulated empirical circumstances, and we have as yet no grounds for believing that these do not hold. What would have to be shown if we are to rule out the deterministic theory is that we could never have any evidence for the truth of such a theory which was not merely evidence for a statistical theory. We could show this if the current scientific knowledge embodied in T_1 showed reason for believing that a theory explaining T_1 would have to be of a certain form, but that theories of that form consisting of universal laws could never be confirmed in such a way to justify our going beyond a statistical theory and adopting it. Thus the evidence could show that certain kinds of parameters ought to enter into such a theory, yet measurements of these parameters could never be made in such a way as to get evidence in favour of the theory which was not merely evidence in favour of a statistical theory. In that case we would have evidence that our well substantiated current theory which only predicted individual physical states with a certain probability could not itself be further explained by a theory which predicted with certainty. The evidence would thus show that T_1 (or another theory with merely statistical laws) provided the most fundamental explanation of phenomena and hence that not all states have causes.

If my analysis of what would be evidence for or against the truth of determinism is correct, then the achievements of modern science give good grounds for believing that determinism is false. For quantum theory is a very well substantiated scientific theory which accounts for a whole host of physical and chemical phenomena. The occurrence of these phenomena is thus strong evidence against any rival theory with universal laws. The laws of quantum theory are statistical in predicting future values of many physical states only with some degree of probability. Thus given a light source emitting photons, an intercepting screen with a slit in it, and a plate beyond the screen, the laws of quantum theory predict only to a certain degree of probability whereabouts on the plate a photon emitted at a given instant will arrive. To explain the phenomena predicted by these statistical laws we could construct a more fundamental theory consisting of universal lawlike statements which explained the subsequent destination of photons by properties which they possessed on leaving the source, their possession of which made inevitable their destination.[1] Yet we have evidence that such a theory could never be confirmed. The evidence is that the whole of mechanics and electromagnetism which is taken over by quantum theory indicates that free subatomic particles such as photons travel along continuous paths and hence that in order to know their subsequent positions we need to know, as well as the surrounding circumstances, their present position and their momentum (which way they are moving and how fast). Yet it is a consequence of quantum theory that the position and momentum of a particle cannot be measured simultaneously to an accuracy of greater than $(h/4\pi)$, where h is Planck's constant. For if we could know the simultaneous values of position and momentum of a subatomic particle, then statements about it could not be written as statements about a wave packet, in which case if it were subsequently put into circumstances where it behaved like a wave, this wavelike behaviour would be a mystery. Wave packets are bundles of waves which interfere so as to cancel each other out except in a small region. Photons and other subatomic particles behave, as is well known, in some circumstances as particles and in some circumstances as waves. There are well-established relations between particle

---

[1] A well-known theorem of von Neumann has sometimes been interpreted as a proof that no more fundamental theory T_3 yielding perfect predictions of all physical states, yet making all the predictions of the statistical theory T_1, can even be constructed, let alone confirmed, for quantum theory as T_1. The most that von Neumann proved, however, is that the basic laws of quantum theory cannot be supplemented by laws containing 'hidden parameters', that is, laws about further properties of physical systems, in such a way as to yield perfect predictions of all physical states, where present quantum theory yields only statistical predictions. (See J. von Neumann, *Mathematical Foundations of Quantum Mechanics*, English edition (Princeton, N.J., 1955) Ch. 4.) But all that this means is that the axiom set of T_3 cannot consist of T_1 and certain other laws as well; it must drop at any rate some of the laws of T_1 and bring in laws about properties of different kinds. T_3 could nevertheless yield all the predictions of T_1 and further predictions as well. (This was shown by Bohm: see David Bohm, 'A suggested interpretation of the Quantum Theory in terms of Hidden Variables', in *Physical Review*, LXXXV (1952) 166–93, esp. pp. 187 f.) Some T_3 must always be constructible, at any rate in the trivial way described on p. 165, from the statistical laws about physical states and their properties deducible from T_1 and put in the form 'n% A's are B'. The fundamental laws of quantum theory are of course normally expressed in a far more complicated notation than this.

parameters and wave parameters which enable us to predict the wave behaviour from knowledge of particle parameters and conversely. ($E = (h/4\pi)\omega$ and $p = (h/4\pi)k$, where E is the energy and p the momentum of a particle, and ω the angular frequency and k the propagation vector of the corresponding wave.) It is a consequence of these relations that the narrower the wave packet (viz. the smaller the region in which the waves of the bundle do not cancel each other out), the wider will be the range of the propagation vectors and so of the momenta of the corresponding particles. Hence the more precisely we know position, the less precisely we know momentum. If we could know both simultaneously for a particle, we could not translate our knowledge into statements about the frequency and propagation vectors of waves. In independent confirmation of the claim that we cannot learn position and momentum simultaneously is the fact that we can show for any instrument which may be proposed for detecting position or momentum that using it to detect one rules out the simultaneous use of that or any other instrument to detect the other.

This ludicrously brief survey of quantum theory should indicate how, given the truth of quantum theory, no theory consisting of universal laws about the paths followed by particles could ever be confirmed by observation. For the evidence is that the theory must take the form of attributing to the particle an initial position and momentum and that, since these can never be measured simultaneously, any theory which predicts behaviour in virtue of these characteristics could never be confirmed. This is because the evidence which we could have in its favour could not be evidence about the paths taken by all particles having such and such position and momentum, since to the accuracy to which we could measure these, particles having any given position and momentum would always take very different paths, and hence their behaviour would only support a mere statistical theory. Hence the evidence is not and cannot be strong enough to justify our going beyond a merely statistical theory and postulating universal laws. Thus the very form of quantum theory as well as ruling out rival theories also rules out any more fundamental theory explaining by universal laws. The evidence in favour of quantum theory with its statistical laws making possible only probabilistic predictions of physical states is thus evidence against any theory with universal laws ever being substantiated. It is thus evidence in favour of a theory with statistical laws providing the most fundamental explanation of observations. Quantum theory has the very exceptional characteristic among statistical theories of ruling out more fundamental non-statistical theories.

Now, although quantum theory is a theory very well confirmed by observations, it may well be that one day it will be shown to be false and replaced by a more adequate theory. But at any stage of science we must draw conclusions from the evidence which we have and not that which we guess we might one day obtain. Next century's theory may explain the physical and chemical phenomena which quantum theory purports to explain today in a way entirely different from that of quantum theory. By it a light source may cause a plate to be illuminated without emitting photons which cross the intervening space. But until such a theory is substantiated by evidence, we must reach our conclusions from the theory which we have.

It should be noted that the indeterminancy of quantum theory concerns not merely subatomic particles, about which a rigorous positivist might take the view that their states are not physical states on the grounds that photons are like forces and fields in not being physical objects. The indeterminancy in the behaviour of subatomic particles produces indeterminancy on the macroscopic scale in the behaviour of objects which quite obviously are physical objects. If we choose a very weak source of light, and put a screen with a slit in it in front of a photographic plate, we can predict only with probability which parts of the plate will be illuminated within the next tenth of a second – photons are not observable, but light and dark patches on a photographic plate are observable. True, most quantum effects are not apparent on the large scale, and we can predict most large-scale effects with virtual certainty. But 'most' is not 'all', and it would be only too easy to construct machines in which quantum effects produced very apparent large-scale effects. One could make a hydrogen bomb, the explosion of which depends on whether an atom of some radioactive substance decayed within some period. Quantum theory can tell us only the probability of such decay. Hence it would be a matter of objective probability whether or not the bomb exploded.

I conclude that the claim of the determinist that 'every event has a cause' is significant, and in the light of my analysis of what would be evidence for or against the claim and in the light of modern scientific theory, that the claim is false. An element of indeterminism is a basic feature of natural processes.

10

DISCOURSE ABOUT THE FUTURE

Michael Clark

WHILE philosophers feel relatively comfortable about talking of the present and the past, some of them feel uncomfortable about talking in just the same way of future events. They feel that, in general, discourse about the future differs significantly from discourse about the past and present, and that these differences reflect a logical asymmetry between the past and future beyond the merely defining fact that the future succeeds, and the past precedes, the present time. The problem is: how can we talk about events which have not yet happened, or at any rate are not yet bound to happen, or whose participants do not yet exist? The effect of these worries has led them to claim to recognise restrictions on our talk about the future which do not govern talk about the past and present. The most famous of these views is Aristotle's. According to one familiar interpretation, he holds that a statement about a future event which is not yet settled, a contingent event in the future, is neither true nor false, even though the statement that the event either will or will not happen is necessarily true. Proponents of this view felt that if a future-tensed statement were already true then the fact that it stated would already be settled. I do not propose to discuss this well-known and much-discussed doctrine of Aristotle's, but I do want to consider some allied views which have been aired recently, and to look at their philosophical significance. Before I look at these, however, it will be convenient to recall three of the main reasons why the Aristotelian doctrine is unpopular. In the first place it is paradoxical to accept that a statement of the form $p \vee \sim p$ is (necessarily) true while claiming that neither of its disjuncts is true. Then there are misgivings about the notion of truth involved: many feel that truth is essentially an attribute of timeless propositions and that it is nonsense to talk of a statement's *becoming* true as you would of Aristotle's views if the event described became inevitable.[1] There is also the difficulty of accounting for the meaning of a future-tensed sentence which may express a statement that is neither true nor false simply because what it states is not yet settled. It could not be said of the sentence expressing such a statement that you know what it means if you know what it is for the sentence to express a true statement. I know the meaning of the present-tensed sentence 'A sea-battle is now being waged' if I know that it can normally be used to make a true statement precisely in the event of there being a sea-battle being waged at present. But I do not know the meaning of the future-tensed sentence 'A sea-battle will be waged tomorrow' simply by knowing that the sentence expresses a true statement if it is already settled that there is going to be a battle: the statement doesn't *mean* that the battle is already settled, otherwise it would not lack a truth-value when the matter was still open – it would be false.

I

The view that statements must be regarded as expressing timeless propositions is obviously likely to lead one to assimilate future to past, and certainly prevents one from saying that the same statement changes its truth-value. In my subsequent discussion I shall ignore this point, since, if acceptable, it would immediately undermine the first account of future-tensed sentences which I want to consider, and there is by no means general agreement that the point is to be accepted.

This first account avoids the first and third difficulties involved in Aristotle's view. It has been elaborated by Charles Hartshorne in a paper in *Mind* called 'The Meaning of "Is Going to Be" ' (Jan 1965). If you want to avoid the paradox of admitting the necessary truth of $p \lor \sim p$ while denying, in the case where p is a future contingent proposition, that either p is true or $\sim p$ is true, there are two obvious ways of doing it. You can deny that the law of excluded middle *is* a necessary truth, but many feel that this is equally paradoxical; or you can accept the view that future contingent propositions (already) have truth-values, which is not an alternative open to someone like Hartshorne who thinks that it implies that the whole of the future is causally settled *now*. To accept such a determinist view is to dissolve the problem of future contingents by denying that there are any

---

[1] Cf. W. and M. Kneale, *The Development of Logic* (Oxford, 1962) pp. 46–54.

contingent events in the future, so removing the need for propositions about them. Hartshorne wants to have it both ways by allowing for contingent future events but insisting (with certain qualifications to be noted) that we cannot assert that they will/will not take place without implicitly ruling out their contingency. That is, he admits contingent future events but not contingent future propositions (unless you count statements like '*e* may or may not happen', which he does admit). He does this by offering the following allegedly equivalent analyses of '*X* will do *A*':

(i) '*X*'s doing of *A* is already determined or settled upon';
(ii) 'there is no longer another possibility for *X* at time *t* than doing *A*';
(iii) 'all the real possibilities allowed by the present causal conditions include *X*'s doing of *A*' (pp. 46–7).

In other words, only of an event which is already causally settled and inevitable should we say that it will happen: of a contingent future event we cannot truly say that it *will* happen since that would be to deny its contingency. To say it will happen is to say it must happen. To deny that it will happen is not to exclude its happening but merely to deny that it must happen. Since it is either the case that an event *e* must happen or not the case that *e* must happen, the law of excluded middle is preserved for the case

$$(e \text{ will happen}) \text{ v} \sim (e \text{ will happen}).$$

We must now distinguish between 'it is not the case that he will' and 'he will not', just as we distinguish between a denial that he must and 'he must not'. And just as my doing *A* is no proof that I had to do it, so the occurrence of *e* is not in itself a proof that an earlier statement that *e* would occur was true.[1]

On Hartshorne's analysis '*X* will do *A*' is false if it is not yet settled that *X* will in the ordinary sense do *A*; but it becomes true if the course of events eventually makes *X*'s action inevitable. Such a statement is either true or false, so that the difficulty about the meaning of a future-tensed statement which might lack a truth-value is avoided.

At first sight Hartshorne's analysis might seem to be subject to the following objection. It might be argued that his analysis is inadequate because it eliminates reference to the futurity of the act *A*, or

---

[1] This view has been formalised by Prior in *Past, Present and Future* (Oxford, 1967) p. 128 ff., where it is extended to other types of future tense. It is not a view, however, which Prior presents in order to endorse.

that, if the analysis is understood in a way which overcomes this inadequacy, then it is circular. To take the first horn of the dilemma: presumably past acts are also already 'determined or settled upon' and if you say '*X*'s doing of *A* is already determined or settled upon' this will not necessarily mean that *X will* do *A*, it allows that *X* has already done *A*. And the alternative analysis that is offered – 'there is no longer another possibility for *X* at time *t* than doing *A*' – is really no better, because it seems to allow that *X*'s doing *A* is a *past* possibility. The futurity of *A* must be made explicit in the analysis, we must talk of '*X*'s future doing of *A*'. But saying this seems suspiciously like saying, in the first case, 'That *X* will do *A* is already determined', and, in the second, 'there is no longer another possibility for *X* than that he will do *A*'. If this is so, we seem to have an infinite regress. '*X* will do *A*' means 'it is already determined that *X* will do *A*', which can only mean 'it is already determined that it is already determined that *X* will do *A*' and so on. If you don't know what Hartshorne means by 'will' to start with, you won't really know when you have seen the proposed analysis: you will know that if *X* is going to do *A* then something is determined, but what is determined will not be clear. Not that the regress prevents '*X* will (or is going to) do *A*' from meaning the same as 'it is already determined that *X* will do *A*'. If this were so then '*p* is true' could not mean much the same as 'it is the case that *p* is true'.

'Determined' can be given rather different senses in the context of the present discussion, of course, but the sense intended by Hartshorne is presumably given in his other alternative analysis: 'All the real possibilities allowed by the present causal conditions include *X*'s doing of *A*.' Here the mention of causal conditions suggests a forward reference and is a step towards a more satisfactory formulation of the analysis Hartshorne intends.

Hartshorne means that a simple future-tensed statement is true only if it is entailed by true present- and past-tensed statements together with true statements of laws of nature. We are not told whether the thesis is meant to apply to other types of future tense ('was going to be', 'will have', etc.). But it would be reasonable to assume that it *is* meant to extend to uses of 'will' apart from those in sentences about future human acts and experiences, say to cases like 'The Tower of Pisa will fall down in twenty years' time'.

What sort of view has Hartshorne put forward and what picture of the future does it present? When he puts forward his analysis he claims to be specifying the 'strictest sense' of 'will' and 'is going to be' as auxiliary verbs: 'We often speak more loosely', he admits (p. 46). We rarely know all the relevant present causal conditions, so that often our statements of the form 'X will do A' mean that all the real possibilities allowed by the present causal conditions *we know about* include A. Or it may be that present conditions do not completely rule out the future act A, but very nearly do, that most of the possibilities include A, and again, he thinks, for practical purposes we say, loosely, that X will do A.

I think his view can be stated simply like this. Admissible uses of 'will' are those where 'will' means 'must'. The strictest sense of 'will' is given by a causal 'must'. The looser senses are expressed by an epistemic 'must' ('must in relation to what we know') or a loose 'must' which is properly used when present conditions make the event in question highly probable. At any rate I shall often use the word 'must' in what follows to express Hartshorne-style analyses.

For ordinary purposes, then, Hartshorne thinks that the looser uses of 'will' are quite acceptable, even desirable, but he believes that a philosopher needs to make distinctions which can be ignored in everyday life. In this way Hartshorne tries to sidestep the immediate criticism of his analysis, that it is simply a false account of the actual meaning of 'will'. But he does not go very far in doing this, for the looser uses I have mentioned seem to be the only additional uses he admits. What he really seems to be doing is eliminating the genuine future tense, rewriting future-tensed sentences as sentences about present conditions, allowing us to talk about the future only in so far as it is already settled by present states of affairs. The looser uses of 'will' that he recognises in ordinary speech are admissible because they too can be re-expressed in terms of what present causal conditions allow. There is no way on his account of affirming the occurrence of a future event which present conditions, or present conditions in so far as we are acquainted with them, do not causally settle or make very probable; all we can say is that the event may or may not happen.

This programme of reducing the describable future to the present is consistent with a determinist view of the future as already completely settled by present conditions, but there would be little point in it if it were not to allow for the picture of the future which Hartshorne urges on us. It is of a future made progressively more definite as time rolls on. Consider next year: as we get closer to it the course of events settles more and more of next year's events, closes more and more possibilities and determines the details of events which in general outline are already inevitable. By the time we reach the end of next year all its events are completely settled and remain so for ever. 'Definiteness', he says, 'is progressively made' (p. 51), 'process is always a narrowing of the "openness" of a given moment of the future, never its widening' (p. 52). And this openness of the future gives us our freedom, the 'creative power to add to the world's definiteness' (p. 56).

However, there are some occurrences of 'will' which are not eliminable in the way Hartshorne proposes, occurrences whose total elimination from our language would impoverish it in a way which is surely intolerable. What on Hartshorne's view could it be to guess or doubt that or wonder whether A will occur? Can I only wonder whether A's occurrence is already settled, or perhaps is already settled so far as I know or is very nearly settled? In the case where I know that A is not settled in any way I am left with no means of expressing my speculation. It is no good trying to eliminate the future tense by saying that I am wondering etc. about the future occurrence of A, for this does not tell us just what I am wondering about it, it doesn't tell us that I am wondering *whether it will occur*.

One way out of this situation would be to restrict Hartshorne's analysis to occurrences of 'will' in categorical predictions like those of the form 'X will do A', which was possibly his intention anyway. The restriction would be an artificial one because we often use such sentences to express guesses, speculations or, when uttered in a hesitant tone of voice, doubts. Aren't guesses a sort of prediction in any case? We should have to distinguish these other uses of the sentences from the more straightforwardly assertive uses of such sentences which Hartshorne seems to have in mind. But even then the restriction would be objectionable. Surely what one man may guess and another man may doubt can be the very same thing that a third man may state about the future. It would be a very peculiar view that allowed you to wonder whether p, doubt that p, perhaps even to guess that p, but not sensibly to state that p.

Moreover, whether they ought to or not, people unquestionably do believe propositions of the sort Hartshorne is excluding, they do believe that events which they will admit are not yet settled (or nearly settled or settled as far as they know) will (contingently) occur and that other events of the same sort will not occur. Perhaps they are irrational. Perhaps Hartshorne would be right if he said that they ought not to assert their beliefs because they are unjustified; but it doesn't follow that we ought not to report their beliefs, to say that X believes that A will (contingently) occur. And it would be quite unacceptable to say that 'will' means or ought to mean one thing in a sentence of the form 'A will occur' and another in 'X believes that A will occur', to say that the statement that A will (contingently) occur cannot be made, but that the object of X's belief, that A will (contingently) occur, can be specified in a belief-sentence.

It is also worth noting that there are other cases, like hoping that fearing that or betting that *A* will occur which are difficult for the analysis. I may know that *A* is not yet settled etc. but still hope for or fear it; in such a case I am certainly not hoping or fearing that *A* is already settled. Similarly, if I bet on a horse, I do not, unless I am cynical, bet that it is already settled that it will win, and even if I thought it was settled I would probably bet simply on its winning. Then what would make me win my wager would be the horse's win, not the fact that the race was fixed. Now Hartshorne does consider the case of a wager. He says:

> The wager when made is more or less likely, or not likely, to win, and hence reasonable or unreasonable, according to the causal probabilities; eventually it has won or not won; suppose it has won, this does not show it to have been true when made, any more than a successful prediction from a law establishes the law . . . [p. 54].

What he seems to be saying is that when in betting I say that a certain horse will win, I mean that present conditions (at least so far as I know) make is causally necessary or at least very probable that it will win. And, even if they don't, I still win the bet if that horse wins. But why should I win in such a case? And if I *do* want to bet that an event is already settled, how do I distinguish it from a bet that the event will (contingently) occur? In fact Hartshorne's account of 'will' allows us to bet about the future only in so far as we are betting about what present causal conditions have settled; bets that contingent events will or will not occur as we ordinarily understand 'will' are simply not expressible.

It is true that the apparent elimination of the future tense can be achieved in these cases by replacing the noun clause by a suitable noun or noun phrase, by saying, for example, that we hope for, fear or bet on *A*'s future occurrence, and playing down what is surely the essentially propositional nature of fearing, hoping and betting.[1] This is the line Hartshorne takes with 'possibly or probably *A* will occur'. But it seems to me to conceal rather than eliminate the future tense; (surely to be afraid of *A*'s future occurrence just is to be afraid *that A will occur*).

Perhaps a philosopher who legislates against categorical descriptions of the future inasmuch as it is not yet (completely, more or less,

---

[1] For a defence of the thesis 'that thinking (in the wide sense which includes wanting, hoping, fearing, etc.) always involves entertainment of a proposition', see William Kneale, 'Intentionality and Intensionality', in *Proc. Arist. Soc.*, Suppl. Vol. (1968) 86–8.

or to our knowledge) settled, will as willingly prohibit speculation about it, since it would in any case be idle speculation. However, there are some facts about the future which are not occurrences or events, but are conditional facts, you might say, which *are* already settled. Suppose someone has put a time bomb in my car and the bomb is due to go off at 8 o'clock. Let us ignore the possibility of further human intervention involving, say, the removal of the bomb. Then surely present causal conditions have ensured that if I am in my car at 8 o'clock I shall be blown up. It is not yet settled, we may suppose, whether I shall be in my car at 8 o'clock, and so not yet settled whether I shall be blown up. But the conditional fact, that *if* I am in my car at 8 I shall be blown up, is irrevocably settled. This is a fact about the future which is already closed and determined and Hartshorne should have no reason to pronounce it unstatable: present causal conditions and the laws of nature guarantee it. But it is difficult to see how it can be stated if we are restricted to using 'will' etc. either in Hartshorne's 'strict' sense or in one of the two looser ways he admits. We do not want to say, 'If Clark must be in his car at 8 he must be blown up.' This sentence doesn't even express something which entails what we do want to say, which is that if as a matter of contingent fact Clark is in his car at 8 he will as a matter of contingent fact be blown up.[1] (There is a concealed future tense in the antecedent of the sentence – 'If Clark is in his car at 8' – which escapes immediate notice through a quirk of English idiom and whose concealment would not survive translation into French.) At best Hartshorne could try to replace noun clauses with noun phrases again, but it is both unclear how he could do it while preserving the sentence's full meaning and doubtful whether it really fulfils his programme.

In short, if we admit only those occurrences of the simple future tense which Hartshorne's account seems to allow, we shall deprive ourselves of the means of expressing doubts, speculations and guesses about contingent events in the future, perhaps even of expressing many of our fears, hopes and bets – and these examples are unlikely to be exhaustive. Even those conditional facts which are already settled by the present course of events will often be unstatable. It is not a very appealing programme.

Whether or not these objections to Hartshorne's analysis are sound, no one is likely to adopt it without having good positive

---

[1] From the fact that it must be the case that if Clark is in his car at 8 he will be blown up, it does indeed follow in virtue of a well-known principle of modal logic that if Clark must be in his car at 8 he must be blown up. But the converse does not hold.

reasons for doing so. Hartshorne himself adopts it because he thinks
it is required if we are to reject a view of the future as causally predetermined in every detail in the present. To the extent that we can
make true statements about what is going to happen, to that extent,
he thinks, the future is already settled. If I say '*X will* do *A*' and what
I say is true, then it is already settled that *X* will do *A*, in other words
X must do *A*. One reason which Hartshorne has for believing this is
that he does not believe that there can be a relation between something that exists now and something which is going to exist, until the
latter comes into existence. He says, 'Truth is some sort of correspondence, and the temporal status of the truth is the same as that of
the correspondence. There can be no timeless relation to something
whose mode of being is temporal, for relation to *X* includes *X*, and
if *X* comes into being, so does the relation.' (*Mind* (January 1965)
54–5.) This is why he thinks true statements about the future must
really be about the present, about what present conditions allow.
Why should we accept this dogma about relations? Doesn't today
precede 17 June 1999 and isn't this a relation between days, one of
which has not yet come into existence? We may grant that a relation
cannot hold between things when one or more of them *never* actually
exists. But this does not exclude from the field of a relation something
which is going to, but does not *yet*, exist. Moreover there are those
who would find even the more modest claim that truth is some sort
of correspondence a dogmatic one.

Another argument which might be used to defend Hartshorne's
analysis by one who didn't like the Aristotelian alternative would be
a variant of the notorious fatalist argument. If a proposition is
already true, it is true whatever happens; so what it states must
already be settled and determined, since nothing that might happen
can prevent this happening. Hence there can be no true statements
about the future which predict *contingent* events. This line of argument
is, however, patently invalid, because it exploits a confusion between two distinct inferences:

(i) It is true that *p*;
therefore it is true that *p* whatever (else) in fact happens.
(ii) It is true that *p*;
therefore it would be true that *p* whatever (else) *could possibly*
happen.

If it is true that *p*, then what it asserts will take place and of course
nothing that in fact is going to happen *will* in the ordinary sense prevent its taking place. But this does not mean that there is nothing
which *could* but won't in fact happen which is capable of preventing

its occurrence. If Labour is going to win the next election, then
nothing which will happen will prevent its winning – if anything
does prevent it, then it won't win. But it doesn't follow that there is
nothing that could, even though it won't, prevent it. When the
event does take place it will have taken place whatever else has in
fact taken place. But it by no means follows that it would have taken
place whatever else might possibly have happened. From the truth
of p we can infer that p-whatever-else-actually-happens. But we cannot infer that if it were (though it won't be) the case that q, then it
would still be true that p. Arguments of this fatalist type have often
been subjected to a considerable philosophical battering and I do
not think that it is necessary for me to prolong my attack. Of course,
successful criticism of such an argument does not go as far as to show
that any form of fatalism or determinism is false, but that is not my
intention here. I merely wish to point out that we are not committed to any such doctrine if we reject Hartshorne's analysis.

Does Hartshorne's analysis, acceptable or not, reflect any logical
asymmetry between past and future? If the analysis is plausible for
the future tense, why not a similar analysis for the past tense? If we
consider present conditions as causal conditions, it is true that it is
reasonable to regard the future as indeterminate in the sense that
not every detail has been causally settled yet. So, given present
states of affairs and the laws of nature, there are many different
detailed courses which the future might take. But equally, given the
laws of nature, if we consider present conditions as effects, there are
many different detailed pasts from which they might have arisen.
There are past events which are contingent with respect to the
present, which are not retrodictable even in principle from present
conditions using laws of nature. As time moves on the events at a
given moment in the future are made more definite but those at a
given moment in the past become less definite. Consider all the
cases of suicide in Britain this year. After the suicides have occurred
there remains evidence of them; the year after, the evidence is
enough to determine precisely who killed himself, but hundreds of
years later, perhaps, the remaining evidence is enough to establish
roughly how many suicides there were but not precisely who they
were. The openness of the future is matched by a corresponding
openness in the past.

We may reject Hartshorne's account of predictive statements, or
insist on a parallel account of past-tensed statements, however, without wholly rejecting the picture of the future which he thinks requires such an account, and we shall still be left with an asymmetry
between past and future. A future event is one which will become

definite with time, a past event one which will be made less definite. This is to be interpreted in the way already explained, of course, and so interpreted will presumably be true provided what Hartshorne describes as determinism (every future event causally settled now etc.) is not true. Now whether *this* asymmetry is a logical one depends on whether determinism is logically impossible. I do not propose to discuss this nor do I even wish to imply that the account of determinism involved is a coherent one. I only want to claim that whether there is such an asymmetry is independent of whether we agree with Hartshorne about the meaning of 'will' and 'is going to be'.

II

Hartshorne's thesis that future-tensed utterances are covertly modal was largely inspired by some remarks of C. S. Peirce, which have been conveniently extracted and reported by Prior in an historical appendix to *Time and Modality* (Oxford, 1957, pp. 111–16). Two main points emerge. In the first place Peirce regards the future as largely indeterminate and refers to the present as 'that Nascent State between the Determinate and the Indeterminate'. He throws some light on what his claim amounts to by contrasting the way in which we can talk of the great tragedians who have acted in New York in the past ten years, where we can draw up a list naming each of the actors we are talking about, and the way in which we can discuss a question like whether current theatrical influences favour the development of men or women stars. 'In order to discuss that', he says, 'we have to go beyond our completed experience . . . and have to consider the possible and probable stars of the immediate future. We can no longer assign proper names to each. The individual actors to which our discourse now relates become largely merged into general kinds; and their separate identities are partially lost.' Similarly, statisticians can estimate that there will be a certain number of suicides in New York the year after next, but it would be improper to ask them for a list of those who were going to commit suicide, because it is probably not yet determinate who they are going to be. 'There is an approach to a want of distinct identity in the individuals . . . who are to commit suicide', says Peirce. Of course, as time goes on the range of people from whom the suicides will come gets narrower until, say, the day before, the identities of most of them are more or less fixed. The near future is presumably more determinate than the distant future; but the past is wholly determinate, for it is, Peirce reminds us, 'the sum of *faits accomplis*'.

The second important point in Peirce is that 'future facts are the only facts that we can, in a measure, control'. We cannot, of course, control every future event; many events, like tomorrow's sunrise, are already settled and must happen in virtue of laws of nature: such events are in principle inferable from the present state of affairs. But contingent events in the future, unlike past ones, are amenable to our control.

Hartshorne has attempted to fill out and make more precise the picture of the future sketched in Peirce's writings by interpreting 'determinate' as 'causally settled'. But there is another and more popular way of developing Peirce's remarks, which concentrates on the points about not being able to name future actors and their 'want of distinct identity'. This alternative view which I want to examine has been espoused in one form or another by Broad, Ryle, Prior and Bernard Mayo, among others. It has been presented in some detail by the last writer in an attractive article which appeared in *Mind* (Jan 1962) called 'The Open Future', and it is to that article that I shall pay most attention.

Like Hartshorne's, Mayo's is a general thesis about future-tensed sentences, although again he confines himself to the simple future tense without saying to what extent the thesis is to be extended to other future tenses. Crudely the thesis is that (simple) future-tensed discourse is always general, because the future is the realm of the contingent or merely possible. As Peirce puts it, with more impressive rhetoric, 'The merely possible is necessarily general, . . . it is only actuality, the force of existence, which bursts the fluidity of the general and produces a discrete unit' (quoted by Prior, *Time and Modality*, p. 114).

Professor Mayo sets about giving a clearer, more exact statement of this idea in order to find some logical difference between future-tensed and past-/present-tensed statements which will explain why doctrines 'that emphatically assimilate future to past' like precognition, reversed causation and fatalism are philosophically suspicious. The problem is to distinguish past contingencies or possibilities (like the possibility that Mary Fitton was the Dark Lady of the Sonnets) from future ones. Mayo points out that past possibilities are those that are already realised, and that the realisation or actualisation of possibilities is a one-way process.[1] And that the difference between actualised and unactualised possibilities is not a merely temporal one he seeks to show by refining a thesis about the nature of our discourse about unactualised possibilities, that is, our discourse about the

[1] He should have said that past possibilities are those that have already been realised *or ruled out*.

future. In the chapter entitled 'It was to Be' in *Dilemmas* (Cambridge, 1954), Ryle maintains that discourse about the future cannot properly contain proper names or referring expressions because, as he puts it, you cannot refer to what you have not got. Mayo claims that you cannot properly make singular statements in the simple future tense, meaning by 'singular statement' one which has a singular term as its *logical subject*. 'The direction of time would be determined by the progressive accumulation of singular statements becoming available to match statements which hitherto had been only general.' (Mayo, in *Mind* (Jan 1962), p. 12.)

At first sight there seem to be counter-examples to this thesis in the form of future-tensed sentences whose subject expressions refer to what we have already got, namely, past or presently existing individuals, as in (S 1) 'Professor Carnap will fly to the moon.' Mayo thinks that the statement expressed by this sentence is really general and is to be analysed in the following way:

$(\exists x)$ (x flies to the moon and x is identical with the present Professor Carnap.) (Cf. p. 13, *ibid.*)

For he holds that it is not the present Professor Carnap whom we have already got who will fly to the moon but a future Carnap who can at present only be specified generally as *someone* identical, that is, personally continuous with, the present Carnap (who is named in the analysis). His analysis means: 'Someone identical with the present Carnap flies to the moon.'

An immediate difficulty about this analysis is that it eliminates future reference altogether, since it is really a translation of 'Professor Carnap flew, is flying or will fly to the moon.' Perhaps this could be remedied by rewriting the first conjunct as 'x *will* fly to the moon', but then it might be objected that it is not true of this future traveller to the moon that he *will* fly to the moon, only that, while he exists, he *is* flying there. The objection is disputable, however. I would rather maintain that while we cannot properly say at the time of the flight that the future Carnap *will* fly to the moon, we can say so before. After all, someone talking about his next, as yet unconceived, child can properly say (guessing) that it *will be* a boy.

Mayo claims that his analysis shows (S 1) really to be general despite the fact that his analysis contains what is admittedly a singular term, '(the present) Professor Carnap'. His reason is that it does not occur as a subject term (see p. 11). Unfortunately we are not told why 'Professor Carnap' is not a subject term; the natural thing nowadays would, roughly, be to take 'is identical with' as a relational predicate with the expressions 'x', 'Professor Carnap' as subject terms. Mayo must mean something special by 'subject term', something which forces 'Professor Carnap' but not 'x' into the predicate part of the analysis. But it is difficult to find out from his paper what he does mean. He tells us that 'a predicate term, in general, can be attached to a number of different subject terms, and a subject term can have a number of different predicate terms attached to it '(p. 10). This is not enough, however, to enable us to distinguish subject from predicate terms. 'Professor Carnap' can be completed by many different predicate terms, including, so it seems, 'Someone identical with . . .'. Mayo seems to have given us no reason for denying that 'Professor Carnap', as it appears in this analysis, is a subject term.

Maybe this deficiency is remediable, perhaps a suitable account of the notion of a subject term can be provided. A more serious difficulty for Mayo's analysis is that, in virtue of a familiar principle of identity,[1] it entails the singular statement '(The present) Professor Carnap will fly to the moon.' So even if (S 1) is really general because it is to be analysed in the way recommended by Mayo, whenever there is a true general statement of the form of (S 1) there will also be a corresponding true singular statement. To this objection Mayo could reply that the sort of identity involved is personal continuity between what are in a sense different temporal slices of the same person, and that the logical identity principle I have invoked doesn't apply to this special sort of identity. Alternatively he might reply that the entailment only holds if we take '(the present) Professor Carnap' as a subject term, which he has insisted we shouldn't. Rather, the expression 'is (identical with) Professor Carnap' is to be taken as a predicate expression meaning something like 'is a Carnapian temporal slice'.

Mayo dubs the general thesis whose refinement he is defending 'the Ryle–Prior–Peirce thesis'. But Prior has disowned Mayo's refinement because he objects to the treatment of Carnap as a series of temporally distinct slices of which the present Carnap is one and the future Carnap who will fly to the moon will (if Carnap does make such a flight) be another.[2] On the face of it proper names of people, cities, mountains, rivers and the like do not seem to be names simply for temporal sections of people, cities, etc. I shall not go on to consider the consequences of Mayo's counter-intuitive claim at this point, since his general thesis that there are no singular statements in the (simple) future tense entails a weaker and more attractive thesis,

---

[1] It is a logical truth that $(x)(y)(Fx \ \& \ x=y. \supset . Fy)$. If anything has a certain property, anything identical with that first thing will also have the property.

[2] 'On the Unity of Professor Carnap', in *Mind* (1964) 268–9.

and any objections I may produce to the weaker thesis will consequently count against the stronger one too.

The weaker thesis is reached by conceding Prior's objection and allowing reference in future-tensed discourse to past and already existing individuals. What the weaker thesis does not recognise is the use of proper names and referring expressions attempting to refer to individuals that will but don't yet exist, individuals we genuinely haven't got (henceforth 'future individuals').[1] We have already got Professor Carnap, and we need not worry, it might be thought, about not having the future Carnap, because he's a pseudo-individual anyway, indistinguishable from the Carnap who exists now. So it is not necessary to defend Mayo's awkward analysis of (S 1) in order to defend this weaker thesis. (The range of the word 'individual' in the thesis is still regrettably unclear. Is the thesis meant to exclude particular reference to next Thursday, or to the twenty-first century, for example? Or can such references be analysed out so that they become incapsulated in verbs and adverbial phrases and do not count as references to genuine individuals?)

The thesis should not in general prohibit the use of pronouns in talking about future individuals, *pace* Ryle, who says:

> While it still an askable question whether my parents are going to have a fourth son, [one] cannot use as a name the name 'Gilbert Ryle' or use as a pronoun designating their fourth son the pronoun 'he'. [*Dilemmas*, p. 27.]

Suppose that two years before Ryle's birth someone had said, 'If the Ryles have a fourth child, he will occupy their spare bedroom', isn't this perfectly meaningful? 'He' is being used here like a bound variable in logic and should not count as a referring expression in any case. The sentence in question means 'If the Ryles have a fourth son, *whoever is their fourth son* will occupy the spare bedroom', and it seems perfectly proper to replace the italicised phrase by the pronoun 'he'. If Ryle had meant simply that 'he' does not strictly designate or refer to the fourth son as a genuine proper name designates its bearer, he would have been right.

Indeed, the notion of a referring expression has never been made very clear and it may well be that we should do better to abandon it. But if any terms are to count as referring expressions, presumably

---

[1] If it is allowed that some parts of predicate expressions are referring expressions, this weaker thesis is not entailed by Mayo's. But my objections to this weaker thesis are just as effective against a weaker thesis which merely excludes *subject* expressions that refer to future individuals.

proper names are. So I shall simply consider the case of proper names, for if the thesis cannot be made out for proper names it surely cannot be made out for any other referring expressions.

Why should it be felt, then, that we cannot make particular reference to future individuals by naming them? Mayo's reason seems to be that perceptual acquaintance is necessary for naming individuals. And as Broad put it, 'We cannot stand in the relation of direct acquaintance to future events, for the same reason which prevents us from robbing a Highlander of his breeks' (*Scientific Thought* (London, 1923) p. 79). Mayo makes the point at the end of his paper when he attempts to elucidate the sense in which we 'have not got' future individuals. 'All statements in the past or present tense can in principle be tied down to sense-experience; they contain referring expressions as well as descriptive ones, or where they do not . . . they occur in a framework of discourse which does typically contain referring expressions. . . . Such referring expressions always carry with them a context of sensation' (*Mind* (Jan 1962) p. 14). Mayo makes his point about referring expressions in general; I shall just consider the case of proper names.

Now it is not at all clear precisely what is involved in a proper name's being tied down to sense-experience. It may mean that we cannot genuinely use a proper name for an individual we are not currently perceiving, or that we cannot name an individual we are neither perceiving nor have perceived and can remember (and that if we attempt to do so the 'name' we use is at best a disguised description). Or it may mean that we cannot *assign* a proper name in the first place to an individual we are not perceiving, or to one we are neither perceiving nor can remember; and, of course, you cannot use a proper name before it has been assigned. On the first and stronger thesis, present-day references to people like Plato and Julius Caesar can never involve genuine uses of true proper names. On the weaker thesis, which is presumably entailed by the stronger, there is nothing to impugn such uses of names like 'Plato' and 'Caesar' at the present time. On both theses, if acquaintance in memory is allowed, it will be possible to refer by proper name to some past individuals but not to any future individuals. Again I shall simply consider the weaker and more plausible thesis, since it is entailed by the stronger, and any objections to the weaker will therefore count against the stronger.

The view we have to consider, then, is that you cannot bestow a proper name without having perceptual acquaintance with its bearer. I think that the line of thought behind this is that although a word may have the syntactical character of a proper name it hasn't been given sense or meaning as a genuine proper name until it has been assigned to a bearer. This means that you can't have a proper name without a bearer and that a statement like 'Homer did not exist' is either necessarily false or contains no genuine proper name – but let us waive this objection. Now in order to introduce a proper name into the language we must know which individual we are assigning it to. We must successfully pick out or identify the individual in question.

There seem to be two suggestible ways of picking out an individual which lacks a proper name in order to give it one.[1] One way is to point out an individual you and the hearer are acquainted with, say in present perception. Another way is to describe it. It must be conceded, certainly, that having *some* true description of the bearer, even if it picks it out unequivocally, will not be enough to enable one to introduce a proper name for it. It is arguable that a couple's as yet unconceived child cannot be referred to by a genuine proper name; if they do use a name for it, it is doubtful whether it is being used as a genuine proper name. Suppose they decide to call their next child 'Pat'. It does seem as if they have failed to name some definite individual, even though the description of it as their next child is sufficient to enable people to pick it out when and if they have another child. At most one individual will satisfy the description. If they have two more children, then the first of these will be Pat. But if they have the second it will be possible for them to say that the second and not the first will be Pat if the first has, say, died through abortion. One feels that, when they used the name 'Pat' before the conception of their next child, the target for the name had not really been selected, although there was now some formula for its selection in due course. It is rather as if a chieftain of a tribe were to decide to bestow a coveted name on the strongest of his as yet unnamed sons, and said, 'I hereby give the name "Hud" to whoever wins a race to the next village.' The proper name has not yet been bestowed on anyone, its target is so far unsettled, even though the description determining the future bearer of the name suffices to pick that particular bearer out in the end. (I ignore the complication of a tie.) The child case is not exactly like this, of course; there does not exist at the time the name 'Pat' is chosen a range of individuals from whom the bearer of the name is to be selected. But when the child which gets the name does exist, at least it makes sense to say that *it* might not have been the referent of the name's initial uses. Perhaps this sort of consideration encourages

---

[1] Cf. J. Searle, 'Proper Names', in *Mind* (1958) 168.

some philosophers to think that successful particular reference to future individuals by means of proper names is not really possible.

However, rare though the use of genuine proper names for future individuals undoubtedly is, it cannot be excluded in general on logical grounds. Consider the case of a canal of a certain determinate type to be built in a certain specified place at a certain time, a canal which a planning committee has already decided to call 'Marley Canal'. The conditions for giving sense to and applying the name are already satisfied before the canal is begun. We know how to pick it out from others and how to reidentify it; and only one canal can satisfy the descriptions given. (Until the canal is begun, picking it out and reidentifying it will be largely a linguistic matter, of course. The question at issue is whether a proper name can be used to achieve this.) When the canal is built nobody will be able truly to say that *this* canal mightn't have been the referent of the first uses of 'Marley Canal', that there might have been some other canal of an exactly similar sort in the same place which would have been the referent – unless he means simply that the committee might have decided originally on a different *name*.

In this case, then, I have supposed the proper name to be assigned to an individual picked out, not ostensively, but by a description of distinguishing properties which tie it down in space and time. It is true that this involves defining a singular term solely by means of a description, but the description is not completely general since it contains references to a particular time and place. It is up to those who think that this is not enough, that you also need to be perceptually acquainted with a particular individual before you can give it a proper name, to say what more you would get from perceptual acquaintance with the canal which you don't get from the prior descriptions and which is needed to give the words 'Marley Canal' meaning as a genuine proper name. Suppose instead that the canal is named in its presence after completion. It is not enough simply to point to it and say, 'I name this "Marley Canal".' It must at least be clear under what general description the object of the pointing falls. What is being pointed to: the shape, the colour, the width of the canal, or the canal itself? This is a familiar Wittgensteinian point. Perhaps in this example it falls a bit flat, because the word 'canal' occurs as part of the name; but somehow it must be clear what sort of thing is being named. And in order to be able to reapply the proper name successfully you must notice sufficient distinguishing properties of the canal. You will know some spatial and temporal property of the canal at least, namely that it is here now. But what more do you get from perceptual acquaintance that you do not get from the descriptions settled by the committee before the canal was built?

Consider the reasons which might be given for denying that the canal can be given a proper name before it exists:

(i) Before it is built, it might be said that the words 'Marley Canal' are only the name of a plan or a project, not of a bridge. But, if the plans contained the sentence: 'The length of Marley Canal is to be 30 miles', this surely wouldn't mean that the length of the *plan* would be 30 miles.

(ii) Until the canal is built there will always be genuine doubt whether there will be a referent for the words.[1] But it can hardly be claimed that there is no conceivable case where we cannot be absolutely sure – so strong is the evidence – that there will exist an individual of the description in question. Of course it will always be *logically* possible that the individual won't exist, but then it is also *logically* possible that the canal we think we are perceiving, however clearly we seem to see it, might not exist.

(iii) If the canal can be named in advance of its existence there is nothing to stop us from giving names to indefinitely many *possibilities*, say to many possible canals that never will be built.[2] But this difficulty can be overcome by requiring that we can only bestow a proper name in advance when we know that there will be an individual to bear the name.

The view that ordinary proper names, and perhaps other referring expressions, must be tied down in sense-experience is, I suspect, a ghost of Russellian atomism. Russell thought that what he regarded as a logically proper name, to be distinguished of course from ordinary proper names, could be given sense only by being linked directly through acquaintance with its bearer without collecting any descriptions on the way. If you knew something only by description, naming it was, strictly, impossible. Hence the feeling that singling out an individual by description isn't really pinning down that *particular* individual in a way sufficient to name it. But it seems to me that the idea that acquaintance can add anything to the sense of a proper name that cannot in principle be given by description is a wrong one.

It would not surprise me enormously, however, if I were wrong in claiming that there is no logical barrier to making particular references to future individuals. But even if I am wrong it is still arguable that even Mayo's strong thesis does not provide us with a *logical* determinant of time direction, a *logical* distinction between past and

[1] Cf. R. M. Gale, *The Language of Time* (London, 1968) p. 184.
[2] Cf. Prior, *Past, Present and Future*, p. 142.

future. For his reason why we cannot refer to future individuals (including future Carnaps) is that such references need to be backed by perceptual acquaintance with the individuals referred to. He leaves it open whether memory of such individuals is to count as adequate backing, but if it is then he must surely allow that it would be possible to name future individuals too if only we could precognise them. Now even if as a matter of fact we cannot have precognitive experience of future individuals analogous to our memory experiences of past ones, even if we have no cognitive access to the future as we have access in memory to the past, it needs a lot of further argument to show that such access is *logically* impossible. And if precognition is not a logical impossibility Mayo can at most claim that it is a contingent matter that we cannot use proper names to refer to future individuals, and it will only be a contingent difference between our knowledge of past and future events that is reflected in our discourse.

Anyone who is sympathetic with a causal theory of memory[1] is likely to want a causal theory of precognition, and he is likely to think that if precognition is impossible it is due to the impossibility of reversed causation. I have no space to argue for these contentions, but it is surely reasonable to suggest that some case could be made out for them. Now if the case were sound, whether precognition was logically impossible would depend on whether reversed causation was logically rather than, say, just physically impossible. It would be rash simply to assume that such causation was logically impossible; quite a vigorous controversy has gone on in recent years over this matter.

Mayo also thinks that his thesis about reference explains the philosophical uncanniness of the doctrines of precognition, reversed causation and fatalism. Presumably his idea is that you couldn't precognise particular events or individuals in the future if you couldn't refer to them, or at least that the experiences wouldn't be fully describable; nor could such events or individuals be said to cause anything happening now or in the past. When we ask why we cannot make such references, the answer is that they couldn't be tied down to sense-experience as can our references to past and present individuals. Now although Mayo is unwilling to say whether or not the required perceptual acquaintance can include memory, it will be rather embarrassing for him if he doesn't include it, because if ultimately the reason why you cannot precognise an individual is

---

[1] By a 'causal theory of memory' I mean any account which postulates as a logically necessary condition for remembering that what is remembered should in some sense cause the ostensible memory.

that you are not acquainted in present perception with it, then this means that we couldn't remember events involving individuals which have since ceased to exist – which we clearly can. Yet if he includes memory in acquaintance the explanation of the impossibility of precognition will be vacuous. For if he includes memory he would surely have to admit that, if we had precognitive experience of future events analogous to our memory experience of past events, that too would count as acquaintance. But to say that precognition is impossible because we have no (precognitive) acquaintance with future events is not to offer any significant explanation. In effect it is to explain the absence of precognition in terms of the absence of precognition.

His thesis will not show why reversed causality is impossible, because the thesis rests on the indeterminacy of our *knowledge* of future individuals and does not involve the claim that future individuals will be indeterminate in themselves. And if it is only our knowledge of them that is indeterminate or general we may not yet be able to say of a future event involving some particular future individual that it will cause some present event, but it doesn't follow immediately from this that it couldn't be true. Mayo wants to explain the impossibility of reversed causation in terms of the impossibility of particular reference to future individuals, which will be explained in terms of lack of precognition. But if precognition depends on reversed causation, as I have suggested above might well be the case, the impossibility of precognition will be explained by the absence of reversed causation. Another circle.

It is not at all obvious how Mayo's thesis undermines fatalism. A future wholly predetermined in its general description is still a disturbing thought; if the only true statements I can make about the future are general ones and their truth at the present time means that the sort of event predicted is unpreventable in every case, this still seems to me to be worrying.

If we confine ourselves to the indicative mood, I do not believe, then, that we shall find any interesting logical asymmetries between past and future directly reflected by general features of tensed discourse. At the end of his paper Mayo mentions the imperative and optative moods, which seem to be especially oriented towards the future. The imperative mood seems necessarily to refer to the future, and wishes about the past, although it is perfectly possible to express them, seem in a sense to be idle. It is arguable that it is once more the absence of reversed causation that accounts for the lack of imperatives to do acts in the past and for the idleness of wishes about the past. And again, whether this feature of our language reflects a *logical* asymmetry between past and future will depend on whether retroactive causes are *logically* impossible.[1]

[1] Several people have made helpful comments on earlier drafts of this paper. I am particularly indebted to Professor A. G. Wernham for his comments on Section I.

11

DUHEM, QUINE AND A NEW EMPIRICISM

Mary Hesse

I. THE DUHEM–QUINE THESIS

As in the case of great books in all branches of philosophy, Pierre Duhem's *Le Théorie Physique*, first published in 1906, can be looked to as the progenitor of many different and even conflicting currents in subsequent philosophy of science. On a superficial reading, it seems to be an expression of what later came to be called deductivist and instrumentalist analyses of scientific theory. Duhem's very definition of physical theory, put forward early in the book, is the quintessence of instrumentalism:

> A physical theory is not an explanation. It is a system of mathematical propositions, deduced from a small number of principles, which aim to represent as simply, as completely, and as exactly as possible a set of experimental laws [p. 19].

The instrumentalist overtones of this become clear from the implications of the denial that theories are explanations. For Duhem an explanation is a metaphysical entity, and science should be independent of metaphysics. But this dictum is not intended, as with the positivists, to dispose of metaphysics as irrational or meaningless; it is rather an assertion of the autonomy and dignity of metaphysics as alone capable of expressing the truth of how things are in the world. Metaphysics according to Duhem is not independent of experience, but its methods are not those of science, and its conclusions stand independently of changing fashions in science. Thus it is for Duhem a grave error to interpret scientific theory as itself providing a metaphysics – a global theory drawn from science such as mechanism is not only false, because science outgrows it by its own methods, but also it is not the kind of theory that could ever be true, because it illegitimately uses the methods of mathematical representation of experimental facts to construct an ontology and to give answers to substantial questions about the nature of the world and of man. But only metaphysics, and in particular a religious metaphysics, can do that. The aim of science must be more modest. A non-interference pact must be established between the domains of science and metaphysics.

Duhem was not the first nor the last philosopher of religion to see the answer to teasing conflicts between science and religion in terms of a complete separation of their spheres of influence, but this is not the aspect of Duhem's thought that I want to discuss here. Indeed, if this were all there were to say about Duhem's philosophy of science it would deserve no more than a minor place in the history of positivism. But his extra-scientific preoccupations did not after all mislead him into so crude an analysis of science itself as his definition of scientific theory would entail. He is saved by a discussion of the observational basis of science that is far subtler than that presupposed by later deductivists and instrumentalists, and paradoxically it is a discussion which can be made to undermine the very foundations of the dichotomy of mathematical theory and explanation, science and metaphysics, that his theory of explanation presupposes.

Most empiricist accounts of science have been based, usually tacitly, on the notion of a comparatively unproblematic observation language. It matters little how this is construed – whether in terms of hard sense data, operational definitions, ordinary language, or what not – the essential point is that there are statements of some kind whose meaning as descriptions of states of affairs is supposed to be transparent, and whose truth-value is supposed to be directly and individually decidable by setting up the appropriate observation situations. It is a long time since anyone seriously claimed that the truth of such statements can be known *incorrigibly*, but most eyes have been averted from the consequences of the significant admission of fallibility of even observation statements, and attention has been concentrated on the way in which meaning and truth-value is conveyed to theories, regarded as in these respects parasitic upon observation statements and clearly distinguishable from them. The consequences for deductivism have been proliferation of a number of insoluble and unnecessary problems regarding the meaning of theoretical statements and the possibility of confirming them, and the result has been a slide into instrumentalism in which, in the end, only observation statements and not theories have empirical interpretation. What that interpretation and its significance is still remains unanalysed.

Duhem introduces two important modifications into this type of classical empiricism. They may be expressed as a new theory of *correspondence* and a new theory of *coherence*.

(i) In his theory of *correspondence*, attention is shifted away from the empirical basis of traditional empiricism to the theoretical *interpretation* of that basis. Duhem sees that what is primarily significant for science is not the precise nature of what we directly observe, which in the end is a *causal* process, itself susceptible of scientific analysis. What is significant is the interpretive expression we give to what is observed, what he calls the *theoretical facts*, as opposed to the 'raw data' represented by *practical facts*. This distinction may best be explained by means of his own example. Consider the theoretical fact 'The temperature is distributed in a certain manner over a certain body' (p. 133). This, says Duhem, is susceptible of precise mathematical formulation with regard to the geometry of the body and the numerical specification of the temperature distribution. Contrast the practical fact. Here geometrical description is at best an idealisation of a more or less rigid body with a more or less indefinite surface. The temperature at a given point cannot be exactly fixed, but is only given as an average value over vaguely defined small volumes. The theoretical fact is an imperfect translation, or interpretation, of the practical fact. Moreover, the relation between them is not one-one, but rather many-many, for an infinity of idealisations may be made to more or less fit the practical fact, and an infinity of practical facts may be expressed by means of one theoretical fact.

Duhem is not careful in his exposition to distinguish *facts* from *linguistic expressions of facts*. Sometimes both practical and theoretical facts seem to be intended as linguistic statements (for instance, where the metaphor of 'translation' is said to be appropriate). But even if this is his intention, it is clear that he does not wish to follow traditional empiricism into a search for forms of expression of practical facts which will constitute the basis of science. Practical facts are not the appropriate place to look for such a basis – they are imprecise, ambiguous, corrigible, and on their own ultimately meaningless. Moreover, there is a sense in which they are literally inexpressible. The absence of distinction between fact and linguistic expression here is not accidental. As soon as we begin to try to capture a practical fact in language, we are committed to some theoretical interpretation. Even to say of the solid body that 'its points are more or less worn down and blunt' is to commit ourselves to the categories of an ideal geometry.

What, then, is the 'basis' of scientific knowledge for Duhem? If we are to use this conception at all, we must say that the basis of science is the set of theoretical facts in terms of which experience is interpreted. But we have just seen that theoretical facts have only a more or less loose and ambiguous relation with experience. How can we be sure that they provide a firm empirical foundation? The answer must be that we cannot be sure. There is no such foundation. It must be admitted that Duhem himself is not consistent on this point, for he sometimes speaks of the persistence of the network of theoretical facts as if this, once established, takes on the privileged character ascribed to observation statements in classical positivism. But this is not the view that emerges from his more careful discussion of examples. For he is quite clear, as in the case of the correction of the 'observational' laws of Kepler by Newton's theory (p. 193), that more comprehensive mathematical representations may show particular theoretical facts to be false.

However, we certainly seem to have a problem here, because if it is admitted that subsets of the theoretical facts may be removed from the corpus of science, and if we yet want to retain empiricism, the decision to remove them can be made only by reference to *other* theoretical facts, whose status is in principle equally insecure. The correspondence with experience, though loose and corrigible, must still be retained, and still remains unanalysed.

(ii) Duhem's theory of *coherence* is indispensable to a satisfactory resolution of this problem. The theory has been much discussed, but unfortunately not always in the context in which Duhem set it, with the result that it has often been misunderstood and even trivialised.

Theoretical facts do not stand on their own, but are bound together, in a network of laws which constitutes the total mathematical representation of experience. The putative theoretical fact that was Kepler's third law of planetary motion, for example, does not fit the network of laws established by Newton's theory. It is therefore modified, and this modification is possible without violating experience because of the many-one relation between the theoretical fact and that practical fact understood as the ultimately inexpressible situation which obtains in regard to the orbits of planets. It follows that neither the truth nor the falsity of a theoretical fact or a lawlike relation connecting such facts can be determined in isolation from the rest of the network. Systems of hypotheses have to come to the test of experience as wholes. Individual hypotheses are not individually falsifiable any more than they are individually verifiable.

Quine, as is well known, has taken up both aspects of Duhem's new empiricism. A bare remnant of empirical correspondence is implied by his dictum that 'our statements about the external world face the tribunal of sense experience not individually but only as a corporate body' – for Quine they do face it; how they face it has come in his recent writings to be a question for a stimulus-response psychology (Quine, 1960, 1968). The coherence of our knowledge is also implied, in the very strong sense (which is never explicitly claimed by Duhem) not only that generally speaking hypotheses cannot individually be shown to be false by experience, but that *no* statement can be; any statement can be maintained true in the face of any evidence: 'Any statement can be held true come what may, if we make drastic enough adjustments elsewhere in the system' (Quine, 1953, p. 43). Because it is doubtful whether we ever want to 'hold a hypothesis *true*' rather than highly confirmed or highly probable, and because I do not here want to beg or examine that question, I shall discuss Quine's claim in a slightly more weakened form than is implied by this quotation. The weaker form, which I shall call the Q-thesis, is that

No descriptive statement can be individually falsified by evidence, whatever the evidence may be, since adjustments in the rest of the system can always be devised to prevent its falsification.

It has seemed to many commentators that to replace the observational basis of science with this shifting network is to open the floodgates to conventionalism, and to a vicious circularity of truth-value and meaning which is in effect an abandonment of empiricism. Popper (1959, p. 78), for example, classes Duhem with Poincaré as a conventionalist. But if by conventionalism is meant, as Poincaré apparently intended in regard to the geometry of physical space, that any given total theoretical system can be imposed upon any logically possible experience, then surely to class Duhem as a conventionalist is a mistake. For neither Duhem nor Quine say anything to imply that a total system is not refutable by experience; indeed that it is so refutable is entailed by their contrast between refutability of individual hypotheses and refutability of the linked system of hypotheses. Once parts of the system have been fixed, perhaps conventionally, there are some extensions of it that are empirically excluded.

But elsewhere Popper (1963, p. 238 ff.) demands something more than this:

We can be reasonably successful in attributing our refutations to definite portions of the theoretical maze. (For we *are* reasonably successful in this – a fact which must remain inexplicable for one who adopts Duhem's or Quine's views on the matter) [p. 243].

The 'holistic argument goes much too far' if it denies that it is ever possible to find out which is the guilty hypothesis. There are, he suggests, three ways in which it may in fact be identified:

(i) We may provisionally take for granted the background knowledge common to two theories for which we design a crucial experiment, and regard the experiment as refuting one or other of the theories rather than the background knowledge. But neither Duhem nor Quine would ever deny this possibility, and it is of course not sufficient to refute Q, since it does not require acceptance of the background knowledge to be anything but *provisional*.

(ii) We may be able to axiomatise the whole theoretical system in such a way as to isolate the effect of a single axiom, which may then be refuted in isolation. But even if we disregard the extreme impracticability of such axiomatisation in the case of most interesting scientific theories, its ideal possibility still does not refute Q, because no axiomatisation can fully account for the empirical applicability of the system, and the correctness of the conditions of application (the so-called 'correspondence rules') might always be called into question to avoid abandonment of any of the axioms.

(iii) Theories need to make successful predictions (to be 'corroborated' in Popper's terminology) as well as being refuted if false. When successful predictions have occurred, Popper seems to suggest, we are more reluctant to abandon those parts of the theory responsible for them, and more willing to locate the responsibility for subsequent refutations in other, less well corroborated parts of the network. Popper's notion of corroboration here as elsewhere is far from clear, but it is difficult to interpret this suggestion in any sense other than in terms of relative inductive *confirmation* of some parts of the system in comparison with others. Some theory of confirmation of the system by experience does indeed seem to be a requirement of the network analysis, and I shall return to this requirement below; but as far as Popper's suggestion goes, he only regards this method of picking out a guilty hypothesis as indicative and not conclusive, and so the method in any case would not refute Q.

The Q-thesis has also recently come under attack from Adolf Grunbaum (1963, ch. 4; 1966). In a series of articles Grunbaum has sought to show that Q is true only in trivial cases in which 'drastic adjustments elsewhere in the system' are construed as allowing *ad hoc* changes in the rules of English usage. Clearly if a hypothesis predicts that roses are red, and they turn out to be black, Q is not satisfied except trivially by interchanging the uses of 'red' and 'black' in observation reports in English. 'Hence', Grunbaum continues, 'a *necessary* condition for the non-triviality of Duhem's thesis is that *the theoretical language be semantically stable* in the relevant respects' (1966, p. 278). He does not, however, claim to give general sufficient conditions for the non-triviality of auxiliary hypotheses or rules which would preserve the truth of a hypothesis H in the face of apparently contrary evidence, nor does he attempt to spell out in detail what it would be for the theoretical language to be 'semantically stable' or for H to remain the 'same hypothesis', arguing only that Quine's suggestion of resort to a non-standard logic must at least be regarded as trivial, as must *ad hoc* changes in the meanings of descriptive terms.[1]

This criticism suggests, therefore, a second requirement for the Q-thesis to be viable, namely some theory of change and retention of *meaning* within the network, in addition to the first requirement of some theory of confirmation.

To summarise these important and pervasive kinds of doubt about the viability of the Q-thesis, it is convenient to quote further from Grunbaum. Discussing Einstein's assertion that any metric geometry can be preserved in the face of any empirical evidence, he says:

> Indeed, if the Duhemian is to maintain, as he does, that a *total theoretical system* is falsifiable by observations, then surely he must assume that the relevant falsifying observations present us with sufficient *relatively* stubborn fact to be falsifying. . . . And if there were no relatively stubborn fact . . . how could the Duhemian avoid the following conclusion: 'Observational findings are always so unrestrictedly ambiguous as not to permit even the refutation of any given total theoretical system'? But such a result would be tantamount to the absurdity that any total theoretical system can be espoused *a priori* (1966, p. 288).

One could earn a quick point against this passage by remarking a *non sequitur* between 'if there were no *relatively* stubborn fact' and 'observational findings are always so *unrestrictedly* ambiguous . . .'. Might there not, one wants to ask, be relatively *un*stubborn facts which were nevertheless not *so* unrestrictedly ambiguous as to warrant the conclusion that any theory might be espoused as true *a priori*? Neither does it obviously follow that if there is no conclusive refutation, any theory goes, for there may be available a theory of relative confirmation. More fundamentally, it should be noted that Grunbaum has almost unwittingly fallen into just the habit of distinguishing the theoretical system from the 'relatively stubborn facts' that are called in question by the Q-thesis. That the facts are

---

[1] *Note added in proof:* Professor Grunbaum has now developed these arguments further in 'Can we ascertain the falsity of a scientific hypothesis?', a Thalheimer Lecture, 1969, to be published by the Johns Hopkins Press.

only *relatively* stubborn does not save him, for the whole thrust of Q
is against the practice of looking in the system for those statements
which can, even relatively, form its basis, and upon which the rest of
the system is propped up. 'Relatively' in this context is always taken
in classical empiricist accounts to imply 'relative to some *more* basic
statements which we could uncover if we had time or necessity'. But
the only relativity of stubbornness that can be allowed in a Q-system
is relativity with respect to the *other theoretical* statements. The
structure is mutually supporting. Where the points of external
support are applied is a subsidiary matter which cannot be decided
independently of the character of the network itself. Grunbaum
might well reply that this leaves the theory completely up in the air,
and removes it from empirical control in just the way he fears. So
we are left with the two requirements of a network theory as
constituting problems for explication:

(i) That some relative empirical confirmation should be provided,
and that without being able to identify any statement of the system
which expresses the evidence incorrigibly.

(ii) That some means of analysing stability and change of
meaning in the network should be provided.

2. CRITERIA OF CONFIRMATION

When faced with a philosophical tangle which seems to involve
logical circularities or contradictions, it is often illuminating to try
to conceive of a mechanism which simulates the conditions of the
problem, and to see whether a self-consistent model of it is possible.
What we need in this case is a machine capable of representing and
theorising about its environment according to the conditions just
described. We can distinguish in the usual way between the hardware and the software of the machine: the machine has a certain
physical constitution, the hardware, which we will assume remains
fixed (the machine is not at present regarded as a structurally evolv-
ing organism), and its software includes a certain system of coding
according to which some of its physical states can be represented in
its own 'language', and the representation perhaps printed on an output
tape, so that the machine is capable of 'reporting' on its environment.
Suppose the machine goes through the following stages of operation:

(i) Physical input from the environment causally modifies part
of the machine (its 'receptor').

(ii) The information thus conveyed to the receptor is represented
in the machine language according to a code present in the machine.

We may assume at this stage that the code is not, at least in practice, infinitely and exactly competent, so that (*a*) if the input is potentially infinitely various, some information present in the receptor is lost at the coding stage, and (*b*) the mechanism may make mistakes in a small proportion of translation of the input into code. The product of this stage will be called the *coded input* (C.I.), and corresponds to the set of observation statements produced by a human investigator as the representation in language resulting from experienced sensory input. Notice in particular that C.I. is not necessarily a complete or accurate representation of the input.

(iii) C.I. is examined for repetitions which yield inductive generalisations, and for more complex patterns which yield theories. If the machine is inductivist it may run through all possible systems of generalisations seeking that which is in some specified sense most probable or most simple. If it is deductivist it may have a small stock of patterns to try out on C.I., rejecting those whose fit is too bad, and retaining those whose fit is 'best' or good enough. In either case it is not necessary that the theory arrived at by the machine should be consistent with *every* piece of C.I., only that *most* of it should be consistent. Moreover, *which* parts of C.I. are going to be consistent with the best theory cannot be determined in advance, but only by examining the theory in the light of the complete C.I., and adjusting it to make the best fit. In other words, no single statement of C.I. is incorrigible relative to a good theory, only most of it must be. There are no epistemologically privileged protocol statements, but the element of correspondence which implies an empiricist check on the theory is still present in the whole set of observation statements. Thus the first requirement of the network model of science regarding the possibility of confirmation can be met by providing (*a*) the empirical check or correspondence element present in the whole of C.I., and (*b*) some principles of probability or simplicity of theories which are used as the coherence element to choose the best theory and modify and perhaps discard some small part of C.I.

Does the Q-thesis hold for such a machine? No C.I. statement (say C_1) is logically immune from correction by the best theory or theories, and therefore if some given descriptive statement S is contradicted by C_1, S can in principle always be regarded as unfalsified by taking C_1 to be itself false. But what does 'false' mean here? It cannot mean that C_1 is false as a direct representation of the input, because all that can be known about this is that a certain small proportion of such C.I. statements are false, not which ones. It must mean false relative to a 'best' theory constructed in the light of the whole C.I. and the internal coherence criteria for construction of theories. If these criteria are sufficiently modified no doubt C_1 could be made consistent with some theory which satisfies them, but it does not follow that this could be done according to any criteria which would be accepted as reasonable for a good theory. However, this limitation on the applicability of Q only highlights the importance for judging 'truth' and 'falsity' of what are taken to be reasonable criteria, and indicates that these are not immediately determined by the input, but are in a sense *a priori* relative to that input. They may, of course, possibly be regarded as modifiable in a second order sense in the light of the type of theories which seem to be successful for large amounts of input, but then the principles of modification would presuppose yet higher-level criteria, and so on. I shall not pursue here the problem of specifying and justifying criteria for 'best' theories, for in the light of current discussion of various kinds of confirmation theory the only thing that is clear is that the problem is turning out to be unexpectedly deep and difficult, and as yet hardly rewarding. But it does seem important to emphasise that some statement of confirmation criteria for theories seems to be a necessary condition of rebutting the charge that the Q-thesis effectively abandons empiricism.

It may seem that this requirement contradicts the claim that is also integral to the Quinean approach, namely that there is no ultimate distinction between the *a priori* and the *a posteriori*, the analytic and the synthetic. Quine himself (1968) has recently willingly accepted that the possession of some 'innate ideas' is a corollary of his network model of language. This is in reply to objections by Chomsky (1968), who curiously reads Quine, not as abandoning empiricism, but as sticking too closely to it in his analysis of sensory conditioning as the foundation of language learning. There is no empirical evidence, Chomsky claims, for the kind of language learning Quine seems to require, rather all the evidence we have (which incidentally is from syntax rather than semantics, and therefore not clearly relevant to the conditions of applicability of descriptive predicates – but let us take Chomsky for the moment at his own valuation) points to the presence of innate, interlingual dispositions to certain standard linguistic principles. Quine's acceptance of this point seems motivated rather by desire to conform to the present state of empirical linguistics and psychology of perception than by general arguments such as have been put forward here. Innate principles which are understood merely as conditions causally operating on sensory data perhaps need not count for Quine as *a priori* principles which refute his conflation of the prior and the posterior. However, we can hardly be content with this understanding of the principles. To remain so would be like accepting a physico-physiological account of the processes which go on when we do sums, and regarding this as excluding rational discussion of the logically systematic principles involved in doing sums correctly. To adapt the favourite metaphor which Quine takes from Neurath, modifying parts of the network while relying on other parts may be like rebuilding a boat plank by plank while it is afloat, but there are right and wrong ways of doing the rebuilding. To provide a normative inductive logic in which the innate principles are systematically explicated does not *preclude* empirical investigations of the scientific and social facts about inductive reasoning, but it tells us more about them, by showing why and under what conditions they can be regarded as rational. There is a close parallel here with the programme of rational decision theory, which may be assisted, but is not determined, by empirical investigations of practical decision making. In the sense of a rational inductive logic, then, the innate principles would be *a priori* relative to the data which they process, but this sense need not be objectionable to Quine, since no claim is made about the eternal immutability of the principles – different external conditions may cause adaptive organisms to modify these principles too.

3. MEANING

The alternative possibility of saving S from falsification, which has been dismissed by Grunbaum as trivial, is to so 'change the meaning of S' that it no longer contradicts the evidence. How can we understand in terms of the machine model the demand that meanings shall be stable in order to exclude trivial satisfaction of Q? We cannot directly and immediately apply the usual empiricist interpretation of 'the meaning of S' as the empirical conditions necessary and sufficient for S to have the truth-value true, because the only criteria of truth we have are relative to the coherence of the system as well as to its empirical constraints. Indeed, the truth- or probability-value of S *relative to the current best theory* may change as additional evidence replaces best theory by another, and that without direct observation of the empirical conditions of satisfaction of S. So in this sense the meaning of S, like its truth-value, is not invariant to accumulating evidence. Is such instability of meaning an objection to the network model?

It can certainly be interpreted in such a way as to constitute a *reductio ad absurdum* of any model of science which attempts to retain an element of empiricism, including the network model. It has been so interpreted by several recent writers in the guise of what has come to be called the 'meaning variance thesis' (Hanson, 1958; Feyerabend, 1962; Kuhn, 1962), and since I want to distinguish the network model from this thesis in important respects, I shall start by stating and examining the thesis itself.

The original context of the meaning variance thesis was an attack upon the deductive model of theories with its accompanying assumption that there is a comparatively stable and transparent observation language, upon which theoretical language is parasitic. It is pointed out, first, that reliance on deducibility in the deductive account of explanation of observation by theory, and reduction of one theory to another, is vain, because there is always a measure of approximation in such inferences, and hence it is always possible for the same data to be 'explained' in mutually contradictory forms by mutually contradictory theories. For example, Galileo's law is not a logical consequence of Newton's theory; in fact it is contradicted by that theory, because the law asserts that the acceleration of bodies falling along the earth's radii is constant. It was possible to hold Galileo's law to be true only because this discrepancy was concealed by experimental error. And yet Newton's theory is held to *explain* the facts about falling bodies in spite of contradicting the experimental law which had been accepted up to then as a description of those facts. Again, Newtonian mechanics cannot simply be reduced by deduction to the more comprehensive relativity mechanics, because relativity mechanics entails, among other things, that space and time are mutually dependent and inseparable dimensions, and that the mass of a body is not an invariant property, but a function of the body's speed relative to whatever happens to be taken as the rest frame. Such consequences of relativity are strictly *inconsistent* with Newtonian mechanics. Similar objections may be made to the alleged deductive reduction of phenomenological thermodynamics to statistical mechanics, and of quantum to classical electrodynamics. Many of these examples involve something even more radical than mere numerical approximations. It is meaningless, for example, to speak of Newtonian mechanics 'approximating' to relativistic mechanics 'when the constant velocity of light c is taken as infinite', or of quantum theory 'approximating' to classical physics 'when the quantum of action h is taken as zero', because it is of the essence of relativity and quantum theory that the respective constants c and h are *finite constants*, having experimentally specifiable values. Moreover, in passing from one theory to another there are *conceptual* as well as numerical changes in the predicates involved: mass as invariant property becomes variable relation, temperature as property becomes a relational function of velocity, atom as indestructible homogeneous stuff becomes divisible and internally structured.

Such examples as these lead to the second, and more radical, part of the meaning variance thesis, namely that deducibility is impossible not only because numerical fit between theory and observation is at best approximate, but also because the concepts of different theories are governed by rules of syntax and use implicit in the respective theories, and since different theories in a given experimental domain in general conflict, these rules of usage are in general inconsistent. Hence explanation of observation by theory, or reduction of one theory to another, cannot take place by identification of the concepts of one theory with those of observation or of another theory, nor by empirically established relations between them. We cannot even know that different theories are 'about' the same observational subject matter, for if the meaning of the predicates of observation statements are determined by the theoretical beliefs held by their reporters, and if these meanings differ in different theories, then we seem to have an incommensurability between theories which allows no logical comparison between them, and in particular allows no relations of consistency, incompatibility or relative confirmation.

The thrust of the meaning variance thesis is therefore primarily against the notion of a neutral observation language which has meaning invariant to changes of theory. But the thesis becomes impaled on a dilemma. Either there is such an independent observation language, in which case according to the thesis its predicates cannot be related deductively or in any other logical fashion with any theoretical language, or there is no such observation language, in which case every theory provides its own 'theory-laden' observation predicates, and no theory can be logically compared with any other. The consequences of meaning variance can be put in paradoxical form as follows:

(1) The meaning of a term in one theory is not the same as its meaning in another prima facie conflicting theory.

(2) Therefore no statement, and in particular no observation statement, containing the predicate in one theory can contradict a statement containing the predicate in the other.

(3) Therefore no observation statement which belongs to one theory can be used as a test for another theory. There are no crucial experiments between theories.

A similar paradox can be derived from (1) with regard to both explanation and confirmation.

(1a) The meaning of a predicate in the pre-theoretical observation language is different from its meaning in a theory which is said to explain that domain of observation and to be confirmed by it.

(2a) Therefore if the theory entails some observation statement, that statement cannot be the same as any pre-theoretical observation statement, even if it is typographically similar to it.

(3a) Therefore no theory can explain or be confirmed by the statements of the pre-theoretical observation language.

That such paradoxes seem to follow from the meaning variance thesis has been taken to be a strong objection to the thesis, and hence strong support for the view, presupposed in the deductive account, that observation statements have meaning independent of theories. On the other hand there is certainly a prima facie case for item (1) of the meaning variance thesis, and the network model itself is committed to a similar abandonment of the theory-neutral observation language. Must the notion of a theory-laden observation language lead to paradox?

First, it may be wondered whether so radical a departure from deductivism as indicated by (2) is really warranted by the argument for (1). Suppose we grant for the moment (1) in some sense of 'the meaning of a predicate' which could be incorporated into deductivism, for example that the predicates of a theory are 'implicitly defined' by the postulates of that theory, which entails (1). Even so, for the paradoxes to go through, a further step is required. It must be shown either (i) that the sense of 'meaning' required to make (2) true is the same as that required for the truth of (1), or (ii) that another concept of 'meaning' is implicit in (2), that for this concept meaning is also theory-variant, hence that (2) is still true, and the paradoxes follow. (i) can be disposed of very quickly. In order to establish (i) it would be necessary to show that the difference of meaning of 'P' in different theories which is asserted in (1) is such as to preclude substitutivity of 'P' in one theory T for 'P' in the other theory T', so that no relations of consistency, entailment or contradiction could be set up between statements of T and T'. If this were true, however, it would also be impossible to speak of the difference of meaning *of* 'P' in T and T', for this formulation already presupposes some meaning-identity of 'P' which is not theory-variant. Hence (1) would be not just false, but inexpressible. What, then, is the relevant identity of 'P' presupposed by the possibility of asserting (1) which will also make (2) false and hence dissolve the paradoxes? Here typographic similarity will clearly not do. We must appeal somehow to the external empirical reference of T and T' to give the meaning-identity of 'P' that will allow substitutivity of 'P' between the theories.

The suggestion that naturally springs to mind within the deductive framework is to take the class of objects that satisfy P, that is, the extension of 'P', and identify the relevant meaning of 'P' with this extension. In pursuit of this suggestion Israel Scheffler (1967, ch. 3) proposes to construe 'meaning' in the classic Fregean manner as having two separable components: 'sense' and 'reference'. (1) may be regarded as the assertion that the sense, or definition, or synonymy relations of predicates differ in different theories, but in considering the logical relations of deducibility, consistency, contradiction, and so on, it is sameness of reference or extension that is solely involved. Difference of sense does not imply difference of reference, hence (2) and (3) do not follow from (1). Thus Scheffler claims to reconcile variance of meaning between theories, and between theory and observation, with invariance of reference and hence of logical relations.

Unfortunately this reconciliation does not work even within the deductive framework. Waiving difficulties about construing sense in terms of definitional synonymy relations, the most serious objection is that 'same reference' is neither necessary nor sufficient for the logical comparability that is required of different theories. It is not *sufficient* because the properties ascribed to objects in science are not extensional properties. Suppose two theories T_1 and T_2 are 'about' two quite distinct aspects of a domain of objects: say their colour relations, and their shapes. It may happen that T_1 and T_2 are such that there is an exact one-to-one correspondence between the sets of predicates of T_1 and T_2 respectively, and that as far as is known T_1 is true of any set of objects if and only if T_2 is also true of it. Then the corresponding predicates of the two theories have the same referential meaning. But this does not imply that the theories are the same. So long as no predicates are added to their respective predicate-sets, no development of T_1 can be either consistent with or contradictory to any development of T_2. In other words, because science is about *intensional* properties, sameness of extension does not suffice for logical comparability. Furthermore, sameness of reference is not *necessary* for logical comparability. Two different theories may make use of different categorisations or classifications of objects: thus Dalton's atoms have different extensions from Cannizzaro's atoms, yet we want to be able to say of some of Cannizzaro's statements that they entail or contradict some of Dalton's.

The network model gives promise of resolving the paradoxes by, first, giving a more subtle analysis of the observation language than that presupposed by deductivism, in terms of which what I have called 'intension' of predicates as well as their extension has a place, and second by allowing a distinction to be made between meanings which are internal to a theory, and meanings which are empirically related. Return for a moment to the observing machine described

earlier. We have already noticed that the meaning of descriptive
statements is internally related to the best theory and its criteria in
something like the way the meaning variance theorists describe. It is
also the case that no simple account of the meaning of descriptive
predicates in terms of their extension is possible in this model, because all we can know about extension is also relative to the state of
the evidence. It may be true or highly probable that P applies to a
given object according to one best theory, but false or highly
improbable according to another theory adopted on different
evidence. There is, however, a relation between machine hardware
and input that does remain constant during the process of data
collection and theory building that has been described. This is the
set of physical conditions under which input becomes coded input.
These conditions do not demand infinite exactness nor complete
freedom from error, but in what has been said so far they have been
assumed sufficiently stable to permit the assertion that a high
proportion of statements in the C.I. are true, though we don't know
which. This stability is sufficient to ensure that trivial changes of
meaning are not resorted to to save theories come what may. Trans-
lated into terms of human language-users, this stability does not
require that they be aware of some transparent empirical relation
between observed properties and linguistic predicates, nor even that
they always entertain the same theories; it requires only that by
learning to apply predicates in an intersubjectively acceptable
manner, they have acquired physical dispositions which are invariant to change of evidence.

To express the matter thus is to invite the comment: does not this
kind of stability entail undue inflexibility in the use of descriptive
predicates? Do not the meanings of our predicates sometimes change
even in this respect under pressure of evidence? In other words, does
not evidence also educate our dispositions? It seems fairly clear from
the history of science that it does. Consider the predicates 'heavy'
and 'light' after Newton's theory had been accepted. It then became
incorrect to use the word 'light' of air, and correct to use the word
'heavy', because in Newton's theory all material substances are
heavy by definition, even if they can be made to cause a balloon to
rise. In such cases there is indeed no substitutibility with retention of
truth-value of 'heavy' before and after the change, and so the
meaning paradoxes seem to arise. But consider the reason why such
a change might occur. In machine terms, we might find that certain
applications in observational situations of a given predicate to
objects of a certain kind were always contradicted by the best theory
for a wide variety of evidence. This would not of course *force* on us a

change of disposition to apply that predicate to those objects under the appropriate input, because we expect a small proportion of such applications to be in error relative to the best theory. But if these errors seemed to be concentrated in an unexpected way around certain predicates, we might well decide to change the use of these predicates to fit better the best theories as determined by the large proportion of other observation statements which are assumed true. It might even be possible to state explicit rules for such changes of use and disposition, depending for example on the small probability values of the observation statements involved relative to the rest of the evidence. But all this of course depends on any particular occasion on the presence of many predicates which are not so subject to change of use. The solution of the meaning variance paradoxes requires that there are always many stable predicates when one theory gives way to another.

The possibility of some change of use according to empirically controlled rules shows, however, that Grunbaum's requirement of 'stability of meaning' to save the Q-thesis from triviality is too stringent. Allowing the sort of flexibility of meaning which has obviously often occurred in the development of science need not open the floodgates to apriorism.

4. SUMMARY

In summary let me try to state explicitly the main principles of the new Duhem–Quine empiricism in distinction from the old.

(i) There is no need to make a fundamental epistemological distinction between the theoretical and observational aspects of science, either in regard to decidability of truth-value, or transparency of empirical meaning. The network of relatively observational statements can be imagined to be continuous with a network of theoretical relationships. Indeed much of the recent argument in the literature which has been designed to show that there is no sharp line between theory and observation has depended upon examples of quasi-direct recognition in some circumstances of the empirical applicability of what are normally called *theoretical* predicates (such as 'particle-pair annihilation', 'glaciation'). The corresponding theoretical properties cannot, of course, be directly observed independently of the surrounding network of theory and empirical laws, but neither can the so-called observable properties. The difference between them is pragmatic and dependent on causal conditions of sense-perception rather than epistemological.

(ii) The corollary is that empirical applications of observation predicates are not incorrigible, and the empirical laws accepted as holding between them are not infallible. A whole theoretical network may force corrections upon empirical laws in any part of it, but not all, or even most, of it can be corrected at once. Moreover, there is no way of telling *a priori* by separating the theoretical from the observational, *which* part may need correction in the light of subsequent evidence and theory.

(iii) Corrections may strongly suggest changes in the conditions of correct intersubjective application of some of the descriptive predicates, and these changes may be made explicitly according to rules which presuppose that other predicates are not subject to change on the same occasion. To save the notion of 'same theory' which is required to avoid the meaning variance paradoxes, there must be some such stability, indeed the majority of descriptive predicates must be stable in this sense, but just as we do not know *a priori* which observation statements will be retained as true in the next theory, neither do we know which observation predicates will retain stability of meaning. Had Aristotle been a Carnapian, 'heavy' would undoubtedly have appeared in his list of primary observation predicates, and he would have held it to be observable that air is not heavy.

(iv) To avoid total arbitrariness in adoption of the 'best' theory on given sensory input, some prior principles of selection of well-confirmed theories, and criteria for shifts of applicability of some observation predicates, must be assumed. This does not seem, however, to be an objectionable apriorism in the context of the new empiricism, since it is always possible that these principles themselves might change under pressure of the evidence in second or higher order network adjustments.

(v) Lurking within many of these elements of the new empiricism is a systematic conflation of certain aspects of the epistemological problem with causal mechanisms. This occurs at the point of what has been called 'coding' of the input into the coded input, and the identification of this process in human observers with the causal process by means of which descriptive language has been learned. Doubtless to the old empiricism this is a fatal circularity in the network model, because the question will immediately be asked: How do we know anything about the causal coding and the input it processes except in terms of the usual scientific method of observation and theorising? And if this in turn is subject to the conditions of the network model is not the regress irreducibly vicious? Similar objection, it will be recalled, was made to Russell's causal account of the reception of sense data. But there is a crucial difference between the aims of the new empiricism and those of Russell. Russell, in common with most old empiricists, was looking for 'hard data'; new empiricists accept that these are not to be had. This, incidentally, suggests that the approach suggested here to the relatively prior principles of data processing, via a search for a rational inductive logic, is a better reflection of new empiricism than is the purely scientific search for invariants of language which Chomsky favours, or for psychological and machine models of human learning with which some investigators replace the study of inductive logic. Such empirical approaches are always open to the regressive argument, and leave unanswered the question of what prior principles they themselves depend on. The approach via a rational inductive theory, on the other hand, has the merit of exploring possible rational strategies in possible worlds, independently at least of the details of actual learning processes. But it provides no assurance like that sought by old empiricists, that our knowledge of *this* world is firmly based, only that *if* we we were given certain interconnected prior conditions, of whose actuality we can never in practice be certain (for example, that the world is not infinitely various), then we could give reasons for our conscious methods of developing science in a world where these conditions obtain. Duhem might hasten to applaud this conclusion as confirming his view that after all scientific knowledge is superficial and transient compared to the revealed truths of a theological metaphysics. We, who do not have this assurance either, must make do with what we have, a poor thing perhaps, but enough.

REFERENCES

N. Chomsky, 'Quine's empirical assumptions', in *Synthese* (1968) 19, 53.

P. Duhem, *The Aim and Structure of Physical Theory* (Princeton, N.J., 1906; trans. Wiener, Oxford, 1954).

P. K. Feyerabend, 'Explanation, reduction and empiricism', in *Minnesota Studies*, III, ed. H. Feigl and G. Maxwell (Minneapolis, 1962) p. 28.

A. Grunbaum, *Philosophical Problem of Space and Time* (New York, 1963).

—— 'The falsifiability of a component of a theoretical system', in *Mind, Matter, and Method*, ed. P. K. Feyerabend and G. Maxwell (Minneapolis, 1966) p. 273.

N. R. Hanson, *Patterns of Discovery* (Cambridge, 1958).

T. S. Kuhn, *The Structure of Scientific Revolutions* (Chicago, 1962).

K. R. Popper, *The Logic of Scientific Discovery* (London, 1959).

—— *Conjectures and Refutations* (London, 1963).

W. v. O. Quine, *From a Logical Point of View* (Cambridge, Mass., 1953).

—— *Word and Object* (New York, 1960).

—— 'Replies', in *Synthese* (1968) 19, 264.

I. Scheffler, *Science and Subjectivity* (Indianapolis, 1967).

12

MEMORY, MEMORIES AND ME

Don Locke

IN this paper I want to discuss two separate problems about memory, connected in that they both have to do with memory as a source or ground of knowledge.

I

The classic theory of memory, one that seems to have been adopted by almost all philosophers from Aristotle to Russell, goes something like this:

> To remember is to undergo a certain sort of mental experience. In particular it is to experience an image, a memory-image, which reproduces some past sense-experience. It might even be said that this image is literally a re-production of the original sense impression which has, meanwhile, been stored away in the mind. This image provides us with the information that we are then said to remember; it is because we have and experience the image that we have the particular piece of memory-knowledge.

This theory, which for obvious reasons has been called the representative theory of memory, has three main features. First, memory is tied to the individual's own personal experience: I remember what happened because I once experienced it in some way, and I remember it by recalling that original experience. Second, memory is tied to imagery: to remember something is to have a memory-image of it. Third, memory is a source of knowledge of the past: I may know what has happened because I now read it in a book, but that is not remembering. If it is a case of memory then I

210

know it because I have the memory-experience; it is my image – or perhaps my having the image – which tells me what has happened and thus provides me with the knowledge.

This representative theory held the field for a long time, but now it seems it has been vanquished at last. Certainly all three of its crucial features have been challenged. First, it has been argued that memory is not restricted to an individual's own personal experience. I can remember that the Battle of Hastings was fought in 1066 without having had any experience, however distant, of that battle. I can remember that $E = MC^2$, but I have no idea of what it would be like to experience that fact. Second, memory does not necessarily involve imagery. I can remember my mother's maiden name, without having an image either of her or of her name. I can remember that $E = MC^2$, but I have no idea of what it would be like to have an image of it. Third, memory is not a source of knowledge, it is itself a type of knowledge. To remember that kumaras are sweet potatoes is precisely to know that kumaras are sweet potatoes, so my remembering that they are sweet potatoes cannot be what gives me this knowledge, cannot be the source of my knowledge. What gives me the knowledge is not the fact that I now remember it, but rather the fact that I once tasted kumaras.

So the representative theory of memory has been replaced by what I will call the contemporary theory, which is that to remember something is to know it, where this is knowledge one has obtained in the past. It need not even be knowledge of the past, so long as it is knowledge acquired in the past. If an astronomer tells me there will be an eclipse in four days' time, then three days later I may suddenly remember that there will be an eclipse tomorrow.

The problem now is to explain why the traditional theory should ever have seemed plausible. The obvious answer is that there are many different types of memory, and that the representative theorists fastened on to just one, neglecting the other possibilities. We can, for example, distinguish between factual memory (remembering that something is the case), practical memory (remembering how to do something), and acquaintance memory (remembering some particular thing). There is a world of difference between remembering how to bake a Pavlova cake, remembering that you baked a Pavlova cake, and remembering the Pavlova cake you baked. You might do any of these without doing either of the other two – you might remember how to bake it by remembering how mother used to do it, without remembering that you once baked one for yourself; you might remember the cake that you baked, without remembering that you baked it; and so on.

The suggestion is that the representative theorists made the mistake of restricting memory to acquaintance memory, for this does seem to presuppose personal experience. I can remember that Los Angeles is in California even though I have never been there, but I cannot remember Los Angeles unless I have been there. Indeed it is part of the definition of acquaintance memory that you can remember some item – a person, a place, an incident – in this way only if you have experienced it for yourself, which is why I am calling it, clumsily, 'acquaintance' memory. In reciting a list of the kings of England I may remember George III but forget George IV, but remembering George III, in this example, is not acquaintance memory, precisely because I never saw George III. To remember something, in the sense of acquaintance memory, you must have experienced that thing, you must remember it because you have experienced it, and also, perhaps, you must remember it as something you have experienced.

Notice that when we say we can remember something, in this way, only if we have ourselves experienced it, this need not necessarily refer to sense-experience, perception. 'Experience' here must have a very wide and rather loose sense, for we can remember things which we have not actually perceived. I remember World War II, even though I was on the other side of the world at the time, inasmuch as I remember news bulletins, rationing, war maps in shop windows, and so on. Indeed it is doubtful whether anyone, even the soldiers in the front line of battle, perceived World War II, as opposed to perceiving various things that happened during and as part of World War II. What is true is that I, or the soldier in the front line, can remember World War II only in so far as we did perceive various things that happened during and as part of that war, and it is in this sense that World War II is something we experienced.

However the main point is that acquaintance memory does involve personal experience of the thing remembered, and it is fairly easy to see why empiricists, in particular, should have ignored other types of memory. For they hold that all knowledge comes, and can only come, from experience, so memory-knowledge must, for them, be knowledge which comes from previous experiences. It is a short, though disastrous, step to holding that memory-knowledge must be knowledge which comes from recalling those previous experiences. The mistake is to think that if all knowledge comes from 'acquaintance', i.e. sense-experience, all memory-knowledge will come from acquaintance memory. The parallel mistake about knowledge in general would be to think that since all knowledge comes from experience, we can have knowledge only of what we experience for ourselves – which would mean that I cannot know anything about California.

But now, if the mistake was to think that all memory is acquaintance memory, the representative theory might at least be accurate as a theory of acquaintance memory, even if inaccurate as a theory of memory in general. Is this so? Do the three central features of the representative theory in fact hold good of acquaintance memory? We have already seen that the first one does, that acquaintance memory, as opposed to memory in general, is restricted to what the individual has personally experienced. So the next question is whether acquaintance memory necessarily involves imagery.

The first thing to notice is that even if I do have an image it may very well not be a reproduction of what I originally perceived. When I remember a certain room and form an image of it, I may 'see' in the image myself sitting there in the room – which is not something I could ever have actually seen, since I cannot get outside my own body. What does seem to be true is that if I remember something by forming an image of it, the image must be dependent on my having perceived that thing. If I form an image of some place I have never seen then no matter how accurate the image, this does not count as remembering that place. On the other hand, forming an image of the room where I base the image on what I saw does count as remembering the room, even if the image is not an accurate reproduction of that room. This brings out how remembering the thing does not consist solely in having an image. If it is to count as remembering it, the image must be based on what I experienced. And, similarly, in so far as a verbal description is based on what I experienced, it too can constitute remembering. Thus forming an image of it is one way of remembering a thing, but it is not the only way.

Suppose, for example, that someone names all the shops in the High Street of his home town, and gives us all sorts of information about them, but says he cannot remember how they looked. Is this not a case of remembering the shops without being able to form an image of them, and so a case of acquaintance memory that does not involve imagery? It might be said that this would be factual memory rather than acquaintance memory, but the point is rather that detailed factual memory of things we have experienced, where the memory depends on the fact that we have experienced them, itself counts as acquaintance memory. If Evans can remember that Jones the Draper's was a musty old Victorian shop, between Thomas the Butcher and Morgan the Baker, remarkable mainly for Jones's beautiful daughter, and so on, then we can and do say that he well remembers Jones the Draper's, whether he has images of it or not. It seems, then, that although having an image of it is one way of remembering an item, it is not the only way. Acquaintance memory does not necessarily involve imagery.

Finally, is acquaintance memory a source of knowledge? For a start, acquaintance memory is not itself a type of knowledge, in the way that factual and practical memory are. For although we speak of knowing a person or a place just as we speak of remembering a person or a place, acquaintance memory cannot be explained in terms of this 'acquaintance knowledge', as we might similarly call it, in the way that factual memory can be explained in terms of factual knowledge, and practical memory in terms of practical knowledge. That is, to remember some fact is to know that fact where you have acquired that information in the past; and to remember how to do something is to know how to do it where you have acquired that skill in the past; but to remember some place is not, as we might at first think, to know that place where you have 'made that acquaintance' in the past. There is a difference between remembering a place and knowing it; I have, for example, spent two days in New York and I remember New York well, but I do not claim to know New York, let alone to know it well. It is also relevant that we do not speak of knowing an incident, scene or situation in the way that we do speak of remembering some incident, scene or situation; and it might well be argued that we remember people or places only in so far as we remember incidents, scenes or situations involving those people or places.

However, if acquaintance memory is not itself a type of knowledge, at any rate it seems that it involves knowledge. I remember Vienna, but I do not think I could be said to remember Vienna unless I also remembered certain facts about Vienna. The question is, then, whether my remembering Vienna could be said to be the source of that knowledge. I do not think it can. A source of knowledge is, presumably, something that provides us with the information we are said to know; the sources of our knowledge are the means by which we come to know the various facts we do know. But my remembering Vienna is not what provides me with my knowledge of Vienna. Rather it is only because I remember, and so know, these facts about Vienna that I can be said to remember it in the first place. The source of my knowledge of Vienna is not my present remembering, but my former visit, and what I then saw.

Thus the representative theory remains unsatisfactory, even when taken to be a theory about acquaintance memory in particular, rather than about remembering in general. I want now to suggest that the representative theory springs not from concentrating on acquaintance memory to the exclusion of other types of memory – although this may be part of the explanation – but rather from a failure to notice a different distinction: that between memory and a memory, or in the plural memories. This is a distinction worth noticing, because it seems to me that those who attack the representative theory and replace it with what I called the contemporary theory, have also failed to make it. My suggestion is that although the representative theory is inaccurate as a theory of memory, it is at least fairly accurate as a theory of memories.

By 'memory' we refer to our ability to do certain things, our ability to remember. By 'a memory' we refer not to what we do in remembering, but to what we remember of something that has happened to us. More precisely, a memory is some item or incident as recalled from your past experience. Thus the first feature of the representative theory is in fact true of memories: they are restricted to personal experience. I may remember the date of the Battle of Hastings, but this is hardly a memory of mine.

What of the second feature: do memories necessarily involve mental images? It is easy to see why it should be thought that they do. The main feature of our memories is that they involve recalling what we have experienced, and this can easily be rephrased as: memories involve recalling our experiences. And this in turn can easily be taken to mean: memories involve reproducing our experiences, in the form of mental images. But is it not possible that we recall some item not visually by forming an image of it, but verbally by going over a description of it? Consider, for example, the case of the two old soldiers who spend hours swapping wartime stories. Surely we can say they are swapping their war memories, regardless of whether they are having mental images? They are going over things again, bringing various incidents back to mind, in short, recalling them. And that is precisely what I said a memory was: some item or incident as recalled from your past experience.

I am not sure about this. There is an important difference between recalling an incident and recalling some fact about that incident. I may remember that I saw Jim break his leg, and in that sense remember his breaking his leg, without recalling Jim breaking his leg. To do that I have actually to bring the incident itself back to mind. Now I am inclined to say that in order to have a memory of some item I must do more than merely remember, or for that matter recall, facts about it; I must recall the item itself. If our two old soldiers are merely repeating well-remembered stories about their war days, without thinking of those days as such, then their stories do not relate memories, however accurate they might be. We are sure they are memories, that the soldiers are recalling their wartime experiences and not merely rehearsing their knowledge of what then happened to them, because they constantly alter and modify and correct and add to their stories, as they remember new details. If the stories come out precisely the same time and time again, and particularly if they cannot add to the details except in such a way as to suggest they are inventing them, then we will probably conclude that they can no longer recall the actual incidents, but are relying solely on their memory that such things occurred. That is, if these stories relate genuine memories, they must be based on the recollection of incidents, and not merely on the recollection of facts.

Now what counts as recalling an item, as opposed to recalling various facts about it? The answer must be, I think, that to recall the item is to remember how it was, not just in the sense of remembering that it was such-and-such, but in the sense of remembering the such-and-suchness of it. The man who remembers that the shop was dark and dirty and musty may be said to remember the shop, but this is not to recall it, to have a memory of it, unless he remembers the dark, the dirt, the musty smell. And, I would say, to remember the dark, the dirt, the musty smell, is precisely to have images of it. If this is so, then memories do necessarily involve mental imagery, inasmuch as to recall some item is to remember how it was, in the sense in which to remember how it was is to have a memory-image of it. This need not mean that memories consist in reproducing our experiences, in the sense of re-creating the original sense-experience. To remember how it looked is not to see a reproduction now, but to think again of what was seen then. However I dare not go further into this difficult topic of mental imagery, so let us turn to the third feature of the representative theory: the claim that memory is a source of knowledge.

The contemporary objection is that memory is not a source but a type of knowledge: to remember that $E = MC^2$ is, in part, to know that $E = MC^2$. But this account clearly cannot apply to our memories, for a memory is not a piece of knowledge. Rather it is – there seems no other word for it – an experience which we have, or sometimes passively undergo – which, of course, is how the representative theory thinks of memory in general. Moreover our memories can be inaccurate, incorrect, perhaps even completely delusive. But can they, on the other hand, also provide us with knowledge? It has been argued that we cannot remember how things were, not even in the sense of having a memory-image of it, unless we already know how they were, so that we know how to form the appropriate image. Thus

One must evidently relinquish any idea that our images in recollecting can be transmitters of information or independent vehicles of knowledge. . . . Any image that may come before the mind will owe its existence to some knowledge which is possessed by the knower independently of the image; and it will be this knowledge which makes it possible for the image to be created at all.[1]

But I think this exaggerates the extent to which we actively and deliberately construct our images in order to illustrate what we already know to be the case. I might, for example, have completely forgotten that Jones was at the meeting and then, going over the meeting in my mind, suddenly recall that he was there. My knowledge that he was there cannot be responsible for the image I have, for until I had the image I had forgotten that he was there.

Moreover this seems to be a case where my memory, in particular my memory-image, provides me with knowledge, i.e. a case where memory is, after all, a source of knowledge. I would not now know that Jones was at the meeting had I not recalled him sitting there; it is only because I now have this clear memory of him sitting there that I know that he was there. Now it might be said that the source of this knowledge is not so much my present memory as my previous experience, the fact that I saw him there at the time. Certainly I would agree that I knew at the time that he was there because I saw him there, and in that case my experience at the time was the source of my knowledge. I would also agree that I now remember him sitting there only because I did, at the time, see him sitting there. But this does not mean that my seeing him there is the source of my present knowledge that he was there, because, as I said, I had completely forgotten it. Suppose, to make the example clearer, someone had asked me whether Jones was present and I had replied, 'No, he wasn't.' It is only now that I suddenly realise, with a shock, that he was there. And how do I know that he was, when an hour ago I had thought that he was not? Because I now remember, have a memory of, him sitting there. It is my present memory, not my past experience, which provides me with this information, for I had forgotten the information provided by my senses at the time.

Indeed, to take a more extreme example, it even seems possible for my memories to provide me with knowledge I did not previously have at all. While going over the meeting I may suddenly realise *for the first time* that Jones was there after all, sitting alongside Smith, though I had not consciously noticed it at the time. Once again my

[1] R. F. Holland, 'The Empiricist Theory of Memory', in *Mind* (1954) 485.

imagery here cannot be dependent on previous knowledge, because I did not know he was there until I had the imagery. Once again my knowledge must be based on or derived from the memory, in that it is only because I have this memory that I know that Jones was there. Once again a memory is the source of my knowledge. No doubt it is only because, in some sense, I saw Jones sitting there that I now have this memory, but that does not make my seeing him the source of my present knowledge. What enables me to know now, when a moment ago I did not, that Jones was present is not the fact that I originally saw him, but the fact that I now remember it. Incidentally this sort of case seems also to conflict with the contemporary theory that to remember something is to know it where this knowledge has been acquired in the past; or to know it because you knew it; or some such. For here is a case where I remember that Jones was at the meeting, without having known it before.

However the main point is that our memories can provide us with knowledge. I am not suggesting that all memory-knowledge comes from memories in this way; that is patently false. I remember that Brutus killed Julius Caesar, that $E = MC^2$, but I have no memories which inform me of these facts. Nevertheless some philosophers seem to have thought that memories are the source of all our memory-knowledge, and we can now see how they might have come to this grossly implausible conclusion. The contemporary theory is that to remember some fact is to know it, where this is knowledge which has been obtained in the past; to remember that fact is to retain your knowledge of it. But when I say I now remember that Jones was at the meeting, I am not asserting merely that I have retained the knowledge that he was there, for in the one example I had forgotten it, and in the other I had not, until this moment, realised or known that he was there. What has to be explained is how I know it *now*, when a moment ago I did not know it, and this is what is explained by the memory I have; my having the memory explains how I now know that Jones was at the meeting.

We now seem to have two questions where before we had but one. There is the question of how someone knows a certain fact to begin with; and then there is the question of how he knows it at some particular moment of time. This distinction need not involve the error of regarding knowing as a datable occurrence; it stems rather from the fact that we can know something at one time and not know it at another – perhaps because we have forgotten it, perhaps because we have not yet learnt it. Now, if we do distinguish these two questions we can see clearly the line of thought that leads to the theory that all memory-knowledge comes from our memories: if our knowledge comes from experience, then if I know some fact it must be because I have experienced something which informs me of that fact; and similarly if I know some fact now there must be something which now informs me of that fact. How do I know, at this present moment in time, that Napoleon died on St Helena? Because I remember it. And so we get the theory that when a person knows something now his knowledge comes from a present experience, namely, a memory-experience.

But fairly clearly one of these two questions is bogus, or at best not a philosophical one. To explain how someone knows a certain fact at all is also to explain how he knows it at some particular point in time. If someone asks how I know that Napoleon died on St Helena, it is a sufficient explanation that I read it in the official biography; we don't need any further explanation of how I know it now, and it is no such explanation to say 'I remember it'. I know it now because I have retained my previous knowledge of this fact, and to say I remember it is, in this case, merely to say that I have retained that knowledge. Of course, there is the question how we manage to retain information, and equally the question how we come to forget things we have learnt, but the answers to these questions lie in psychology or neurology, not in the philosophy of mind or the theory of knowledge. So it seems that the idea that memories are the source of all our memory-knowledge arises as an answer to a non-existent problem: the problem of what informs me of some fact when I remember it. The truth is that, where remembering amounts only to not having forgotten there is nothing, nor any need of anything, which informs me of the fact in question.

But although the representative theorist would be mistaken in thinking there must always be some experience which explains how we know a fact at some particular point in time, as opposed to knowing it at some other point in time, we should not go to the opposite extreme and think that such a question never arises. For sometimes it does, as in those cases where a person has forgotten what he once knew, or where he now realises for the first time something he had not previously known. In these cases we do want to know what gives him this knowledge now, since he did not know it before. And in these cases, as in our earlier examples, a person's memory-experiences, his memories, can provide an answer. Thus the representative theorist thinks, wrongly, that there must always be some experience which explains how a person knows certain facts now, as opposed to knowing them at some earlier time; he sees, correctly, that a person's memories can explain why he now knows certain facts, when before he did not know them; and so he concludes that memories always provide such an explanation, that memories are the source of all memory-knowledge.

This is a mistake, as I have insisted, but it is equally a mistake to think that memories cannot be a source of knowledge. In our examples the person's memories are what provide the person with the information that he is then said to know; his memories are what enable him to know something which he would not otherwise have known. Certainly I would not know that Jones was at the meeting unless I had been there and, at least in some sense, seen him there, but this is what explains my memory of him sitting there, not my knowledge. I know what I now do not because I saw him then, but because I remember him now. Memories *can* be a source of knowledge – which is not to say that they always are, much less that they are the sole source of our knowledge of the past.

So far I have interpreted the claim that memory is a source of knowledge in a relatively strong sense. I have taken it to be the claim that memory can provide us with knowledge which, but for the memory, we would otherwise not have had; that memories can provide us with information we would not otherwise have known. This is what happens in our examples: were it not for my present memories I would not now know that Jones was at the meeting. But the claim might also, and more favourably, be interpreted in a weaker sense. One of the things that interests us in the theory of knowledge is the question of grounds or evidence. It is sometimes said that if what we believe is to rank as knowledge at all, it must be based on such grounds or evidence that knowledge is justified true belief and that grounds or evidence are what provide the necessary justification. But even if this is not so – and personally I doubt whether it is – the question of grounds or evidence remains an important one. For when we assert that someone knows something we are, among other things, asserting that that something is true, is the case. So when the assertion of knowledge is challenged, one of the things we have to do is provide evidence that what is said to be known is indeed the case. This, in philosophical discussion and in ordinary conversation, is often the point of the question: 'How do you know?', and we can define 'evidence' in the sense I am using the term as anything which provides an answer to this question asked in this way, i.e. anything that shows or helps show that what is said to be known is in fact true. Evidence in this sense also constitutes grounds, in that anything that indicates that something is true is also at the same time a reason for believing that it is true.

Now the claim that memory is a source of knowledge might be taken to mean not so much that our memories provide us with knowledge, but that they provide or constitute evidence that what we claim to know is the case, and thus provide or constitute grounds for believing that it is the case. Certainly one major reason for insisting that memory is a source of knowledge is the fact that it is often an entirely sensible and adequate answer to the question of how I know something to say that I remember it: 'How do you know that John broke his leg?' 'Because I remember him breaking it.' If memory were but a type of knowledge this should be no more informative than 'I know it because I know it', but there is no such oddity here. However, this need not mean that my memory is the source of my knowledge, in the strong sense that it is what provides me with the information that John broke his leg. I know it because I was there at the time and saw it happen, and it was this rather than my present remembering that explains how I came to know it. I might, for example, know that he broke his leg, and know it because I was there at the time, without being able to remember him breaking it. In very much this way I know that, as a young child, I travelled on an aeroplane, though I cannot now remember the journey. So when I say I know John broke his leg because I remember him breaking it, I need not be saying that it is my present memory which informs me of this fact in the way that, in our earlier example, it was my present memory which informed me that Jones was at the meeting after all. I may simply be saying that my present memory provides evidence that what I claim to remember is in fact so, and thus provides grounds for believing that John did indeed break his leg.

Notice, however, that the evidence is not that I remember *that* it happened, but that I remember it happening. It would be no explanation of how I know that Napoleon died on St Helena to say that I remember that he did. This is merely to repeat that I know it, not to explain how I know it. Factual memory does not provide evidence or grounds for believing because, as we have seen, factual memory is already a type of knowledge; in this case to remember it *is* to know it. But it would be very different if I were to remember Napoleon dying on St Helena; that would indeed be evidence that he did die there. Our memories can serve as evidence or grounds because, as we have also seen, memories are not pieces of knowledge. Rather they are experiences, in some sense of that vague term, which can provide us with evidence or grounds. To remember something happening is not to know it any more than to see it happen is to know it, but both seeing and remembering can provide grounds for believing that it did happen, for accepting some fact as a fact, and therefore for accepting it as knowledge.

Another point to notice is that although my memories can provide us with evidence that what I claim to know is true, it need not be that my own belief is grounded on that evidence. I might believe it already, quite independently of the evidence of the memories I have. Or, on the other hand, I might be unsure about what has happened, and in that case my memories could provide grounds for my own belief. Thus, for example, it might be only because I dimly remember, through an alcoholic haze, throwing a bottle and the sound of tinkling glass, that I believe that I broke the window.

However the main point is, in short, that our memories can provide evidence for what has happened in the past. This is hardly a surprising conclusion. Ordinarily, remembering something happen is perfectly good evidence that it did happen. It is just the sort of evidence that the law courts like to rely on, for if someone remembers something happen he was there when it happened, and eye-witnesses make the best witnesses. Moreover the evidence seems to be evidence of the familiar inductive sort. People do not normally have memories of things which did not happen, and it is because they do not that remembering something happen is evidence that it did happen. The strength of the evidence depends on the reliability of the particular person's memory, and the more inclined he is to inaccurate or delusive memories, the less good the evidence is. If mistaken memories turned out to be very common, if people were continually having memories of things which did not happen, then memories would cease to provide evidence for what has happened.

However, there is a possible source of confusion here. Normally we are not said to remember something unless it is so. I cannot remember that the Battle of Hastings was fought in 1173 any more than I can know it; I might think or believe it, but I cannot be said to remember or to know it unless it is a fact. Similarly, though I think this is more arguable, we cannot be said to remember something happening unless it did happen. If this is so – and I assume for the sake of argument that it is – then it can easily seem that memory provides us with very special evidence, or perhaps something more than evidence. For if I cannot remember it happening unless it did happen then, it seems, the fact that I remember it happening provides absolutely conclusive evidence that it did happen.

But this is a mistake. The point is rather that if remembering it happen entails that it did happen, then we have to agree that it did happen before we can agree that it is remembered; 'I remember x' will depend on x, rather than the other way around, just as 'I remember that p' depends on p, rather than the other way around. The best way of avoiding this difficulty would be to speak not of what the person remembers, but more neutrally of what he seems to remember or ostensibly remembers. Thus the evidence is not that he actually does remember it but that he seems to remember it, and when he tells us what he remembers he is telling us what he ostensibly remembers. My remembering John breaking his leg is evidence that John did break his leg, not because we would reject my claim to remember it if it were shown that it did not happen, but because people do not normally seem to remember, have memories of, things which did not happen.

In fact our memories characteristically provide evidence or grounds in this way. It is quite common for us to appeal to our memories, the various items and incidents we remember, in order to establish that something happened and to explain how we know it happened. Thus on the weaker interpretation the claim that memories are a source of knowledge is even more obviously and generally true than it is on the stronger interpretation.

So, to sum up: although the representative theory is inadequate as a theory of remembering in general, it does seem fairly accurate as a theory of memories in particular. Our memories are restricted to what we have experienced for ourselves; they seem, in some way, to involve imagery; and they can and do provide us with knowledge of the past, both in the strong sense of sometimes providing us with information which we would not otherwise have known, and also and more frequently in the weak sense of providing grounds or evidence in support of our claims to knowledge. In the past philosophers have almost universally accepted the representative theory because they failed to make the crucial distinction between memory and a memory. It seems to me that much the same mistake is made by those contemporary philosophers who suggest that memory is nothing but a form of knowledge, that memory cannot in any way provide us with knowledge of the past.

II

This discussion of memories providing evidence of what has happened leads me now to another problem which arises in the classic discussions of memory. It is held that as well as providing us with knowledge of the past, memory also, and more particularly, provides us with knowledge of our own pasts, and thus of our own selves. Other people know from the colour of my hair or the sound of my voice, or by assiduously tracking me down from place to place and time to time, that I am the one who broke the window. But this is not how I know it. I know it from memory; I know that I am the one who broke the window because I remember breaking it. Thus memory provides us with knowledge of self-identity in a way that it does not provide us with knowledge of the identity of others. Memory provides each of us with a special privileged insight into his own identity. My question now is whether this is so, and if so, how so.

Certainly I would not agree with those, such as John Locke, who have suggested that memory determines personal identity, in the sense that for X and Y to be the same person is for X to remember doing what Y did, and vice versa. This clearly will not do. The fact that I have forgotten doing something does not mean that I am not the person who did it, nor does the fact that I ostensibly remember doing something mean that I am the person who did it. What is true is that memories provide evidence of personal identity, just as they provide evidence of other things. If I now remember a window being broken then that is evidence that a window has been broken; and similarly, if I now remember breaking a window, that is evidence not just that a window has been broken, but also that I am the one who broke it.

Nevertheless this does not indicate that memory provides us with a special insight into our own identities. For first of all, our memories can provide evidence of the identity of other people in exactly the same way. If I remember breaking the window then that is evidence that I am the one who did it, but equally if I remember Jones breaking the window then that is evidence that he is the one who did it. And secondly, there is nothing privileged about the evidence of my memories; it is certainly not private evidence in any sense of being evidence which I alone can have or can use. Anyone who knows that I remember breaking the window has just the evidence I do that I am the one who broke the window. There is, however, more to be said about this, but I am going to keep the cat in the bag for a moment or two longer, so that I can let it out at the appropriate time.

The point so far is that a person's memories provide evidence, evidence for everyone and anyone, of personal identity, his own and other people's, in just the way that they provide evidence of other things. But notice now that a person's memories can provide evidence in two rather different ways. First of all, if a person ostensibly remembers something happening then that is evidence, though not conclusive evidence, that it did happen. And secondly, if a person ostensibly remembers something happening then that is evidence, though not conclusive evidence, that he was there when it happened, that he witnessed or experienced it happening. For as we

have seen, acquaintance memory – and our memories are a particular form of acquaintance memory – is restricted to what a person
has experienced for himself. Therefore in so far as a person claims or
seems to remember something happening, so far he claims or seems
to have experienced it happening, and to have been one of those who
were there when it happened. Thus the fact that I ostensibly remember the house burning down is not only evidence that it did
burn down, but also, and in much the same way, evidence that I was
one of those present at the time. That is, it is evidence to the extent
that people do not normally remember things happening which did
not happen, or at which they were not present. The extreme case of
this is where I remember not so much something happening, as
actually doing something: if I remember breaking the window this is
evidence not merely that I was there when the window got broken,
but that I am the one who broke that window.

This brings out how our memories can and do provide evidence of
our own identity in a way in which they cannot provide evidence for
the identity of others, and other people's memories cannot provide
evidence for our own identity. This evidence of self-identity is not so
much the fact that I remember *it*, as the fact that *I* remember it. If it
is my memory, then it is evidence that I was there. Other people's
memories can, in the same way, provide evidence for their identity,
but although what I remember may provide evidence for the identity
of others, the fact that it is my memory cannot.

This shows, then, that memories provide evidence of a sort that is
restricted to self-identity. But we have still to discover how each of us
might have a special insight into his own identity, for, as we have
seen, anyone who knows I have these memories has precisely the
evidence I do that I am the person who has witnessed various
incidents and done various things. We can now go back to the cat I
left in the bag. The evidence of my memories, if it is evidence at all,
is evidence for anyone and everyone, but although the evidence is not
private in that sense, I am nevertheless in a privileged position with
regard to that evidence. For I can, and usually do, know that I
remember something happening, just in virtue of the fact that I
remember it; I do not have to find out that I remember it in the way
that others do have to find it out. If I remember breaking the
window then that is evidence that I am the one who broke the
window, and, moreover, I am in a privileged position to know of this
evidence. For since the memory is mine I do not have to find out that
I remember breaking it, as others do have to find out that I remember it. They may have to ask me; I do not have to ask me. To take a
parallel example: the fact that someone has a blocked nose and a sore

throat is evidence that he has a cold. It is, moreover, evidence available to all, in the sense that anyone who knows that I have a blocked nose and a sore throat has just the evidence I do that I have a cold. But I am in a privileged position with regard to that evidence, a privileged position to know that I do have a blocked nose and a sore throat. For I do not have to find these things out in the way that others do.

Thus my conclusion is that each of us knows his own identity in a way that he could not know the identity of anyone else, and in which no one else could know his identity. This is a consequence of two facts. Our memories provide evidence of what has happened, and in so doing also provide evidence of personal identity, our own and other people's. But they also provide evidence of the past history of the person whose memories they are, and so provide evidence of the identity of this person with some person in the past. The only person whose identity can be established in this way is the person whose memory it is. So this is the first fact: memory provides evidence of self-identity in a way that it does not provide evidence for the identity of others. Perhaps I should remind you at this point that to say that memory provides 'evidence' of self-identity is only to say that the fact that someone remembers something happening provides support for the claim that he was there when it happened, and so provides grounds for believing that he was there when it happened, and also provides support for his claim to know that he was there when it happened.

The second fact is that each individual knows of his own memories in a way that he does not know the memories of others. This means not that he has evidence of his own identity which no one else can have, but rather that he knows of that evidence in a way that others do not. So, it is in this way that our memories provide each of us with a special insight into his own identity: our memories provide evidence of our own identity in a way they cannot provide evidence of the identity of others; and we know of this evidence in a way we cannot know of the equivalent evidence for the identity of others.

I want now to defend this position against certain criticisms, implicit and explicit, in chapter 4 of Sydney Shoemaker's *Self-Knowledge and Self-Identity* (Ithaca, N.Y., 1963; all references to this book). For although Shoemaker seems to reach very much the same conclusion, namely that each of us knows his own identity in a way he could not know of the identity of anyone else, his explanation of this is very different. According to Shoemaker our knowledge of self-identity differs from our knowledge of the identity of others, not because of any special feature of the evidence it is based on, but because it is not based on evidence at all. He does not deny that memory, or at any rate sincere memory claims, can provide evidence of personal identity. On the contrary, he explicitly argues (ch. 6, sections 5, 8) that it does, and that this evidence constitutes what he calls a criterion, i.e. *non-inductive* evidence, of personal identity. Thus, according to Shoemaker, the fact that someone remembers doing something is, and logically cannot fail to be, evidence that he is the one who did it – which is not to say that memory provides logically conclusive evidence of personal identity. But Shoemaker's point is that if memory does provide a criterion, it is one which applies generally to all cases of personal identity. There are no special criteria of self-identity, distinct from the criteria we have for the identity of others.

As against this I want to say that although memory can provide evidence of the identity of others, there is also a way in which it can provide evidence of self-identity and only self-identity, i.e. evidence for the identity of the person whose memory it is. I am not entirely happy with Shoemaker's argument that the evidence of our memories is non-inductive evidence, and I am even less happy about his use of the term 'criterion'. Certainly criteria have come to be all things to all philosophers, but it seems to me an odd use of the term to suggest that the fact that I remember the house burning down is a criterion of its having burnt down. However I am, for the sake of argument, going to waive these objections and adopt Shoemaker's terminology. So putting my point in those terms, I want to say that memory does provide a criterion of self-identity distinct from the criteria we have for the identity of others. Which is precisely what Shoemaker wants to deny.

In the chapter we are considering Shoemaker hopes to show how it is that philosophers have come to make the mistake of thinking there are special psychological or first-person criteria of self-identity. The source of this error is that when I assert, on the basis of memory, that I have performed a certain action in the past, I do not base this judgement on the usual bodily criteria of personal identity. That is, when I assert, on the basis of memory, that Jones broke the window, I establish that it was Jones by reference to such things as that it looked like Jones, acted like Jones, spoke like Jones. But when I assert, on the basis of memory, that I broke the window, I do not establish that it was me by reference to such things as that it looked like me, acted like me, spoke like me. This suggests that the judgement must be based on some special non-bodily psychological criterion, in particular a memory criterion. But, Shoemaker argues, the explanation is not that it is based on non-bodily criteria, but that it is not based on criteria at all. Let us look at his arguments.

There are, I think, two. The first is simple enough, indeed rather too simple. It is that when I assert, on the basis of memory, that I have performed a certain action in the past, this judgement does not rest on identity criteria, nor does it need any identity criteria to rest on, because it is not an identity judgement in the first place. That is, when I say 'I broke a window yesterday' this is not an identity judgement at all, and so does not stand in need of identity criteria, either bodily or psychological. Now this is correct as far as it goes, but it does not go very far. Perhaps 'I broke the window yesterday' is not an identity judgement and so does not require identity criteria, but it certainly seems to entail and be entailed by, an identity judgement, viz. 'I am the person who broke the window yesterday.' The important question must be whether this judgement is based on identity criteria, and if so what those criteria are. The puzzling thing is that Shoemaker has virtually nothing to say about such judgements of self-identity, but contents himself with his relatively minor point that first-person past-tense memory statements are not identity judgements. Yet for that very reason this point can hardly throw any light on the question of whether there are special psychological criteria of self-identity.

Of course it may be that Shoemaker wants to deny that a judgement like 'I broke the window yesterday' does entail an identity judgement, a judgement of self-identity. At one point he does say that 'first-person past-tense statements seem to contain identity judgements' (p. 129), but he is there setting up a view he wants to attack, the view that such statements assert the identity of a 'present self' with a 'past self'. And he later says 'it is a mistake, or at any rate very misleading, to say that they always express identity judgements' (p. 135). He brings this out by comparing 'I broke the window yesterday' with 'That novel is lewd': neither of these statements express identity judgements. For 'we cannot say in general that judging that a novel is lewd is judging that it is identical with something, and neither can we say in general that judging that one did a certain thing in the past is judging that one is identical with a "past self" ' (p. 136). But this is a misleading comparison since, as Shoemaker allows, 'I broke the window yesterday' does assert, among other things, the persistence of an individual through time. It would, therefore, have been more accurate to compare it to 'That novel was banned in 1905', and it seems to me that we can say in general that judging that a novel was banned in 1905 is judging that it is identical with something that existed in 1905, and similarly that judging that one did a thing yesterday is judging that one is identical with something that existed yesterday. I am not sure what Shoemaker wishes to deny when he says that 'I broke the window yesterday' does not 'express' an identity judgement, but if he means it does not entail one, I think he must be mistaken. And, to repeat, the question is whether this identity judgement is based on criteria, and if so, what those criteria are.

So let us turn to the second argument. Shoemaker wants to say that although a statement like 'I broke the window yesterday' – and presumably this includes statements like 'I am the one who broke the window' – may be based on memory in the sense that I remember breaking it, such statements are nevertheless not based on memory in the sense that memory provides evidence or a criterion for their truth. There are thus two different senses in which statements can be based on memory, and Shoemaker seeks to distinguish these two senses by distinguishing two different sorts of memory statement, which I will refer to as 'memory-reports' and 'memory-conclusions'. A memory-report is based on memory in the sense of being a description, report or expression of what is remembered, as when I say 'A tall blond man robbed the store yesterday' because I remember a tall blond man robbing the store. A memory-conclusion, on the other hand, is based on memory in the sense of being a conclusion from what is remembered, as when I say 'This is the man who robbed the store yesterday' because this man is tall and blond, and I remember just such a man robbing the store. Shoemaker maintains that it is only if a statement is based on memory in this second sense, i.e. is a memory-conclusion, that it can be based on memory in the sense that memory provides evidence for that statement.

The point of this distinction for Shoemaker is that if a memory statement were an identity judgement based on evidence or criteria of personal identity then, he says, it could not be a memory-report. It would have to be a memory-conclusion in the way that, in our example, 'This is the man who robbed the store yesterday' is a memory-conclusion based on criteria of personal identity. But, as Shoemaker goes on to argue, 'I broke the window yesterday' may very well be a memory-report, and therefore not a conclusion based on identity criteria. Rather it is an assertion that I did something in the past which is not based on the usual bodily criteria of personal identity, not because it is based on unusual non-bodily criteria, but because it is not based on identity criteria at all. There are thus two parts to the argument. The first is that memory cannot provide evidence for a memory-report, so that if a statement is based on memory-evidence it must be a memory-conclusion. The second is that statements of what I have done, where I remember doing those things, are memory-reports, because they are not based on memory-evidence in the way that memory-conclusions are.

So, to begin with the first stage of the argument, Shoemaker is allowing that memory can provide evidence for something else which is thus a conclusion from what is remembered: if I remember a tall blond man robbing the store, then that can be evidence that this man, who is tall and blond, robbed the store. But, Shoemaker argues, memory cannot provide evidence for what is itself remembered: if I remember a tall blond man robbing the store, then that cannot be evidence that a tall blond man robbed the store. Remembering something cannot provide evidence for that something, though it may provide evidence for something else. Of course this runs completely counter to my argument in the first section of this paper, that our remembering does provide evidence that the things we remember did happen, but then Shoemaker's position is prima facie implausible. We have seen that this is just the sort of evidence that law courts like to rely on.

Shoemaker's argument is that since 'I remember that p' entails p in virtue of the word 'remember', 'I remember that p' cannot be evidence or grounds for p. This is a puzzling argument, and I am not sure that I have understood it correctly, since for a start it is perfectly clear that the fact that A entails B, even if only in virtue of the meaning of 'A', does not prevent A being evidence or grounds for B. On the contrary, the fact that someone is my uncle is extremely good evidence that he was not an only child. But whatever the argument may be, it is clear enough that Shoemaker has failed to make two important distinctions. First, there is the distinction between remembering that something is the case and remembering something happening. We saw that remembering that something is the case is not evidence that it is the case: remembering that Napoleon died on St Helena is not evidence that he did die there. But remembering something happen is evidence that it did happen: remembering John breaking his leg is evidence that he broke his leg. Second, there is the distinction between genuinely remembering, in the sense that we cannot be said to remember something unless it is so, and ostensibly remembering. It is only in the former case that 'I remember p' entails p, but where we are talking about the evidence of our memories, it is ostensible remembering we are talking about. So I do not see that Shoemaker's argument affects my claim that remembering can provide evidence for what is remembered.

The second stage of the argument is that first-person past-tense statements about what I have done in the past, where I remember doing it, are memory-reports rather than memory-conclusions, and therefore not based on evidence or criteria of identity at all. Now we can, to begin with, agree with Shoemaker that a statement like 'I broke the window yesterday' is not based on identity criteria because, as we have agreed, it is not an identity judgement at all. But what about 'I am the one who broke the window', which is an identity judgement, a judgement of self-identity? It seems at first sight that this will be a memory-conclusion of the same sort as 'This is the man who robbed the store'. Certainly I remember breaking the window, but can I be said to remember being that person, the person who broke it? Surely that I am that person is something which follows from what I remember, rather than something I remember as such? For how can the claim that I, here and now, am a certain person be a report merely of what I *remember*? It seems it must be a memory-conclusion.

Shoemaker would have to deny this. His test of whether a statement is a memory-report is that if a memory-report 'turns out to be false it follows that the person who made the statement mis-remembered, or had a mistaken memory (assuming that he made the statement honestly), whereas if a statement that expresses a conclusion from memory turns out to be false it does not follow that the speaker had a mistaken memory, since he might have remembered correctly but drawn a false conclusion from what he remembered' (p. 133). On this test both 'I broke the window yesterday' and 'I am the person who broke the window' turn out to be memory-reports rather than memory-conclusions. For if either statement is false it follows that I have misremembered or had a mistaken memory; it cannot be that I correctly remember breaking the window but draw the false conclusion that I broke it or that I am the one who broke it. So Shoemaker would have to say that 'I am the one who broke the window' is a memory-report like 'I broke the window yesterday', and not a memory-conclusion like 'This is the man who robbed the store'.

Nevertheless this argument turns on Shoemaker's account of his distinction between a memory-report and a memory-conclusion, and I think we can see that this distinction is not what he thinks it is. Suppose, for example, that I claim to remember Jones breaking the window, as opposed to remembering someone breaking the window and then concluding from various things that it was Jones. In such a case 'Jones broke the window' looks like a memory-report – a description, report or expression of what I remember – rather than a conclusion from what I remember. Yet it fails Shoemaker's test of a memory-report: if this statement is false it does not follow that I have misremembered or suffered a mistaken memory; if it turns out that the window was broken by someone else who looked very like Jones, and whom I mistook for Jones, we would not then say that I had misremembered. But if 'Jones broke the window' is not, on Shoe-maker's test, a memory-report, it is not a memory-conclusion either. We would hardly say that I had drawn a false conclusion from what I remembered; my mistake was rather one of misidentifying the man at the time the window was broken.

What this shows is that it is not the case, as Shoemaker thinks, that if a memory-report – a description, report or expression of what you remember – is false, it must be that you misremembered. Rather, what Shoemaker takes to be a test of memory-reports is in fact a special feature of remembering your own actions. That is, where I remember someone else doing something it is possible that I am mistaken about who that someone is, without it following that my memory is at fault. But where I remember actually doing something, then if I am wrong about who did it my memory must be at fault. It turns out, then, that the distinction with which Shoemaker is actually operating is not, as he says it is, the distinction between 'statements that are based on memory, in the sense of being . . . descriptions, reports or expressions of what the speaker remembers, and statements that are based on memory in the sense of being conclusions from what is remembered' (pp. 132–3). Rather it is the distinction between remembering other things happening, and remembering you yourself doing things. So Shoemaker does not need his long argument that statements of what a person remembers doing can be memory-reports. They are precisely the sort of statement his test of a memory-report is devised for. I think Shoemaker would have noticed this if only he had stopped to consider whether a claim to remember someone else doing something could, like a claim to remember doing it yourself, be a memory-report and not a memory-conclusion. For clearly it can.

Even so we can now see clearly what Shoemaker's point is. When I claim to remember Jones breaking the window, the question may arise of how I know it was Jones. It may be that someone did indeed break the window as I remember it happening, but that it was some-one else whom I mistook for Jones. But when I claim to remember breaking the window, there can be only one person who did it as I remember it happening, and that person is myself. If it was not me who did it, but someone else, then my memory is entirely mistaken. To put it another way, when I remember someone else doing something, two questions can arise: did it happen as I remember it happening? and was it who I think it was? But where I remember doing something myself, the two questions become one; it cannot be that it happened as I remember it, but that I wasn't the one who did it. We can put the point quite simply by saying that when what I remember is actually doing something then I do not need to identify the person I remember doing it. Thus Shoemaker says, 'It will not be the case that the speaker first knows that someone broke the front window yesterday and then discovers that that person was himself. If what he remembers is that *he* broke the window, then for him the question "Am I the person who broke the front window?" cannot arise.' (p. 135).

The point that emerges from all this argument, then, is this: where I remember doing something in the past there is no question of my identifying or misidentifying the agent in question, whereas where I remember someone else doing something, questions of identification and misidentification do arise. This is why Shoemaker insists that 'I am the person who broke the window', where I remember breaking it, cannot be a memory-conclusion based on identity criteria in the way that 'This is the man who robbed the store' is. On the contrary, 'I am the person who broke the window', where I remember breaking it, is, according to Shoemaker, a judgement that does not rest on identity criteria at all, either bodily or psychological.

But now let us ask why, when I remember breaking a window, the question of identification or misidentification does not arise. Notice first of all that the assumption is that my memory is correct, that I do not suffer from a mistaken memory. If we were dealing with ostensible remembering, then the question 'Am I the person who broke the window?' certainly can arise, even for the person who is remembering. The question then is, in effect, did it happen as I remember it happening, are my memories of it correct? But given that my memory is correct, then the question of who it was does not arise for me. And the reason why it does not arise is that it is already settled. Given that I remember doing something, and given – as Shoemaker is implicitly assuming here – that I do not suffer from a mistaken memory, then the only person it could have been is myself. Just as I cannot perform your actions and you cannot perform mine – though I might do things instead of you and you might do things on my behalf – so I cannot remember performing your actions and you cannot remember performing mine – though I might seem to remember doing something which in actual fact you did. This is of course an analytic truth, and one that follows not so much from what it is to remember as from what it is to be a particular person.

However, none of this shows that my memories cannot provide evidence, and non-inductive evidence if you like, of my own identity. It shows only that where you already have all the evidence that is necessary to establish a person's identity, you don't need any more. The interesting question in this situation is not what further evidence I need, for I need none, but rather what evidence I already have. So how do I know that I am the person who broke the window, where I remember breaking it? The answer is obvious: because I remember breaking it. This is the evidence I have to back up my claim to be the window-breaker. So I can see nothing in Shoemaker's argument to show that memory cannot provide evidence of self-identity, evidence which we can use in establishing our judgements of self-identity.

Nevertheless I do not necessarily want to be committed to the conclusion that judgements of self-identity, based on memory, will be memory-conclusions rather than memory-reports. Earlier I suggested that perhaps they are, since it seems that any judgement that some person, here and now, is the person who did something in the past must be a conclusion from what is remembered rather than something that can be remembered as such. But I can see that it might well be argued that when I remember doing something what I remember is, precisely, being that person, the person who did it, and that this sort of identity judgement is, therefore, a memory-report rather than a memory-conclusion. I am not sure about this and I would need a clearer account of the difference between the two before I made up my mind. But I would feel no qualms if the conclusion were that such identity judgements were memory-reports, for I have already rejected Shoemaker's argument that memory cannot provide evidence for the truth of a memory-report.

My own conclusion remains the same as it was, that memory provides each of us with a special insight into his own identity, inasmuch as our memories provide evidence of our own identity in a way that they cannot provide evidence of the identity of others; and we know of this evidence in a way that we cannot know of the equivalent evidence for the identity of others. I now add to this the further point that *if* Shoemaker is right – and, as I have said, I have my doubts about it – in arguing that memory provides non-inductive evidence or a criterion of personal identity, then he is wrong in arguing that memory does not provide a criterion of self-identity distinct from the criteria we have for the identity of others, and also wrong in claiming that judgements of self-identity cannot be based on just such a criterion.

In the discussion following this paper several people urged on various grounds – the possibility of memories being inherited, the possibility of clairvoyance or E.S.P., the possibility of people splitting like amoebae so that one remembers the history of someone he is not now identical with – that it is only a contingent fact that if I remember doing something, then the person I remember doing it must be myself. If I were to accept this, as I feel inclined to, then many of the points I offer as conceptual truths will have to be interpreted as contingent truths, most notably of course my conclusion that memory provides evidence of the rememberer's identity in a way that it cannot provide evidence for anyone else's identity. Personally I do not mind allowing that this evidence is dependent on the contingent fact that only I can remember my past, just as I feel inclined to say that the status of memory as evidence generally depends on the contingent fact that people do not normally remember things happening which did not happen. Nor do I think that this particular contingency need affect Shoemaker's argument that it is a conceptual truth that sincere memory claims provide evidence for the truth of what is claimed. It does, however, have the effect of making 'I am the person who broke the window yesterday' a memory-conclusion rather than a memory-report.

13

DREAMING

Martha Kneale

IF my argument here is successful, it will follow that this paper should have been included in the first volume of this series, *The Human Agent* (Royal Institute of Philosophy Lectures, 1966–7); for I want to contend that the topic of dreams belongs to philosophy of mind rather than to theory of knowledge.

It has been supposed that the study of dreams belongs to the theory of knowledge because there is an ancient argument for radical scepticism which begins with the premiss that dreams occur. I shall first outline this argument and try to show that it is not so powerful as has sometimes been supposed. I shall then consider what I believe to be an extreme reaction to the sceptical argument, the view of dreaming put forward by Professor Norman Malcolm[1] under the influence of Wittgenstein. I shall try to show that this view is mistaken; and finally I shall consider what seem to me to be the philosophically interesting questions raised by the occurrence of dreams.

The first occurrence of the sceptical argument, as far as I know, is in Plato's *Theaetetus*, where Socrates examines the view that knowledge is perception, a view identified by him with Protagoras' theory that everything is for man as he thinks it is. He finds it an obvious objection to this theory that people in dreams and madness have false perceptions.[2] Theaetetus admits this and continues:

I cannot deny that people in madness or in dreams have false opinions, as when some think they are gods and others that they are winged and in sleep imagine themselves flying.

[1] *Dreaming* (1958).   [2] *Theaetetus*, 158A.

236

Socrates then reminds Theaetetus of a puzzle about dreaming and waking of which, he says, he must often have heard before:

> What proof could we give if anyone were to ask us now whether we are asleep and dreaming everything we think or awake and really talking to each other?

Theaetetus replies:

> I don't see what proof we could give. For they correspond to each other in all respects like strophe and antistrophe. There is nothing to prevent it seeming to us in sleep that we say to each other what we actually are saying to each other now. And when we seem in a dream to relate a dream the correspondence is extraordinary.

It is a curious fact that philosophers, as soon as they begin to talk about dreams, or at any rate as soon as they begin to talk about them for the sake of constructing sceptical arguments, are given to making statements of great extravagance, if not of downright falsity. Theaetetus asserts here that dreaming and waking correspond *exactly*. If this means that every incident in a man's waking life is reproduced in his dreams and vice versa, it is downright false. But perhaps all that it means is that any incident in waking life *may* be reproduced in a dream, and this is in fact the premiss needed for the sceptical argument.

Socrates proceeds to add another extravagance:

> Since the time in which we are asleep is equal to the time in which we are awake and in each state the soul maintains that the opinions then present to it are entirely true, we are saying this to be the case and that to be the case each for an equal time and each with entire confidence.

I find it difficult to believe that the ancient Greeks spent twelve hours out of each twenty-four in sleep (in fact we have good evidence to the contrary in Plato's *Symposium*), and even if they did, it is very unlikely that they dreamt all the time they were asleep, so that Socrates is considerably overstating his case.

Philosophers are conservative creatures, and we find Descartes several centuries later repeating essentially the same argument. In *Meditations* I he notes, like Plato, that there are no certain marks (*indices certains*) by which one can tell whether one is awake or asleep, and in a brief recapitulation of the argument in the *Discourse on Method*, Part IV, he endorses Theaetetus' opinion that everything that can occur in waking life can also occur in sleep:

> Considering that all the same thoughts that we have when awake can also come to us when asleep without a single one of them being

true, I resolved to feign that everything which had ever entered into my mind was no more than the illusions of my dreams.

He has here by implication added another extravagance. *Everything* that occurs to us in a dream is false. All is illusion. I shall have occasion to examine this proposition later on. Descartes himself does not stick to it, for he states at the end of Part IV of the *Discourse* that we may in dreams have some thoughts which are true:

For if it happened even in sleep that one had some very distinct idea, if, for example, a geometer found some new proof, his sleep would not prevent it from being true.

We can gather from the quotations so far given a rough idea of what may be called the traditional account of dreaming. According to this, when we dream we are in sleep accepting as true certain propositions which are, for the most part, false. These are expressed in, or accompanied by, imagery of various sorts and they may also occasion emotions. The contents of the beliefs, that Theaetetus is flying or that Descartes is sitting by the stove, are false but the believing or imagining are themselves real and so are the emotions which they arouse. It is the fact that most of the propositions accepted in dreams are false that gives rise to the sceptical argument. This may be set out as follows:

Premiss 1: Anything that occurs in waking life may occur in a dream.

Premiss 2: When I am dreaming, I think I am awake.

Conclusion 1: Therefore, although I am convinced that I am awake, I may in fact now be dreaming.

Premiss 3: At least most of the propositions accepted in dreams are false.

Conclusion 2: Most of the propositions I now accept may be false.

Many people, and I think not only philosophers, have found the sceptical argument disturbing. Do we really know that we are awake now and, if so, how? The classical answer, as given for example by Descartes and Leibniz, is that we apply the coherence test. Looking back on our lives, we find that our waking life forms one coherent whole, while our dreams are a number of disconnected fragments which rarely link up together. We notice that it is not at all true, as Socrates suggests, that we maintain one set of propositions while awake and another set while asleep. We maintain (with a number of obvious qualifications) one set while we are awake and a number of different sets while we are asleep. The *Peter Ibbetson* situation does not arise in real life. There is, therefore, no possibility that I am dreaming now while what I remember as a dream is part of one continuous life.

Professor Malcolm maintains that the coherence test is inadequate because we might, after all, dream that we apply it and find it satisfied.[1] In other words, we might, while dreaming, tell ourselves that we are awake. This is true. So we do, sometimes. Nevertheless, using the coherence test, supplemented by one other, I think we may be pretty sure that just now we are awake and not dreaming that we are deciding that we are awake. The other test is this. This stretch of experience of mine began with waking up this morning and, generally speaking, when I am awake I can remember the last time I woke up, but dreams do not as a rule begin with anything like waking. They just mysteriously begin. It is true that there is such a thing as false awakening, i.e. the waking from a dream into another dream. But if my waking this morning was a false awakening, then the dream I am having now is the comparatively rare type of dream which is contained within another dream. It is most implausible to suppose that this very solid and coherent stretch of experience is in fact a rare type of dream. My present experience has *all* the marks of waking experience as compared with the dreams that I remember.

At this point the sceptic may perhaps say that I may be dreaming and therefore in such a state of muddle that all my memories of what my previous dreams were like are unreliable. But here he overplays his hand. He can secure the premiss for his argument only by supposing that my memory is more or less reliable. Otherwise, what reason should I have for supposing that I dreamt at all? The sceptic, as sceptics often do, is trying to have it both ways. In order to secure the essential premiss for his argument, i.e. that dreams occur and that they are to some extent delusive, he has to assume that memory is on the whole reliable and that the distinctions that we draw are sound; but when it is pointed out that if this is so there can be no reasonable doubt that I am now awake, he tries to maintain his argument by casting doubt on the reliability of memory and saying that our original distinctions are confused. If the sceptic can maintain his case only by throwing doubt on his original premiss, need we pay so much attention to him?

I believe that philosophers have paid too much attention to sceptical arguments connected with dreams and too little to the nature of dreams themselves. This, I think, is the case with Malcolm; for he undoubtedly regards it as a merit of his view that it does not allow the sceptical argument to get under way, and although he

---

[1] *Dreaming*, ch. 17.

does not confess to it, I feel that a certain neurotic fear of scepticism makes him think that desperate measures are justified to deal with it. His desperate measures take the form of denying what has seemed obvious to all philosophers from Plato downwards, i.e. that we do some thinking, believing and feeling while we are asleep. All that we do, he says, is to dream that we do these things. Descartes's mathematician could not have discovered a new proof during sleep. He could only have dreamt that he discovered it. This can be summed up by saying that according to Malcolm no mental activities or passivities other than dreaming itself occur during sleep, and, if he is right, the sceptic cannot even begin his argument, for his premises are either false or nonsensical. His first premiss, that anything that can occur in waking life can occur in a dream, is false; for we neither do nor suffer during sleep any of the ordinary things we do in waking life and, especially, since we do not believe anything, we cannot be deceived. The second premiss, that when I am asleep I think I am awake, is also false; for I do not think at all while I am asleep. The third premiss, that most of the propositions accepted in dreams are false, is not even false; for since no propositions are accepted during sleep, the question of their truth or falsity does not arise.

Most people will find Malcolm's position paradoxical, and since much has already been written in criticism of it, all I will do by way of refutation is to consider the classic case which overthrows the theory. This is the case of Coleridge, who did not merely dream that he composed a poem beginning 'In Xanadu did Kubla Khan a stately pleasure-dome decree' but did in fact compose such a poem in a dream. We have the poem before us and we have Coleridge's own testimony as to how it was composed. This account is in the third person but it is obviously an adaptation of his own words:

> The author continued for about three hours in a profound sleep, at least of the external senses, during which time he had the most vivid confidence that he could not have composed less than from three to four hundred lines. On awaking, he appeared to himself to have a distinct recollection of the whole and, taking his pen, ink and paper, instantly and eagerly wrote down the lines that are here preserved.[1]

We all know what happened next. The gentleman from Porlock called on business, and when he had gone Coleridge could no longer remember the remaining lines. Now, according to Malcolm's argument, this famous story must be false, for he holds that no mental

---

[1] *Collected Works of S. T. Coleridge*, ed. Hartley Coleridge, I 296.

activities other than dreaming can occur during sleep, and composing
a poem is a mental activity. To my great surprise he does not, in fact,
consider the case, but if he did he would, I think, have to choose between two accounts, both of which are open to strong objections. He
might say (and this is in line with what he says about mathematical
proofs alleged to have been discovered in dreams)[1] that Coleridge
before he went to sleep was unable to compose the poem but after
waking up found that he could do so. In other words his sleep may
have had some causal connection with the composition of the poem,
but it was not simultaneous with it. This is in disagreement with
Coleridge's own testimony. It was his memory, not his inspiration,
which he felt was disturbed by the gentleman from Porlock.

Alternatively Malcolm could say that, in so far as Coleridge did
compose *Kubla Khan*, he was not completely asleep, but awake in a
certain way, like the people mentioned by Aristotle who see lamps
and hear cocks crowing while sleeping.[2] This suggestion has some
support from Coleridge himself. He was in a profound sleep, he says,
'at least of the external senses', which implies that in a certain other
way he was not asleep. But this way out, which is the more plausible,
has two disadvantages for Malcolm. First, it makes his main thesis
uninteresting, because true by arbitrary definition, i.e. he is just
ruling that if we have good evidence for mental activities occurring
during what we should normally call sleep, then we are not to call
it sleep. In the second place, scepticism may rear its ugly head again
not in the form 'Perhaps I am now asleep and dreaming' but in the
form 'Perhaps I am only half-awake and things are not what they
seem', for it is well known that people half-asleep misinterpret the
stimuli of which they are in some sense aware, e.g. they hear thunder
but it is woven into a dream as gunfire.

It seems then that neither of Malcolm's possible explanations of
the Coleridge case is satisfactory and that we might just as well
accept what Coleridge said at its face value. He did compose *Kubla
Khan* in sleep and he remembered so doing. We are bound in the face
of the evidence to admit that mental activities other than dreaming
may occur during sleep, and since, for all we have shown so far, one
of these mental activities may be believing, the sceptical case may
still be stated. Malcolm's exceedingly short way with the sceptic is a
failure, but since the sceptic is not all that formidable, this does not
very much matter.[3]

---

[1] *Dreaming*, p. 39.　　　　　　　　　　[2] Ibid., p. 30.

[3] The intervention of Mr Vesey produced a riposte to this argument from
Professor Malcolm, which consisted in fully admitting the facts but denying their
implications. The nub of his reply, as far as I understand it, is to allow that

I now want to turn to another line of investigation which is nearer to what I think philosophers should have been doing about dreams instead of inventing extravagant sceptical arguments and equally extravagant theses to confute them. I want to raise the question, 'Does dreaming in fact involve believing?' Plato and Descartes, as we have seen, obviously thought that it does, and many other philosophers have shared their opinion. I give an example from a very recent philosophical work, Professor Armstrong's *Materialist Theory of the Mind*:

> For most people the core of dreaming seems to be the having of perceptual experiences. These perceptual experiences involve belief. This belief is entirely unselfconscious. It is a taking for granted.[1]

Others, too, who have studied dreams, but not as philosophers, have shared this view. Freud says, 'Since a dream that shows a wish as fulfilled is *believed* during sleep, it does away with the wish and makes sleep possible.'[2] Nathaniel Kleitman, who has studied dreams as a physiological psychologist, says that the dream is 'a manifestation of low-grade thinking',[3] and if he is using 'thinking' as it often is used, to mean the formation of opinion, he too holds that dreams involve belief. This view, then, has been and is very widespread, but it has recently been questioned by some philosophers who maintain that dreaming is not so much like thinking, in the sense of the having or forming of opinions, as like free imagining. I can give no quotations, as I have met the view explicitly only in conversation, but perhaps Wittgenstein's cryptic remarks in *Zettel* 396 ff. are an expression of it.

Here then are two views of dreaming. Some say that it is a kind of believing; others that it is a kind of imagining, very much like daydreaming, as indeed our language suggests. Philosophers who think that dreaming is like imagining sometimes combine this with another view about dreaming which neither entails nor is entailed by it. This is the view that the thoughts we have during sleep have no truth-value, i.e. are neither true nor false. To maintain it would be another way of undercutting the sceptic's argument, for if the

---

Coleridge remembered composing *Kubla Khan* during sleep but to deny that 'remember' is here used with its usual grammar. My reply would be to ask Professor Malcolm when, according to him, *Kubla Khan* was composed. If he says that this occurred during Coleridge's sleep, then 'remember' is after all being used with its usual grammar; if he says that this occurred after Coleridge's waking, this amounts to what I have above called his first way out and is open to the same objections.

[1] P. 303.   [2] *Collected Psychological Works*, v, 678.
[3] 'Patterns of Dreaming', in *Scientific American* (Nov. 1960) 85.

thoughts we have in sleep are neither true nor false, then they cannot be false. But it would be a mistake to suppose that this would *follow* from the fact that dreaming is like imagining, for when we are imagining, it is very often the case that we have thoughts which are true or false and, moreover, we know which they are. For instance, I might have a day-dream that I am a millionaire living in York-shire. This involves two propositions, one false and one true and I know perfectly well which is which. What is true about imagining is that it cannot involve error, for to be in error is to believe a false proposition and in imagining I do not believe the propositions I entertain. If, then, there is a case for holding that our thoughts in dreams lack truth-value, it cannot rest on the premiss that dreaming is like imagining. Another argument, however, can be put forward for this view which may be put non-technically as follows: only thoughts which are about existent objects have truth-values. The thought, for example, that Mr Pickwick visited Eatanswill during an election has no truth-value, for there was no such person as Mr Pick-wick. Some philosophers have held that if a thought is to have a truth-value, it must be *entirely* about existent objects, while others have held the rather different view that if what would normally be called the subject of the thought exists, then the thought has a truth-value even if the other objects about which the thought is do not exist. Thus, according to the former view, the thought that Lord Melbourne visited Eatanswill will lack truth-value, as there is no such place as Eatanswill, while according to the latter it would be false, since Lord Melbourne undoubtedly existed. Let us apply this to dreams. According to the first and stricter view, many of our dream-thoughts will lack truth-value, for we may very well dream that we see Mr Pickwick, Apollo, or some other fictional or mythical character. On the less strict criterion, it would seem that nearly all our dream-thoughts have truth-value, for we generally dream in some sense about ourselves and we exist. We could deny this only by maintaining (as I have heard it maintained) that the 'I' of the dream is never identical with the dreamer, which seems very im-plausible and to conflict with a very common way of reporting dreams, e.g. 'I dreamt that I was dining in Christ Church Hall', where the speaker is not conscious that the two uses of the word 'I' refer to two different persons. The last example shows that even on the stricter criterion some dream-thoughts may have a truth-value. I conclude then that there is no reason for holding that no dream-thoughts have truth-value, and I now turn to the independent ques-tion, 'Do we believe when we dream or do we merely imagine?'

The answer to this question seems to be an unexciting 'Sometimes one and sometimes the other'. Philosophers in the past had one good reason for thinking as they did that all dreaming is believing. Dreaming is almost always involuntary like believing, while imagining is very often voluntary. But, although good, this is not a conclusive reason, for not all imagining is voluntary. We sometimes cannot help imagining things, e.g. possible disasters, although we would much rather not. There is, however, a conclusive reason for holding that some dreaming is believing, which is the intense relief (or, less often, regret) that we sometimes experience on waking. 'Thank goodness', we say, 'it was only a dream.' This is not the relief we feel when we have at last succeeded in shaking off a frightful imagination, but the relief of knowing that the thing was not *real* after all. I think that belief is especially characteristic of the dreams of children. This seems to be Freud's view, for it is of children specifically that he makes the remark I quoted above. As we grow older it seems to me that our dreams are more like imagining, although they are not for the most part under voluntary control. We do not often take them very seriously. The most dire events are encountered with remarkable sang-froid and correspondingly we experience little relief on waking up. In fact I feel inclined to say that in a good deal of our adult dreaming we know in a sense that we are dreaming and this prevents belief in the dream events. There is indeed a kind of dream, which we are not all capable of having, in which the dreamer fully knows that he is dreaming. This is called a lucid dream. Interesting accounts of lucid dreaming are to be found in Professor Broad's *Lectures on Psychical Research*[1] and again in Miss Celia Green's recent book, *Lucid Dreaming*.[2] Lucid dreaming is very like imagining and, like imagining, it is partly voluntary. The lucid dreamer is, as it were, telling himself a story in which he himself is the hero. He is quite aware of the fact that he is dreaming, and it is interesting to note that a dream sometimes becomes lucid because the dreamer applies the coherence test and finds that it fails. Miss Green quotes an account by an unsophisticated subject which also illustrates the phenomenon of false awakening:

> Twice or more during childhood I remember apparently waking up from a dream and then discovering I had not done so because I could not turn on the light. I recognised in the dream that I was still asleep (because of not being able to turn on the light).[3]

When I say that the normal adult dreamer knows in a sense that he is dreaming, I don't mean that he is having a lucid dream, but

[1] Pp. 162 ff. [2] (Oxford, 1968.)
[3] Ibid., p. 118; cf. also pp. 144–5.

rather that if he could, without waking up, ask himself the question whether he were dreaming or not, he would tell himself that he was. He knows that he is dreaming rather in the way that I know that I am reading when I am absorbed in a book. I don't say this to myself, but if someone were to ask, I should say 'Yes, I am reading.' The two states share the same paradoxical feature, i.e. that they cannot be recognised by the one who has them for what they are without ceasing to be what they are. If I tell myself that I am reading, I shall cease to read absorbedly. Similarly, if I tell myself that I am dreaming, I shall either wake up or the dream will turn lucid.

To sum up this section, I should say that dreaming is sometimes a kind of believing and sometimes a kind of imagining.

I now want to raise a consequent question. When dreaming is a kind of believing, must our dream-beliefs necessarily be false, i.e. are we necessarily in a state of error? Descartes, you will remember, explicitly denies this at one stage. He says, citing the case of a mathematician constructing a proof, that we may have some true beliefs in dreams. For Descartes, then, 'I dreamt that p' is perfectly compatible with the truth of the proposition that p. Some philosophers, including Descartes in his first position, would deny this, and so does Malcolm,[1] although of course he cannot state this in the form that all our dream-beliefs are false. Now who is right? I am not asking whether we do have true beliefs in dreams, but merely whether we could. I cannot see why not. It seems to me that Descartes is right in his second position. A mathematician may state a true mathematical proposition to himself in a dream. But, we may be inclined to say, there must be *some* error in a dream. The *a priori* proposition he accepts may be true, but he will be believing, falsely, that he is writing on the blackboard or expounding it to someone else. But need he? Suppose that he is used to thinking mathematically in imaginary symbols. He will dream that he is doing this and he will be doing just this. Again, may not someone be lying with his eyes closed, hearing the windows rattle, and dream that he is lying with his eyes closed hearing the windows rattle? I think that we have some evidence that this happens in the fact that often people who have demonstrably been asleep deny that they have. Perhaps they have been dreaming all the surrounding circumstances accurately. In the case of such wholly true dreams, the dreamer himself cannot tell that he has been asleep and dreaming, but others can. There are many well-known signs of sleep, e.g. snoring, which can be used by others although not by the sleeper. Of course we often know that we

---

[1] *Dreaming*, p. 66. See, however, p. 68.

have been dreaming because we recognise on waking that the beliefs we have just been having are false. I am not denying that most dream-contents are false. What I want to deny is that there is a necessary connection between dreaming on the one hand and falsity and error on the other. Dreaming is our thinking in sleep, and because it occurs during sleep it naturally enough contains falsehood and error and even extravagant falsehood and error, but this is not part of the definition of dreaming.

I hope that this examination of the nature of dreaming has shown that there is neither the need for nor the possibility of any extravagant undercutting of the sceptical argument.

I now want to make some brief comments on some recent empirical investigations of dreaming and to consider what implications, if any, they have for the philosophy of mind.

It is a disadvantage of Malcolm's view of dreaming that if taken seriously it would discourage research into the temporal correlations which seem to hold between dream experiences and brain events that can be recorded by the electro-encephalograph. On Malcolm's view, it is absurd to ask when in physical time a dream occurred,[1] but the exciting results of Dement, Kleitman, Jouvet and others depend on the supposition that there is an exact correlation between brain events as recorded by the E.E.G. and certain experiences. The evidence is in a certain sense necessarily indirect, as the dream-content is experienced only by the dreamer, while the tracing of the E.E.G. pattern can be observed only by the experimenter, but it is nevertheless such evidence as would be accepted by most practising scientists. Recent researches into dreaming are well reported in a popular form in *Sleep* by Gay Gaer Luce and Lucius Segal.[2] It seems to me that the most interesting results are as follows:

(i) There are at least two different kinds of dreaming. The one occurs in what is called Stage II sleep and is the drowsy kind of dreaming we experience when, for example, falling asleep over a book. The other is called R.E.M. dreaming because accompanied by rapid eye movements. It succeeds our deepest kind of sleep and is

---

[1] Ibid., ch. 13. Miss H. Ishiguro has pointed out to me that the scientific philistinism of which I am here complaining is not necessitated by Malcolm's characteristic view of dreaming as a unique state not identifiable with thinking, imagining, etc., but only by the statement quoted in the text, which seems itself to result from a muddle between such events as dreaming that one jumped over the moon and jumping over the moon. If one asks when the latter occurs, the answer is obviously 'Never', but there is no reason why Malcolm should not, like anyone else, ask when the former occurred and answer the question by using Kleitman's techniques.

[2] (London, 1967.)

accompanied by brain states which in some respects resemble waking brain states. For this reason some investigators call the sleep in which it occurs paradoxical sleep. I say *at least* two kinds, for lucid dreaming may be yet a third kind. Unfortunately the correlation between lucid dreaming and E.E.G. records has not yet been investigated, as far as I know.

(ii) R.E.M. dreaming is connected with the hypothalamus, a comparatively primitive part of the brain, and occurs at a fairly primitive level both on the evolutionary scale and in the individual life. Such lowly creatures as opossums, rats and cats show the E.E.G.s characteristically connected with R.E.M. dreaming, while infants and new-born kittens spend a considerable proportion of their time in R.E.M. sleep.

(iii) Deprivation of R.E.M. sleep has a particularly bad psychological effect, and a person suffering from it will make up by extra R.E.M. sleep when left undisturbed.

This last fact suggests that R.E.M. sleep and therefore dreaming have some biological usefulness. Kleitman indeed is careful to point out that this conclusion is not absolutely necessary as regards human beings. We may simply become addicted to dreaming as to cigarette smoking and therefore be irritable when deprived of it.[1] But when we take the facts about animals and infants into account, this suggestion seems implausible and the hypothesis of biological usefulness gains strength. To a neurophysiologist engaged in physiological investigation it will seem natural to suppose that the biological usefulness of the dreaming state lies in the chemical or electrical condition of the brain which accompanies it, and that the actual dream, the conscious state which occurs in human beings at least, is an epiphenomenon, a mere accompaniment of some state necessary to the health of the brain. This suggestion is implicit in a passage from Luce and Segal, who philosophise from time to time in the course of reporting their material:

A dozen years ago we might have observed the agitation of vivid dreaming and inferred that the body was reacting to the inward images of the mind. Today it is quite as possible to take the opposite view – that dreams are manufactured by certain physiological cycles that are independent of the individual's history.[2]

This may be so, but I think it is part of the philosopher's job to consider whether it is necessarily so on the evidence we have. Can we suppose that the *conscious* experiences we call dreams have any

[1] *Scientific American* (Nov 1960) 88.
[2] *Sleep*, p. 168.

evolutionary significance? This is part of a large question not so often discussed now as it once was: 'Has consciousness itself any evolutionary value and, if not, why has it arisen and survived?' In the case of dreams the question is peculiarly difficult, for their apparently random and often absurd nature makes it natural to regard them as by-products of a physical process. Freud, as we all know, has nevertheless produced an elaborate theory which gives dreams, as conscious processes, an important biological function, guarding sleep and providing an outlet for the drives suppressed during waking life. For a variety of reasons, which it is impractical to expound here, I have doubts about this Freudian theory. I should like to offer, very tentatively, an alternative suggestion about the evolutionary usefulness of dreaming. What advantage has the dreaming creature over a possible non-dreaming creature? Simply this. In dreaming the connections set up in the pursuit of goals in daily life are broken and new connections randomly suggested. The dreaming creature is thus less at the mercy of conditioned reflex and mere habit. It is able to spot new connections and, in a word, to learn. It may be objected that the connections thrown up in dreams are so bizarre that they could not be of any practical use. This is obviously so of most of them, but it is notorious that nature is indefinitely wasteful and if one in a million of the connections thrown up in dreams should suggest a new insight or a new way of reaching a desired goal, the dreaming creature would still have an advantage over the one whose consciousness is restricted to those connections encountered in actual waking life.

The last section of this paper has necessarily been tentative and sketchy. I wish to present it merely as a specimen of one of the ways in which I should like philosophers to treat of dreams.

14

MORAL KNOWLEDGE AND MORAL PRINCIPLES

J. B. Schneewind

WHAT is the function of moral principles within the body of moral knowledge? And what must be the nature of moral principles in order for them to carry out this function? A specific set of answers to these questions is widely accepted among moral philosophers – so widely accepted as almost to constitute a sort of orthodoxy. The answers embody a view of the place of principles within the body of morality which crosses the lines between cognitivism and non-cognitivism. Though I have put the question in cognitivist terms and shall discuss it in those terms, I think a similar question and a more or less parallel discussion could be given in non-cognitivist terms. Perhaps the time-honoured debate between the two positions can be suspended, at least temporarily, while we examine, not the nature of morality, but its structure.

The generally accepted view of moral principles consists of four main points. First, moral principles must possess a high degree of substantial generality. Generality of logical form is not sufficient; moral rules have this type of generality, but principles must in addition be applicable to a wide variety of cases and circumstances. They must, I shall say, be relatively context-free; unlike 'One ought to help old ladies crossing busy streets', which is relevant only to a fairly limited set of situations, 'One ought to help people in need' is applicable to an indefinitely large number of kinds of case, and can, so far, be a principle. Second, these moral principles must allow of no exceptions, nor can they rightly be overridden. Unlike moral rules, such as the one telling us to keep our promises, which may rightly be broken or suspended in certain circumstances, the principles of morality must always hold and always be binding. Third, moral principles must be substantive and not merely formal. It must, that is, be possible to derive answers to specific and detailed moral questions from a moral principle by applying it to the facts giving rise to the questions. This is the feature which critics of Kant's ethics have frequently said is missing in his formulation of the moral law; its absence is fatal to its claims to be the principle of morality. These three features mark what, for convenience, I shall call a classical moral principle. When we add a fourth feature to these three – relative context-freedom, unexceptionability, substantiality – we have what I shall call a classical first principle. The fourth feature is that the principle must be foundational or basic. Other principles, rules, or particular judgements may derive their validity from a first principle, but it must be an originating source of the authority of lower-order parts of morality and must not in turn depend on other moral judgements or principles for its own binding power. It must possess prior or basic validity or authority or truth, not derived or dependent power.

This view of moral principles rests – at least in part – on the claim that if there is to be such a thing as genuine moral knowledge, then there must be at least some true classical first principles. It is this claim which I propose to examine. There are a number of inter-related arguments in its favour. The first, which is tied to the three features making a principle a classical moral principle, is that there must be such principles if any reasons for or against particular moral judgements, or less context-free rules, are to be sound. There must be classical moral principles, that is, according to the first argument, if it is to be possible to reason about moral problems. Building on this position, two further arguments are used to show that these principles must be first principles. One is an attempt to show that first principles must exist if morality is to constitute a rational and coherent system; the other is an attempt to show that first principles must exist if morality is to be more than a merely hypothetical or possible system – if it is to be genuine knowledge, then, the argument goes, we must know the truth of at least one classical first principle. I shall sketch these arguments briefly and indicate why they seem to me to be unsuccessful in establishing their conclusions.

The attempt to show that there must be classical moral principles if reasoning is to be possible about moral matters proceeds on the assumption that the reasoning needed in morality is purely deductive. Now if the only generalities available as premises for such reasoning were rules to which exceptions could be made, or which could be overridden, then one could never be certain that a particular case to which a rule applies is not one of the anomalous ones. Then it would always be possible to assert the general premiss – the rule – and the fact-stating minor premises, and yet deny the conclusion. But then no reason at all would have been given, on this view, for the particular moral judgement asserted in the conclusion. Hence, if it is to be possible to give reasons for moral judgements, there must be some exceptionless principles.

An explanation can of course be given along these lines of the reasoning involved in applying rules or practical principles to the cases where they are relevant, and similar explanations can be given of the many other ways in which we actually think about moral problems – drawing comparisons with similar cases, using analogies, considering what some ideal or admired person would do. Our procedures may, however, be given another interpretation, according to which to adduce a principle may be to give a good reason for doing a certain act, and to apply a principle may be to subsume a case under it in deductive fashion, even if the principle allows of exceptions. For in morality, it may be argued, as frequently in law, we have to do with rebuttable subsumptions. When a relevant and acceptable principle has been adduced, a reason has been given for doing the act it dictates in the circumstances. The burden of proof has thereby been shifted to anyone who thinks that the act ought not to be done. It is open to an objector to give reasons for thinking the case in question to be exceptional; but if no such reasons are given, then the act dictated by the principle remains the act that ought to be done, since it is the act for doing which the best reason has been given. In the absence of definite grounds for thinking the particular case exceptional it would be foolish to take the logical possibility of its being exceptional as a serious reason for doubting that it ought to be done. Similarly it would be foolish to take the bare logical possibility that I might be hallucinating now as a serious reason for thinking that I am not now perceiving my surroundings correctly. We are, therefore, not compelled to interpret the procedures we use in thinking about moral problems as aiming at the production of logically conclusive reasons for or against moral assertions; and so the argument to show that there must be classical moral principles if there is to be reasoning on moral matters collapses.

The next step in the argument is an attempt to show that there must be classical *first* principles if morality is to be rational and coherent (and rationality and coherence are clearly necessary if morality is to be essentially a body of knowledge). The line of thought I shall consider is in fact used to prove an even stronger claim: it is used to prove that there must be one and only one first principle. It is a simple argument. No rational, coherent system can contain contradictions. But if there are a multiplicity of rules and principles, they are liable to become involved in conflicts over particular cases. These conflicts are the equivalents of contradictions among assertions, and it cannot, therefore, be admitted that they are the final truth about morality. It follows that there must be a method of resolving them. There must, then, be a principle in terms of which any conflicts arising between or among relatively context-bound principles can be resolved. There can be only one such principle, for if there were more than one the same sort of conflict could arise again. This principle must be completely context-free, since it must be capable of being applied to any kind of situation. And, finally, it must be supreme in authority, for it may be called upon to adjudicate disputes involving any other principles within the morality over which it reigns. Hence, it must be able to override any other principle and no other principle must be able to override it. And this being so, the authority of other principles must depend on their being allowed to dictate by what is plainly the first principle.

This line of thought – if I may make an historical comment – is of great importance in classical utilitarianism. It enabled Bentham and J. S. Mill to give reasoned support to the utilitarian principle as the one candidate that could fill the requirements for being the classical first principle, without relying on any premises drawn from the content of the accepted morality. The line of argument they invoked is epistemological, yet, if sound, it establishes a principle which can be used to override any common-sense rule or principle, even if no conflict of principles has arisen. For the argument establishes the total supremacy of the conflict-resolving principle and therefore justifies its use in any context.

Yet I think the argument is not sound, for two reasons. First, to say that there are conflicts of rules and principles in specific cases is not to say that there are contradictions in morality which destroy its coherence. Just as there may be good reasons for believing each of two incompatible factual assertions, so there may be good reasons for doing each of two incompatible actions. We may be in a position in which we are unable to tell which of the two assertions – if either of them – is really true and we may similarly be unable to tell for which of the two actions – if either – there are ultimately better reasons. It might in such cases be *morally* desirable to have a principle which would always resolve such conflicts, but even if it were this would not show that the existence of such a principle is a necessity for the cognitive status of morality. Second, even if there were some conflict-resolving principle (or perhaps I should say, even if there is one), it would not follow that such a principle must be the first principle of morals, in the desired sense. From the fact that a given principle is supreme in resolving conflicts it does not follow that it must be supreme in every context. To suppose that it does follow would be like supposing that every decision and rule agreed upon by a happily married couple depends on the authority of the divorce court, since that court has the final word in settling all their affairs if they cannot settle them by themselves. An authority to settle difficulties may conceivably be restricted to doing just that, and its interference in normal cases, where no other conflict of principles or rules is involved, may be totally unwarranted. Any principle established with the help of this argument might simply be as it were a moral ambulance, not for everyday use, having the right of precedence only in emergencies and not in the ordinary run of events. I do not say that this is the correct view: I mention it only as an alternative possibility which militates against this particular argument.

The last set of considerations to be examined leads to the conclusion that there must be some classical first principles, but does not allow the conclusion that there can be only one. It embodies an argument that frequently leads to intuitionism or 'Cartesianism' in ethics, and though it is extremely old it has a perennial appeal, appearing even in the thought of those who do not intend to draw intuitionist conclusions from it. Thus Professor D. H. Monro, a defender of naturalism, writes that 'we settle moral questions by appealing implicitly to some general principle', and this principle serves as a major premiss to enable us to deduce from a minor, factual, premiss a particular moral judgement. 'There does not seem to be any way of testing this [major premiss]', he continues, 'except by an appeal to some further principle about what is right or what ought to be the case.'[1] This is the way the argument usually begins. It continues with the threat of an infinite, and vicious, regress of moral principles, each one used to support the one to which we have just appealed. The conclusion is that there must be some principle which can be known to be authoritative or true without needing further moral support, and which can give support to the lower-order principles which have been adduced to prove the particular judgement. But such a principle answers to the description of a classical first principle.

This argument presupposes the strict deductive model of giving reasons, which we have already touched on. More interestingly, it presupposes that there is a context-free order of dependence among moral propositions, so that if a particular judgement or a rule or principle ever depends on another then it always does. Since it seems

---

[1] D. H. Monro, *Empiricism and Ethics* (Cambridge, 1967) p. 8.

undeniable that we frequently settle particular moral questions by appeal to general principles, and support these by showing that they follow from still more general principles, the conclusion of the argument follows quite obviously. Yet the assumption that there is a context-free order of dependence, though rarely discussed by moral philosophers, is to say the least doubtful. It has been attacked, in rather different ways, by C. S. Peirce and other pragmatists, and more recently by J. L. Austin. They have argued that the distinction between knowledge which depends on being inferred and knowledge which is independent of inference is not one which can be drawn simply in terms of the content or the degree of generality of the knowledge. It is a context-bound distinction. What is for me dependent on some other information need not be so for you: that your name is Jones may be known by me through a complicated inference, and if so my knowledge depends on the premises of the inference, but presumably the knowledge of your name is not thus dependent for you. Similarly, time can make a difference: presumably after years of friendship my knowledge of your name is not dependent on the premises from which I first inferred it. In fact I might now adduce my knowledge of your name as evidence that those premises themselves were true. This point applies as well to moral as to factual knowledge. What is a matter of moral perplexity for one person need not be so for another, and hence a moral assertion which is in need of support, and is dependent for its authority on a further principle, need not be in this position for everyone alike. I may change my mind about a particular class of cases under the influence of a principle I have always accepted; but I may later come to see that this class of cases also falls under a different principle which I have not previously accepted, and may come to accept the principle as showing more clearly the justification for my judgement of the class of cases. Moral philosophers, whatever their theoretical programmes, have in practice always recognised that allegedly basic moral principles depend no less on fairly specific moral propositions than on the other sorts of grounds that have been offered for them; a principle that led to the conclusion that truth-telling was usually wrong, and torturing children normally permissible would be rejected, no matter what kind of proof it might have. But if general principles may sometimes depend on particular moral judgements, and particular judgements sometimes on general principles, then there is no impersonal, necessary order of dependence within the realm of moral knowledge, and we are not compelled to conclude that there must be classical first principles.

So far we have discussed arguments to show that there *must* be classical first principles. Could it simply be that there just *are* such principles? There seem to be two difficulties with this. One is the problem of finding any candidates which fit the requirements for being a classical moral principle. The principles that operate in daily life seem generally to allow of exceptions or of being overridden, and the candidates proposed by philosophers fail, either – like Bentham's version of the utilitarian principle – for the same reason, or – like Kant's formulation of the moral law – because they are only formal. But even if some such principle were to be found, there would remain the problem of whether it would be a *first* principle in the required sense. And here the difficulty seems to be insurmountable. For it is a defining characteristic of moral directives, as contrasted with those of law, tradition, custom, or manners, that none of them can be always relieved of the need to be justified. If particular moral assertions need at times to be justified, so too do moral principles. The facts seem to be that we give reasons for particular judgements in terms of principles, and also that we justify principles in terms of particular judgements. If in different types of situation and in response to different problems we use both procedures to justify moral directives, then it cannot be claimed that in fact there just are principles which never receive support and always give it. To say that there must be some acceptable classical first principles is to insist on forcing the facts to fit a theoretical model.

The epistemological arguments we have considered do not force us, then, to adopt the view that there must be classical first principles if there is to be moral knowledge. There may well be other important arguments to show that there must be principles of this sort if a given morality is to be viable, and it would be interesting to discuss the question of the extent to which, and the ways in which, the above arguments could be rephrased to fit a non-cognitivist view of morality (how can moral attitudes guide conduct if they are not coherent? and how can they be coherent if they are not ultimately based on one fundamental attitude?). Yet as one of the considerations leading to the belief in classical first principles is that there is no other model for understanding moral knowledge than the one which involves commitment to them, I should like to devote the remainder of this essay to a very rough sketch of a different way of viewing it, one which does not involve this commitment.

The model of knowledge which I shall use for discussing morality is the scientific model. It is almost inevitable that a cognitivist view of morality should stress the resemblances between science and ethics; yet to do so is not necessarily to escape from a demand for classical first principles. The ideal of reasoning, and the correlated ideal of knowledge, behind the belief in classical first principles, is a geometric and deductive ideal, and frequently leads to intuitionistic positions. But it can also lead to certain varieties of 'scientific' morality. Thus, Herbert Spencer's moral theory is essentially a deductive system based on a single classical first principle. What is supposed to be distinctively 'scientific' about it is that the principle is allegedly derived wholly from the discoveries of the positive sciences. J. S. Mill's version of utilitarianism is less wholeheartedly scientific than Spencer's view: Mill does not think that the single basic principle of morality can be scientifically proven. But every moral problem and every other rule of morality can, under the supervision of the utilitarian principle, be given purely scientific treatment (or will be susceptible of it, when the social sciences have matured). Still, one need not fall back on classical first principles when one attempts to show that morality can be understood along the lines of a science. There is at least one other way in which science can serve as a model, a way pointed out in certain of its aspects by John Dewey. It may be argued that what is scientific about morality is neither some basic principle or principles on which it rests, nor its reliance on special sciences for most of the premises on which moral reasoning proceeds, but the general structure of its contents and its methods. Moral beliefs show the same kind of susceptibility to systematisation, criticism, revision, and re-systematisation that factual beliefs show. There are analogues to theory and data among our moral beliefs, and these can be understood as related in ways like those in which theory and data are related in the sciences. If we can show that this way of understanding morality is feasible, we shall have undercut the argument claiming that the model which commits us to classical first principles is the only possible one.

Principles of morality function in some ways like the formulations of laws which scientists propose. There are, at any given time, a number of specific judgements, rules and ideals, the correctness of which we have no hesitation in affirming. Formulations of moral principles serve to systematise and generalise these beliefs, and in doing so they articulate what may be called the spirit of our morality. They pick out the aspects of our less general beliefs which are not tied to specific circumstances and which would remain constant in a variety of situations. This enables them to express the point or rationale of specific moral convictions. And this in turn enables us to carry out a critical and explicit projection of our moral beliefs to new kinds of problem and new combinations of circumstances. The formulation of a principle to cover classes of cases where we know the rights and wrongs, and the application of the principle thus formed to the solution of difficulties which arise where we have no firm convictions, are analogous, in a rough but fairly clear way, to the formulation of a law to cover a set of well-established data and its use to predict results of new combinations of causal factors.

We must avoid taking too simple a view of this procedure, either in science or in morality. Recent work in the philosophy of science shows that it is misleading to think of each formulation of a scientific law as operating in isolation from every other formulation. Laws are expressed in the context of general theories, and they, as well as many of the concepts involved in assembling the data of the science, must be understood within that context. Similar points hold of morality. I do not mean to suggest that philosophical theories of ethics occupy the position of general theories in the sciences. What occupies the analogous position is rather the general world outlook – typically a religious outlook, or a non-religious world-view still conscious of its non-religiousness – in which a morality is embedded. A large part of the terms and beliefs of these general metaphysical views of life and the world are inseparably intertwined with what we tend to think of as distinctively moral beliefs. The very concepts by which we pick out subjects for moral predication may be rooted in religious or metaphysical propositions, and these in turn may be unintelligible without their evaluative and moral implications. Thus it will take a whole set of moral principles, understood against a metaphysical background, to articulate our moral beliefs adequately and to provide an intelligible and applicable projection of them to new problems. These complex interconnections give rise in morality to a phenomenon comparable to the use in scientific practice of 'theory-laden' observation terms. Many terms employed in the description of particular things and events carry strong theoretical implications, so that in using them we are committed to accepting certain scientific laws. Similarly, many of the terms used for describing our commonest actions and social relations have moral implications built into them. Those who use them are by that fact committed to at least the prima facie acceptance of certain moral directives: to say, e.g. that I am 'married to' so-and-so is to imply my acceptance of a directive against having sexual relations with anyone else. The moral implications of terms like this have been called 'practice-defining rules', and contrasted with 'summary rules'. It is not necessary that a comparison of moral principles with scientific laws should force us to accept the view that all moral principles are of the latter type. But it must equally be borne in mind that the vocabulary embodying practice-defining rules is itself open to alteration and in this respect like the theory-laden terms used in scientific observation.

If the relations between fact and theory in science are complex, so is the way in which the acceptability of a theory depends on the data it organises and the predictions it warrants. Laws that unify a large body of well-established facts and empirical generalisations, that enable us to make successful predictions over a wide range, and that suggest numerous points for further fruitful experiment and theory-construction, are not easily abandoned. A well-founded theory cannot be overthrown by the negative results of a single 'crucial experiment'. Logically speaking, it is always possible to defend a formulation of a law from a counter-instance by explaining the instance in terms of an *ad hoc* hypothesis, or by treating it as due to faulty instruments, bad observation, freakish accident, etc. In terms of the economy and strategy of research this is not always a bad move to make. It is only when the amount of evidence that must be avoided instead of absorbed grows fairly large, when the original theory becomes cumbrous and difficult to use because of the qualifications and adjustments needed to make it fit the evidence, that serious exploration of alternative theories takes place; and the existence of some viable alternative theory is needed before an accepted view will be abandoned. A new theory, if it is of the most attractive kind, will explain the evidence which told in favour of the older view – perhaps recasting it in a new terminology – and it will explain as well what was anomalous or required special hypotheses from the older standpoint. It will enable new areas of investigation to be developed and new types of prediction to be successfully made. It will, in short, perform the same functions as the replaced theory, but better.

If the study of the history of science is still at a comparatively early stage of development, the study of the history of moral systems has hardly even begun. At this point it can only be proposing a hypothesis to say that the pattern of thought revealed in studies of 'scientific revolutions' may be useful as a guide in investigating the development of norms and values. Still, even a rudimentary knowledge of history may allow us to see how this pattern could be relevant. Moral systems are used, not to predict, but to direct and evaluate conduct. They can fail to operate in any number of ways, as scientific theories can fail. Yet accepted systems have a definite value in virtue of the fact that they are widely accepted: they give shape and coherence and predictability to large segments of life, and they are therefore not lightly to be abandoned. Hence no single failure is likely to suffice to overthrow an accepted morality. As in the case of reasonably good theories, it is likely to take an accumulation of difficulties before serious investigation of alternatives occurs. These difficulties may arise from a number of causes. There can, for instance, be failure of relevance to prevalent problems. A morality developed within one type of social or economic situation may be carried over while technological or financial changes occur which effectively alter the nature of the society in which people accept it; and in the new situation the old directives may simply fail to cover recurring problems generally felt to be important. In such circumstances a morality also may fail by giving guidance which is not specific enough, or which it is not feasible to expect people to follow. R. H. Tawney's well-known discussion of the failure of the medieval church to provide an adequate set of precepts for action in a developing capitalist economy gives illustrations of these points. Either the types of monetary transaction vital to a capitalist economy were not covered by any of the standard directives or else they were covered by directives involved in concepts like that of usury and just price which it was no longer feasible to apply. People simply could not live in accordance with the dictates implied by those terms, and were forced to find new ways of organising their actions. Another kind of difficulty with a moral code arises when a change of circumstances transforms a once coherent set of practical demands into directives that repeatedly require incompatible or self-defeating actions. This is the sort of situation involved in what R. K. Merton calls 'anomie', where (roughly) socially acceptable goals can only be reached by breaking socially acceptable rules; and there are other types as well. Still another kind of difficulty with a moral system arises when the religious or metaphysical outlook with which it is involved ceases to be widely accepted: its categories may then cease to seem relevant to the daily problems people face, and therefore its judgements may be increasingly wide of the mark.

Complaints of these kinds about an accepted morality have often been answered by its defenders with the claim that the fault lies not in the moral code but in the social system which is changing in immoral directions, or in the weakness of men, which makes them less willing than usual to expend the effort needed to live up to moral demands, or in the faithlessness of men, which leads them to abandon the revealed truth, or in any of an innumerable variety of factors which allow one to admit the failure of the system to give useful guidance but to cling to the system nonetheless. As in similar cases where counter-evidence to a well-based scientific law is presented, this procedure has a definite justification. But in morality, as in science, it is not always used. There are times when abandoning a moral principle seems more reasonable than continuing to claim that it is true despite the numerous exceptions and qualifications it requires. And the abandonment of one principle is likely to involve repercussions in other parts of the system: the controversy over the morality of birth-control may be mentioned in illustration, touching as it does on the nature of the family, the function of sexual relations and the permissibility of pleasure, the place of women, the authority of various institutions, etc. In this connection it would be interesting to investigate the part played, in basic moral change, by the availability of some alternative system of morality, which would incorporate what is still held to be true in the old view while advancing to new insights on the points of difficulty in that view.

These brief comments may indicate some of the ways in which the structure of morality is like the structure of science, and may point towards an interpretation of moral principles and moral knowledge which does not force us to a belief in what I have called classical first principles. It may help to clarify the hypothesis being suggested if I add one or two further remarks.

The claim that morality is 'cognitive' and that we now have some moral knowledge is not the claim that all our moral convictions as they now stand are true or justifiable. We do not think any such implication to be involved in the claim that we have knowledge of geology or physics or mathematics. We are aware that many of the particular opinions and theories we now hold in these disciplines will eventually be discarded as mistaken, but we have no hesitation in claiming knowledge within these fields nonetheless. The situation is the same as regards morality. I have suggested that moral principles can be supported by showing that they provide adequate articulation of less general moral beliefs which are at a given time held without doubt. I do not mean to imply, however, that the beliefs to which we are at this moment committed are beyond criticism – far from it. Our morality has been derived from many sources and shaped by many influences. It is moreover deeply involved with our factual and religious or metaphysical beliefs. There is no guarantee that it is free from inconsistency, error, or superstition, either on the purely moral plane or in its non-moral involvements. Though it is bound to be our main starting-point in thinking about practical matters, we must assume that progress and improvement in moral knowledge are possible. This is no more, and no less, than we must assume in every area of thought where truth is an aim. Most moral philosophers, however, have thought of moral progress chiefly as the progressive improvement of the human race – as a slow growth in the degree to which men live up to the demands of morality. Few have considered the possiblity that moral progress may consist primarily in the growth of moral knowledge. One reason for this may have been their acceptance of the presuppositions that lead to a demand for classical first principles. For on that view, if we do not now know at least the first principles of morality, we cannot really know anything of morality (though of course our opinions may be true). But if we already know the first principles of morality then whatever progress is to be made in our knowledge of the subject (discounting that which will result solely from the improvement of scientific knowledge) must be comparatively minor. The view being put forward here in opposition to this places no such block in the way of contemplating the improvement of even our most general or most cherished principles.

Does this view leave open the possibility that moral knowledge might be, or become, esoteric, the possession of a small group of experts? This did happen to scientific knowledge, yet we do not wish to grant that it could occur with respect to morality. Nor, indeed, are we required to grant it. Any claim to know something must be open to assessment by the relevant group of those qualified to judge. In the case of morality this group consists of those who are able and willing to live their lives – to the usual extent – under the guidance of moral directives understood as such, and not taken simply as customs or taboos or religious commands or positive laws. It is a necessary, if not a sufficient, condition of the justifiability of any claim to knowledge that those who are competent to judge should come to agree with the claim when they investigate it in the proper manner. Moral claims are no exception, and the disagreement of informed and thoughtful moral agents with our own moral assertions gives us a reason for being less confident of them. Still, disagreement, even when the reasons for it are given, is not refutation, and one defence of controversial opinions which must be admitted does leave an opening for the charge of esotericism. It must, I think, be granted that some people really are more insightful and sensitive, morally speaking, than others, and that these people may possibly be ahead of the majority in their grasp of the morality of a particular kind of action. But the distinction between insight and delusion – between wisdom and charlatanry – is no less real than that between science and quackery, and it involves the same basic point: eventually the community of competent judges will come to accept the one and reject the other, if it looks into the matter with sufficient care.

Our moral principles, then, must articulate our unshakable convictions and provide us with adequate guidance for future

decisions. In addition they must be capable of calling forth agreement
in a potentially unlimited community of moral agents. How can we
be sure enough of any principles, under such stringent conditions, to
claim that we know they are correct? Well, of course, our scientific
theories and hypotheses must survive similar tests, and we manage
to make this claim about some of them. And after all the quest for
moral knowledge did not begin yesterday. The moral principles most
of us accept have had to survive a fair amount of testing and sifting in
the course of time. There is therefore a fair amount of evidence to show
that they can give acceptable guidance and can form the nucleus
of a moral community. To say that we *know* some of them to be
correct is to express our reasoned confidence that they, or something
very close to them, will, of those available for consideration, come
out best in relation to all the evidence, future as well as past. It is also
to express our decision, at least for the present, to hold to these
principles despite any objections to or difficulties with them. This
decision need be no more irrational than similar decisions made by
scientists. The principles that we decide, in this fashion, to maintain
are the ones we consider basic. The theory of classical first principles
involves mistaking this kind of decision for a discovery that certain
principles are basic because of their own inherent nature.

15

IS A RELIGIOUS
EPISTEMOLOGY POSSIBLE?

Terence Penelhum

THOSE who despair of the possibility of proving the existence of God tend, naturally, to hold that knowledge of God's existence and of those religious claims that depend upon it can only be had, if it can be had at all, through some direct religious awareness or insight. On this view appeals to authority or to revelation rest on appeals to such insight, if it is agreed that the credentials of the revealing authority cannot be established by the methods of natural theology. It is common for debate between believers and sceptics who share this despair about the possibility of proof to take on an air of hopelessness and unreality because of a fundamental epistemological cleavage: on the one hand the believer has an allegedly cognitive experience and on the other the sceptic lacks and suspects it. I want in this paper to scrutinise some aspects of this division. I shall not do much to mitigate the pessimism of my earlier statements, since I think the division really is, in certain critical ways, an unbridgeable one. But it is worth while to come to a clearer understanding of its nature than I think some philosophers have. What follows has been influenced by reflection on recent controversies about the meaningfulness of religious discourse, but is not intended to be a contribution to them. Some of the best-known contributions, however, seem to me to have made the epistemological cleavage I have referred to seem even worse than it is.

The reason that so many despair of the possibility of proving God's existence, and other claims that depend upon it, is of course the apparent failure of the traditional theistic arguments. The confidence with which this despair is proclaimed is surprising if one reflects that no number of failures, however large, entails the impossibility of an enterprise; but no doubt if the failures show anything this is

263

what they *tend* to show. It is quite common for theologians to try to
make a virtue of necessity by producing reasons why failure to prove
God's existence is to be expected – for example, that a proof compels
assent to its conclusion, and God does not compel human assent to
his existence. This is a highly dubious argument, since it entails that
it is not possible for someone to have something proved to him yet
manage to avoid accepting it, which surely pays far too high a com-
pliment to human reasonableness. But I do not want here to question
the common view that God's existence cannot be proved; I shall,
with apologies to some present, assume it to be true. I want rather to
examine a little more carefully what it comes to, and what some of its
implications are.

Suppose someone holds that it is not possible to prove God's
existence, or to prove any statement about God that presupposes it.
Obviously such a person is likely to mean that these statements
cannot be proved if one starts from premises that do *not* presuppose
it. He is not likely to be moved by the production of a proof which
starts with premises that do presuppose it. While I do not wish to
argue this here, I do not think it wise to try to dismiss such cases by a
tight definition of what a proof is. Even so, the belief that God's
existence cannot be proved will hardly be shaken if only arguments
like this are produced as counter-examples. I would like to express
this in a slightly more rigorous manner, and without using the rather
inappropriate notion of presupposition. I shall call a statement a
'theistic statement' if it is a statement that one cannot know to be
true without also knowing that God exists. A statement that one *can*
know to be true without knowing that God exists I shall call a 'non-
theistic statement'. The epistemological pessimism about proving
God's existence and proving statements that presuppose it can now
be expressed as follows: it is not possible to produce a proof of God's
existence, or of any theistic statement, using as premises only non-
theistic statements. The arguments of traditional natural theology
are, or are based upon, attempted proofs of the kind which this
principle excludes.

Let us give a name now to the belief that such probative enter-
prises are doomed to failure. I would like to call it (borrowing and
misappropriating a term from Professor Gareth Matthews)[1] 'theological non-naturalism'. The first thing to notice about it is that a
theist can be a theological non-naturalist as well as a sceptic, and
many theists are. The second thing is that the position needs much

[1] Gareth B. Matthews, 'Theology and Natural Theology, in *Journal of Philosophy*,
LXI (1964) 99–108.

more clarification than it normally receives before its implications can be understood.

Why might someone say that certain premises cannot serve to prove a particular conclusion? There are at least two possible reasons. He may think that the premises are not themselves true, or at least not known to be true, even though, if they *were* known to be true, they *would* be sufficient to show conclusively that the conclusion was true. Or he may think that even if they were known to be true, they would *still* not suffice to show conclusively that the conclusion was true. Now to say that conclusions of a certain kind cannot be proved from premises of a certain kind is not, so far, to decide between these reasons. It is merely to say *either* that the premises will not be known to be true, *or* that even though true they would not suffice to show the conclusion conclusively to be true, *or* in some cases, both. This ambiguity enables someone who takes the position that theistic statements cannot be proved from non-theistic premises to re-examine the truth of the premises whenever it looks as though they would, if true, serve to render the conclusions true – a move which in view of the importance of the subject-matter it is tactically advantageous to make from time to time. Theological non-naturalism, however, as I have so far defined it, also enables someone to say that there are certain non-theistic statements which would, in his view, be sufficient to prove some theistic conclusions but which happen as a matter of fact not to be true, or are not known to be true. Many of those who have rejected particular proofs of God's existence seem to take this position. At least a good deal of the time in Hume's *Dialogues* (during the discussion of evil, for example) it seems to be implied that although the world as we find it does not contain the features which would serve to show, with the conclusiveness that Cleanthes argues for, that the world was designed by a benevolent intelligence, this might be shown conclusively if only the world were different – e.g. better in certain ways. This is a common enough position, and one, again, which many theists also take, recognising and indeed emphasising that a world which *needs* God may not be one the examination of which will prove that he is there. This position implies that a proof is an argument which conclusively shows its conclusion to be true, but it does not define this conclusiveness in terms of entailment; this is surely correct, it being only a rationalist dogma that p cannot show q to be true conclusively unless p entails q.

Let us now imagine ourselves undertaking an inquisitorial exercise. Let us imagine ourselves asking some particular theological non-naturalist a series of questions designed to elicit from him *what* non-theistic statements he would regard as sufficient to prove a theistic conclusion, if only he knew them to be true. Would he think that the occurrence of a certain number of medically inexplicable cures at Lourdes would show that God cared for the sick? Would he think that the fact that certain mediums had conversed with departed spirits who had told them that God had preserved them from death would show that God does preserve men from death? Suppose, more radically perhaps, that it came to pass that all persons who let atheistic statements escape their lips were stricken dumb? Suppose that every Sunday night the stars in the sky over London formed themselves for three hours into the letters of the sentence PRAISE THE LORD? Suppose it were the case that every innocent sufferer of whom he had knowledge had his or her character greatly improved by suffering? As these questions, however fanciful, proceeded, one might very well expect disagreement among respondents over the probative value of this or that imagined fact, and one might also expect individuals to hesitate in their interpretation of one or another of them. But sooner or later one might expect a parting of the ways among those we have so far classed as theological non-naturalists. Sooner or later it would appear that some of them would be prepared to agree that there are some non-theistic statements which, if only they were true, would be sufficient to prove that some theistic statement is true, whereas for others of them there are in fact *no* non-theistic statements which, even if true, would be allowed by them to be sufficient to prove any theistic conclusion. I shall call the latter sort of theological non-naturalist a 'radical' theological non-naturalist. For him no non-theistic statement whatever, however much it reported a world different from the one we in fact live in, would be allowed to show conclusively that God existed. From this it would follow that for him no theistic statement could ever be known to be true by anyone except through an appeal to some other theistic knowledge already possessed by that person, or through direct religious insight of some kind. Theistic statements are simply not, on this view, capable of indirect proof (i.e. proof through non-theistic statements). Someone, on the other hand, who adopts the less radical view that even though theistic statements cannot in fact be proved from non-theistic ones, this is merely because the premises that would prove them are not premises anyone will ever know to be true ones, is admitting that it is possible to envisage situations which could in principle be known to obtain by someone who did not know that God existed and yet could serve, if they only did obtain, to prove to that person some truth about God. Someone who merely says that God's existence cannot be proved does not make it clear which view he holds, and may not, of course, have thought about it.

But it is of some consequence to see that these two views are possible. For radical theological non-naturalism comes to the thesis that without direct religious insight *nothing* could make it irrational to refuse to accept any theistic conclusion. And this view places theistic statements in a very over-privileged, or very under-privileged, position indeed. Whereas saying that there are some things that would make it irrational to refuse to accept theistic conclusions, but that these things are things we cannot know to be the case, is to place them on a footing quite like that of propositions of many other kinds. There is nothing epistemologically odd about a class of propositions which cannot be shown to be true merely because the facts that would serve for this are not available.

The purpose of much traditional natural theology was to show that in the face of certain facts which could be ascertained by some-one who did not already know that God existed, it is irrational to deny that he does. The theological non-naturalist denies that there are actually facts accessible to such a person of which this is true. The radical version of theological non-naturalism insists that there *could be* none. Of course, once again, someone who thinks that there could be some in principle, but are not, need not mean by this that these facts would *entail* some theistic conclusion: only that any other logically possible explanation of these facts would be an irrational one to prefer. Someone who wavers over a particular example is presumably trying to decide whether or not it would be irrational to prefer some stretched non-theistic explanation of those imagined facts to the theistic one that it is alleged would be proved by them. Now how does one decide whether the theistic choice is or is not the only rational one in such circumstances? Is one left with the shocking subjectivity of what it seems reasonable or unreasonable to accept as sufficient to establish some conclusion? Or are there general criteria that one can use to determine one's decision?

There are two general considerations which would decide the matter, but which I suggest should be put aside. One simple way to justify radical theological non-naturalism would be to prove that God could not exist. This one could do by showing that the concept of God contains contradictions. If one could do this one could justify a negative evaluation of any and every suggested probative premiss. I have had to assume without demonstration that this move is not available. I will merely point out that it is not, of course, a move that all atheists are committed to; for the atheist, though committed to the moderate form of theological non-naturalism, can reject its radical form, since he can hold that there are propositions which, were they only true, would show that God existed; they might be the contradictories of propositions which he does think are true and show in his view that God does not. Another general sort of consideration that could be brought in in some instances is that the concept of God has built into it certain attributes which show that if God existed the fact imagined in the alleged probative proposition would never be the case. It might be said, for example, that a world in which outspoken atheists were struck dumb would not show on pain of irrationality that God existed because even though we might be frightened in such a world into accepting that God existed, the concept of God is the concept of a being free of malevolent bursts of temper; so if we succumbed to these phenomena we would be calling some other less admirable being by too complimentary a title. Objections of this sort might very well defeat particular imagined inferences; but they would not undermine more than a modest number. For unless one were to adopt the quite indefensible position that the world we have is the only one which God, if he exists, could have created, it will never be impossible to think up descriptions of better worlds in which it might be less obviously rational to deny his existence than it is in this one.

Another general consideration that suggests itself is that the conclusion that some theistic statement is true is a very *important* sort of conclusion to draw, and therefore one on which it is proper to withhold one's judgement for as long as one conceivably can. This looks like a counsel of prudence in favour of refraining from jumping to theistic conclusions, and might seem to weigh against the intrinsic stringency of any imagined inference. But it is not so very clear which way prudential considerations ought to sway us in these matters. We can brush aside the suggestion that prudential considerations are enough to tell us which way to draw our conclusions. But if, *ex hypothesi*, there is some need to look for others, there seems no good reason to exclude prudential ones. But if one admits them at all, then they seem to be distinctly double-edged. Against the claim that theistic beliefs have such far-reaching practical implications that they ought not to be adopted unless the evidence is compelling is the simple counter-argument, which all readers of Pascal know, that these beliefs have such far-reaching practical implications that one had better *not fail* to adopt them unless there are cogent reasons for not doing so. The importance of religious claims should certainly make us look at them hard. But looking at them hard is not the same as looking at them sceptically.

A more plausible general consideration is that of economy and complexity. It seems obvious that some account of an apparently probative fact that does not involve reference to divine agency or divine wishes is a more economical account than the one that would be implied if the fact were allowed to prove divine agency or divine wishes. It may *seem* obvious, but it becomes less so on reflection. Against the apparent economy of non-theistic accounts of some imagined facts one has, first, to weigh their intrinsic implausibility in the very striking cases, and the coincidences and anomalies that give rise to it. The sorts of cases that would offer themselves as likely candidates for probative status would require a good many explanatory epicycles, as it were, to account for them naturalistically. One has, then, to weigh the economy of the naturalistic account (in the sense of its relative parsimony with entities) against its theoretical complexity. But in addition to this one has to weigh it against the vague but recognisable claims of explanatory depth. The man who accepts that certain facts would prove God's existence or agency need not deny that naturalistic accounts of them can be given, but he will deny that they escape a fatal superficiality. And he will argue that the appropriateness of a standard in one field does not guarantee its force in another. These considerations are very vague and general, but I think recognisable. In order to decide between them one must confront, one by one, test cases that involve them, and give up hope of settling them at a higher level of generality. For it is hard to see what general epistemological considerations can be brought to bear upon them, except those that depend on a decision about the truth or falsity of the very theistic claims the imagined facts are supposed to prove or fail to prove.

We do seem, then, to be unable to escape very easily from individual judgement that this or that inference from some imagined non-theistic fact to some theistic conclusion would constitute a proof of it, or would not; that it would or would not render that conclusion overwhelmingly likely, or show it to be true conclusively, or put it beyond reasonable doubt. None of these are evaluative expressions that it is easy, or even perhaps possible, to define very exactly – as one can see if one reflects for a moment on how hard it would be to define the notion of overwhelming likelihood in terms of frequency. Yet if he cannot demonstrate logical contradictions in the concept of God, a radical theological non-naturalist is also forced back upon justifying his stance by reference to a series of individual judgements that this, that, or the other premiss would fail to prove a theistic conclusion. Yet this would supply him with no grounds for his negative position, since he would never, presumably, be prepared to say what premises would be free of the inadequacies that he claimed to detect in the ones he rejected. And without such preparedness his position is wholly arbitrary. The situation, therefore, appears to be that when presented with a series of allegedly probative imaginary premises, and asked whether they would or would not put theistic conclusions beyond reasonable doubt, we do not have any non-question-begging general principles to appeal to in reaching our decisions; yet it is still irrational to insist that *no* imaginary premiss whatsoever could have the required probative force. We may bewail, if we wish, having to depend on individual judgement without the aid of general principles, though life is very often like that; but we should bewail much more loudly any *a priori* insistence that this judgement must always be exercised in one direction. There is no good reason to think that we could not, with a little ingenuity, think up some non-theistic statements which would serve, if true, to put some theistic conclusions beyond reasonable doubt. So theistic statements are not immune to indirect proof in principle, even if the outlook for proving them in practice is completely gloomy. The facts as we know them may not be sufficient to prove them, but it is irrational to insist that nothing *could*.

If this is true, let us now look at the disagreement between the believer and the sceptic. Both can agree that a certain indirect proof of God's existence, or of some theistic statement, would be a sound one. Both may further agree that although it would be a sound one the premises of it are not true, or not known to be true, to anyone who does not already know that God exists. The sceptic, who does not have knowledge that God exists, will now justify his scepticism by pointing out that inductive considerations make it very unlikely that such premises will ever be true, or will ever be known to be true. The world as it is is not such as to provide us with such a proof, as Hume showed us so convincingly in the *Dialogues*, and ordinary inductive considerations make it very unlikely indeed that it will change radically enough to do so, as Hume reminded us in his essay on *Miracles*. The believer, on the other hand, thinks he knows that God exists. He may still not think it any more likely than the sceptic does that the world will provide the material for a sound indirect proof of this fact. On the other hand, if his knowledge (or supposed knowledge) of God's existence is brought to bear on the matter, it is not irrational *for him*, since he is *ex hypothesi* not restricted to ordinary inductive considerations, to take a different view of the likelihood of the world's providing it from the one the sceptic takes – a point which I take Hume to have recognised when he confines the conclusion of his argument about miracles to the claim that miracles cannot be established so as to form the foundation of a system of religion; given the basic propositions of such a system the likelihood of a particular miraculous event could reasonably be assessed differently. Furthermore, whatever position the believer may take about the likelihood of some probative events coming to pass, the fact that he considers himself to know that God exists enables him, if he wishes, to prove to his own satisfaction all sorts of other theistic conclusions – if he combines non-theistic premises, which the unbeliever could also accept, with theistic ones which he can claim to know independently. The proofs that may result from this will naturally be rejected by the sceptic, since they will depend on premises some of which he will deny to be true; but if the believer really *does* know their truth, and his arguments have all the other prerequisites of good proofs, they will *be* good proofs in spite of the sceptic's objections. They will just not convince him. Such in-group exercises are by no means pointless; I take it that arguments like this are not uncommon in theological disputes between theists. For example if one theist wishes to prove to another that *p*, he may be able to show that some scriptural text states or implies that *p*. This is something that the sceptic could agree to. He can then combine with this minor premiss some major premiss to the effect that the text in question has divine authority. These two together will prove that *p*, for anyone who knows both the major and the minor to be true. The sceptic will reject it because he will deny that the major is true, or at least that it is known to be. But *if* the theist constructing the proof and the theist for whom he constructs it *do* know that the major is true, then they have a sound proof of *p* and the sceptic is wrong. Of course all this requires direct rather than indirect knowledge that propositions like this major premiss are true.

I have spoken so far only about *proving* propositions about God. It is obvious enough that even though they *may* expect certain probative statements to turn out in the long run to be true, many Christian theists do not look for this. So I will turn for the present to a closely allied question, that of the possibility of *verifying* theistic statements. This notion has been discussed a good deal recently in the philosophy of religion because of the writings of John Hick,[1] and of those sceptical critics he has tried to answer.

In his theory of the eschatological verification of theism, Hick attempts to give a general account of what it is to verify a proposition, and then argues that Christian theists, contrary to the views of some of their recent critics, are in a position to say what would verify their beliefs. The assumption common to the critics and Professor Hick appears to be that it is necessary to hold that they are able to do this in order to maintain that these beliefs are intelligible – or, if I

[1] See particularly ch. 8 of *Faith and Knowledge*, 2nd ed. (Ithaca, N.Y., 1966).

may use the opaque jargon favoured in these controversies, 'factually meaningful'.

I cannot examine in detail here all of Hick's analysis of the concept of verification itself. There are two major points in it that I should comment on here. First, he says that verifying is an *action* that people perform, e.g. by making observations or performing experiments. While this is largely true, Hick's own theory requires, I think, that it be qualified. The fact that a claim that someone has made is verified does entail that there is someone for or to whom it is verified; but it does not entail that there is anyone *by* whom it is verified. It may be verified *by events*, which the person to whom it is verified recognises as having this import. Second, and much more fundamental, Hick stresses the distinction between verification and 'logical certification or proof'. To verify *p* is not necessarily, he argues, to establish some other proposition or propositions that *entail p*, but only to establish that there is no ground for rational doubt as to the truth of *p*. This he insists can be done by producing facts which remove all grounds for rational doubt about *p*, even though they do not entail *p*. This seems to me clearly part of the concept of verification. But the contrast with proof is erroneous, since it seems to me part of the concept of proof also, and I have assumed this throughout.

Let us distinguish between direct and indirect verification. This is not easy to do in wholly general terms, but easy enough with examples. A shopkeeper may say that his calculations indicate that there 'must' or 'should' be £32 3s 5d in the till; he may then ask his assistant to verify this by counting the money that is there. In this case a claim or tentative conclusion is verified by someone's independently ascertaining the truth of that which is tentatively asserted in this conclusion. This seems a natural enough candidate for the title of direct verification. On the other hand, there do seem to be cases where one verifies some claim or assertion that *p* by ascertaining the truth of something else, *q*, which is sufficient to establish that *p*. I can verify the claim of my Member of Parliament that he spoke in favour of the abolition of income tax in the Commons by reading the appropriate issue of *Hansard*. The doctor can verify the detective's theory that the victim was dead before midnight by determining the condition of the corpse. In these cases what one ascertains in the process of verifying *p* is not *that p*, but *that q*, which in turn puts *p* beyond reasonable doubt. These cases I would call cases of indirect verification. And they seem at least as common as cases of direct verification.

There are very great affinities between indirect verification and indirect proof. I do not wish to suggest that the concepts are interchangeable (for what concepts are?), but I would suggest that in some cases they can be used interchangeably, and, more significant than this, that if some statement, q, would be sufficient in a proof context to *prove* that p, it might very well be sufficient in a verification context to *verify p*. (I incline to think that the choice of expression is dictated not by the epistemological weight which q would carry, which would be the same, but by contextual circumstances of a different kind.) Given these likenesses, we can add another dimension to the positions I have called moderate and radical theological non-naturalism. A theological non-naturalist must hold that no theistic statement can be verified by reference to any set of non-theistic statements, however large. That is to say, he must hold that if any non-theistic statement is offered as a verification of some theistic claim, it is either a statement that is false or that we do not know to be true, or it is a statement which, even if it *were* true, would fail to place the theistic claim beyond reasonable doubt. For if he were not to take this view of it, he would have to say that that statement would serve as the premiss of a sound *proof* of some theistic claim, which he cannot admit. Now such a person might very well believe that there are statements which, if they were true and were offered as verifications of some claim that the theist makes, *would* verify that claim; he might believe that theistic statements are not indirectly verifiable merely because he does not think these verificatory statements are true, or known to be true. On the other hand, someone might hold that no non-theistic statement whatever, even if true, would serve to verify any theistic claim. This view is of course what I would have called radical theological non-naturalism. Another but less clear way of putting this would be to say that theistic statements are in principle incapable of indirect verification. Both the moderate and the radical theories are open to theists as well as to sceptics, if they are prepared to insist that theistic statements can only be known to be true by direct religious insight of some sort. Without going through the corresponding arguments, I would like to suggest once again that radical theological non-naturalism is in this case, as in the case of proof, an arbitrary thesis, incapable of being justified except by arguments that beg critical questions about the truth or falsity of the theistic claims themselves.

Even if the moderate version of theological non-naturalism is true, it would not show that someone who already knew by direct religious insight that God existed could not verify some claim that he or another theist made about God by ascertaining the truth of some non-theistic statement and combining this knowledge with the prior knowledge of God which he has. In combination, these two things might very well be enough to place some claim about God beyond reasonable doubt. But here again the sceptic, lacking the knowledge of God that would be needed, would not be able to subscribe to the conclusion of this in-group exercise. Verifications of this sort, or apparent ones, are nevertheless frequent in the lives of believers.

Let us turn back to the fact that the sceptic and the believer alike could agree, even if moderate theological non-naturalism is true, to the existence of some non-theistic statements which would, if they were true, serve to verify claims about God. They may both agree, and the sceptic will insist, that it is highly unlikely that they will ever turn out to be true. At this point it is of great interest to consider Hick's doctrine of the eschatological verification of theism. He argues that it is an integral part of the Christian tradition that those belonging to it have expectations of a future existence in which the ambiguous experiences of our present life will be supplanted by experiences which will clearly serve to verify Christian claims about God, or put them beyond reasonable doubt. It is not wholly clear to me whether Hick intends that these predicted experiences could in some cases be described in wholly non-theistic terms or not. I am uncertain, that is, whether he thinks that those experiences which believers expect include some which, though enough to verify the claim that God exists, could be recognised by someone who did not know that God existed, or whether he does not think this. His theory was offered as part of a quite different sort of debate, about the meaningfulness of theistic claims. But I have some inclination to think that the original purposes of his contribution to that debate would make him welcome the suggestion that at least some of the future experiences which he claims would verify the existence of God would be experiences which could be reported in non-theistic terms. If this is correct, his theory can be the source of suggested non-theistic statements that would, if they were to turn out in the eschatological future to be true, serve to verify Christian theism. Then believer and sceptic alike might agree that if the world *were* to be transformed in the future so that these experiences took place, Christianity would be verified. They would of course not agree about the likelihood of this transformation. What sort of transformation would it have to be, and can it be described in non-theistic statements?

Mere survival of death, as Hick points out, would not be enough. For mere survival of death might be an unexpected and surprising natural fact and nothing more. What is needed to verify Christian theism is a future community of persons whose relationship to one another represents the sort of fulfilment of human personality indi-

cated in the gospels, and who experience communion with God as
revealed in Christ. In this last sentence I have merely paraphrased
Hick and not interpreted him. As the statement stands it looks quite
obvious that anyone who predicted that this state of being will come
to pass would be making what I have called a theistic statement –
one that could not be known to be true by anyone who did not know
that God existed. I incline to read Hick otherwise; but aside from
the issue of interpretation, let us ask whether something couched in
non-theistic statements could have the same verificatory value. It is
not as difficult as it sounds. If we say that there will be a community
of persons infused by grace, over whom Jesus will return to reign as
the Son of God, obviously we make a theistic statement. Suppose,
however, we say that there will be a community of persons whose
personalities are *as they would be if* they were infused by grace, i.e.
manifesting love and righteousness, that Jesus will rule over this
community in the manner in which the Son of God would, i.e. in love
and forgiveness, *and* that they would describe this community as one
infused by grace and ruled by the Son of God? These statements
could be known to be true by someone who did not know that God
existed. At least they do not *entail* that God exists. I would suggest
that if someone were to find himself in a world in which these non-
theistic predictions turned out to be true, he would be irrational if
he did not take this as verifying the claims of Christian theism with
which these predictions are associated.

An objection is natural here, especially in the light of familiar mid-
century debates about religious discourse. It is natural to protest
that these non-theistic statements contain references to grace and to
the Son of God, and that these are religious expressions. This is not a
relevant objection, however. It would only be an objection to a
theory that was supposed to use the fact that such eschatological predictions can be made as a way of explaining the *meaning* of the basic
Christian claims about God. In spite of his disclaimers, Hick has
been criticised for allegedly trying to 'give meaning retrospectively'
to Christian discourse by reference to a future crux;[1] and it is obvious that such an enterprise would be circular if one's description of
the future verifying circumstances was nearly precise enough to constitute a possible verification. But all that is claimed here is that the
predicted circumstances are of a sort that could be recognised to obtain by someone who did not *know* that God existed – not that they
could be recognised by someone who did not *understand* the claim
that God exists.

[1] This criticism is made by R. W. Hepburn, in 'From World to God', *Mind*,
LXXII (1963) 42.

I would suggest that the believer and the sceptic could and should agree that such a future world would verify the claims that Christians now make about God, that indeed it would be irrational to deny that it would, even though the coming of such a world would not *entail* the truth of those claims. (This outcome of the doctrine of eschatological verification is only possible if one admits that the claims are intelligible, and that understanding them is a condition of understanding the predictions to which they give rise.) Although they could and should agree about this, it is very obvious that they will not agree about the likelihood of these things coming to pass, since the likelihood is dependent entirely upon whether or not one already has knowledge of God's existence and intentions.

To sum up so far: I have assumed without argument the common view that God's existence cannot be proved from non-theistic premises. I have distinguished two versions of this, which I have called moderate and radical theological non-naturalism. The moderate view holds that there are no premises of this kind that we can know to be true which would serve to prove God's existence, or any other theistic statement; but it allows that there might be some non-theistic statements which would serve to prove such conclusions if only they *were* known to be true. The radical view denies that there are any non-theistic statements whatever which, even if true, could prove such conclusions. I have argued that the radical view is an irrational view, so that both believers and sceptics should be able to agree upon some, or some set of, non-theistic premises which, if true, would prove theistic conclusions without the further aid of theistic premises. The choice of some set of non-theistic premises as being probative ones would involve, no doubt, accepting an inference which sacrificed economy and perhaps achieved explanatory depth, but it could not be based upon a prior choice between these two considerations at a general level, for such a choice would lack a justification unless critical questions were begged. The probative force must be seen to lie in the examples themselves. The decision that some example, if true, would have the force of a proof, however, is not itself a concealed appeal to specifically religious insight. And to insist that no non-theistic premises whatever could be probative would be completely arbitrary unless independent knowledge of the incoherence of theism could be drawn upon to support it. Parallel considerations can be made out in the case of the verification of theistic claims. Here, even though there may be no non-theistic facts which we can know to be true which *do* put these claims beyond reasonable doubt, both believers and sceptics ought to be able to agree that certain situations (which could be reported in non-theistic statements) *would* serve to do so. I have suggested that some of the eschatological predictions of the Christian tradition are, as John Hick has claimed, in this category. In both cases, however, the believer and the sceptic will take a different view of the likelihood of the probative or verificatory statements ever turning out to *be* true. And the difference will be traceable to one source: the presence or absence of alleged independent knowledge of the truth of religious claims. For someone without such knowledge only standard inductive considerations can be relevant to the question of the likelihood of any of the probative or verificatory statements coming true, and these considerations alone count firmly against them. For someone who has this knowledge a variety of possibilities are open. While he will no doubt find proofs and verifications of theistic statements time and again by combining secular facts with religious ones he claims to know, he might take the same view the sceptic does about the likelihood of anything happening which would suffice to *prove* God's existence or God's love to those who do not know of them already. On the other hand, he might, with his supposed knowledge of God, feel that in certain cases the standard inductive considerations have to be weighed against what he knows of God's purposes, and might take a view of their likelihood which is opposite to the sceptic's. Many believers would side with the sceptics over the likelihood of events occurring in this life which would suffice to prove God's existence without the aid of theistic premises. But most would take the opposite side (and in my view all *ought* to take the opposite side) from the sceptic on the eschatological predictions. Their alleged independent knowledge of God and his purposes would override the inductive considerations to which the sceptic is confined and make them predict these fulfilments with confidence.

There is, then, or should be, an area of theoretical agreement between believers and sceptics; but it is also obvious that on the practical level the deadlock is complete. For those who do think they have independent religious knowledge of God and those who do not think they have must, on pain of irrationality, take quite opposite views of the likelihood of the agreed indirect verification of God's existence coming to pass. The theoretical assumptions that they may share are not sufficient, it would seem, to allow useful debate between them on the basis of agreed standards. Can this deadlock be broken down?

In a way obviously it can, and often is. People are converted, i.e. those who do not have the alleged independent knowledge of God come to believe that they do have it; and people who used to think they had it change their minds about its genuineness. But this is not the outcome of debate according to agreed standards. For if we are right that there are no indirect proofs now to be had, conversion will be a process of inducing in someone the religious insight that he so far lacks. Doing this to someone is (usually) a matter of preaching to him. If one has theistic knowledge then no doubt one is correct in interpreting what happens when a man is preached at as being a process of revealing to him what he has not so far seen by putting him in a position where he can see it. But if one is sceptical of the truth of theistic claims and judges them by the standards one would use for assessing procedures that lead to knowledge in areas where one does claim to know something, it is clear that preaching appears as a set of dubious persuasive devices designed to cloud the judgement and induce belief by putting aside normal requirements of objectivity – devices to which the rational man would not submit any more than he would to mob oratory. Similarly the attempts to convince believers that their alleged insights are illusory, even if they work, seem bound to commit the genetic fallacy and to depend on applying to religious beliefs standards which those who hold them can quite rationally insist do not apply to them. The deadlock is typified by the debates which rage about the cognitive significance of religious experience. No amount of psychological knowledge of the genesis of such experience can (or should) show to someone who considers himself to know of God's presence that such experience cannot be revelatory, yet no amount of insistence that it is a form of cognition can (or should) convince someone who does not think he knows of God's presence that it really is. No community of standards exists which would enable the kind of agreement which I argued earlier to be possible in imagined cases, to be arrived at for the experiences that the world in fact *does* offer. The deadlock is deepened by the fact that the believer and the unbeliever each has at his disposal, if he wishes to use them, explanatory devices for accounting for the alleged blindness or gullibility of the other.

In another way, of course, the deadlock can resolve itself: by each side resting on its laurels and waiting to see if the eschatological predictions come off. This, however, is a frivolous suggestion, for the believer at least. It seems that the only course is for each to do what it is rational to do given the knowledge that he has, or thinks he has, or lacks. The believer must preach; the unbeliever must try not to listen too hard but can either attack what he hears or wait and see without conviction.

Of course we can say what *would* resolve the deadlock – the actual occurrence of one of those transformations in our world which would, by mutual consent, serve to prove indirectly that God does exist. In other words, a sign.

But a sign is not to be looked for, because a sign would compel assent to it. This, at least, is often said. But I think it is far from obvious. Some signs might compel assent in that they might frighten people into acceptance of God's existence; and perhaps it is contradictory to suggest that an all-good deity would resort to signs of this sort. But I am speaking here of something that would make it unreasonable for someone who knew of it still to doubt whether God exists; and I am quite unable to see that everything that would qualify for this description would compel belief in God. This would only happen if people were rational enough not to refuse to believe something they did not want to believe when the evidence leaves no grounds for rational doubt; and many people are not like this. Many are radical theological non-naturalists. To remove rational grounds for dissent is not to compel assent. If only it were! There is an allied difficulty here which is worthy of mention. It is hard to see how unbelief can be treated as blameworthy if there are rational grounds for doubt. A sign that removed those grounds would make unbelief necessarily blameworthy. Those who hold that unbelief *is* always blameworthy are either driven to saying that there are already conclusive signs, or, more usually, driven to say (or hint) that in fact all men have direct knowledge of God independently of such signs and therefore do not need them even though they pretend to bewail their absence – that they have knowledge of God and smother it, so that all unbelief is a form of self-deception. I think the theological temptation to argue this way is due to the fact that it is *not* true that conclusive evidence compels belief.

This is enough to show, I think, that a world in which conclusive signs of God were to be had could still be a world in which faith was called for. For such a world could quite easily be a world in which most men did not accept the signs and those who did had to live among them. Remember again we are talking only of that which would put religious claims beyond reasonable doubt. What, however, about *this* world, in which, we have assumed, such conclusive evidence is not to be had, and only direct knowledge of God seems available, if any knowledge of God whatever is? Surely I have persistently misdescribed this world by saying that the believer is one who thinks himself to have such direct knowledge? Surely it is part of the concept of *faith* that he does not think he has *knowledge*? Well, it is certainly part of a major theological tradition to insist that faith and knowledge are exclusive, so that faith only exists where rational doubt is possible (though it is part of that same tradition to insist that some religious claims can be matters not of faith but of knowledge). While I am not wholly convinced that my account of the relation between belief and unbelief could not be transposed into the key of this tradition, it will be clear that it has run counter to the division on which this tradition insists. The extravagances of 'encounter' theologies have been due largely to the attempt to give a different account of the believer's conviction from the one which is available to someone who regards faith merely as the acceptance of propositions on less than sufficient evidence. It seems to me that it is more promising to try to define what faith is in terms of the possession, or, in neutral language, the conviction of the possession, of direct knowledge of God when others insist, and insist correctly, that there is no indirect knowledge of God. The conflicts to which those who have faith are said to be prone would naturally arise if the secular knowledge that the man of faith shared with the sceptic was easily attained, was constant, made insistent demands on his attention, and was frequently unpleasant, whereas the religious knowledge which he considered himself to have was fragmentary, intermittent, and easy to brush aside, and was not regarded by most of his fellows as being knowledge at all. But I do not think there is time now to describe the confrontation of the believer and the sceptic all over again.

INDEX

281

74
75
76
79
8
83
86
88